D1106561

DANIEL WAY   JON PROCTOR

GUN THEORY

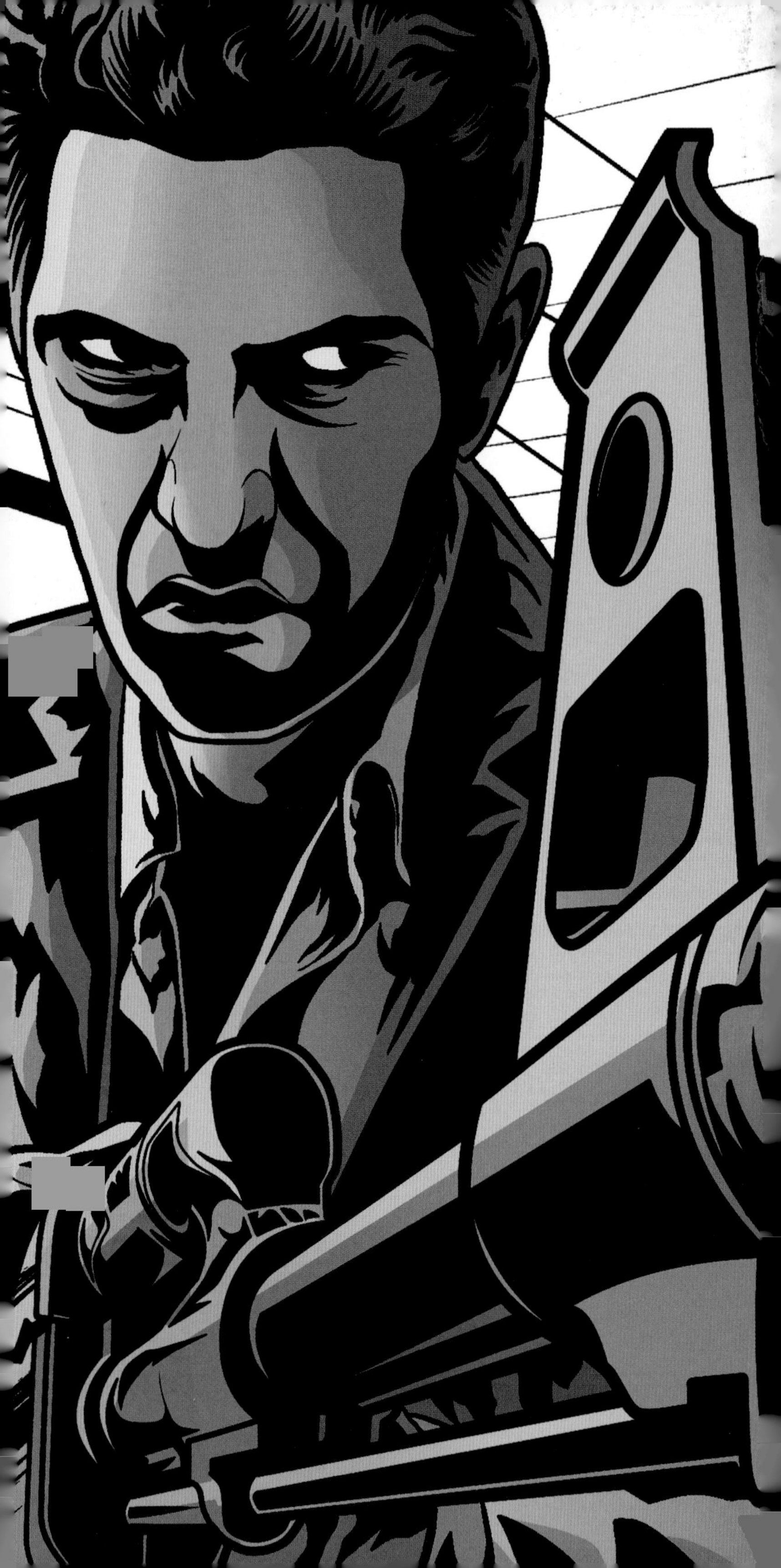

GUN THEORY

SCRIPT

DANIEL WAY

ART

JON PROCTOR

PRESIDENT & PUBLISHER
MIKE RICHARDSON

EDITOR
DANIEL CHABON

ASSISTANT EDITOR
IAN TUCKER

DESIGNER
ETHAN KIMBERLING

DIGITAL ART TECHNICIAN
ALLYSON HALLER

Gun Theory

Published by Dark Horse Books
A division of Dark Horse Comics, Inc.
10956 SE Main Street
Milwaukie, OR 97222

DarkHorse.com

International Licensing: (503) 905-2377
To find a comic shop in your area, call the Comic Shop Locator Service toll-free at (888) 266-4226.

First edition: December 2016
ISBN 978-1-61655-657-0

10 9 8 7 6 5 4 3 2 1

Printed in China

Neil Hankerson, Executive Vice President | Tom Weddle, Chief Financial Officer | Randy Stradley, Vice President of Publishing | Michael Martens, Vice President of Book Trade Sales | Matt Parkinson, Vice President of Marketing | David Scroggy, Vice President of Product Development | Dale LaFountain, Vice President of Information Technology | Cara Niece, Vice President of Production and Scheduling Nick McWhorter, Vice President of Media Licensing | Ken Lizzi, General Counsel | Dave Marshall, Editor in Chief | Davey Estrada, Editorial Director | Scott Allie, Executive Senior Editor | Chris Warner, Senior Books Editor | Cary Grazzini, Director of Specialty Projects | Lia Ribacchi, Art Director | Vanessa Todd, Director of Print Purchasing | Matt Dryer, Director of Digital Art and Prepress | Mark Bernardi, Director of Digital Publishing | Sarah Robertson, Director of Product Sales | Michael Gombos, Director of International Publishing and Licensing

Library of Congress Cataloging-in-Publication Data

Names: Way, Daniel, 1974- author. | Proctor, Jon, artist.
Title: Gun theory / script, Daniel Way ; art, Jon Proctor.
Description: First edition. | Milwaukie, OR : Dark Horse Books, 2016.
Identifiers: LCCN 2016029179 | ISBN 9781616556570 (hardback)
Subjects: LCSH: Comic books, strips, etc. | BISAC: COMICS & GRAPHIC NOVELS / Crime & Mystery.
Classification: LCC PN6728.G84 W39 2016 | DDC 741.5/973--dc23
LC record available at https://lccn.loc.gov/2016029179

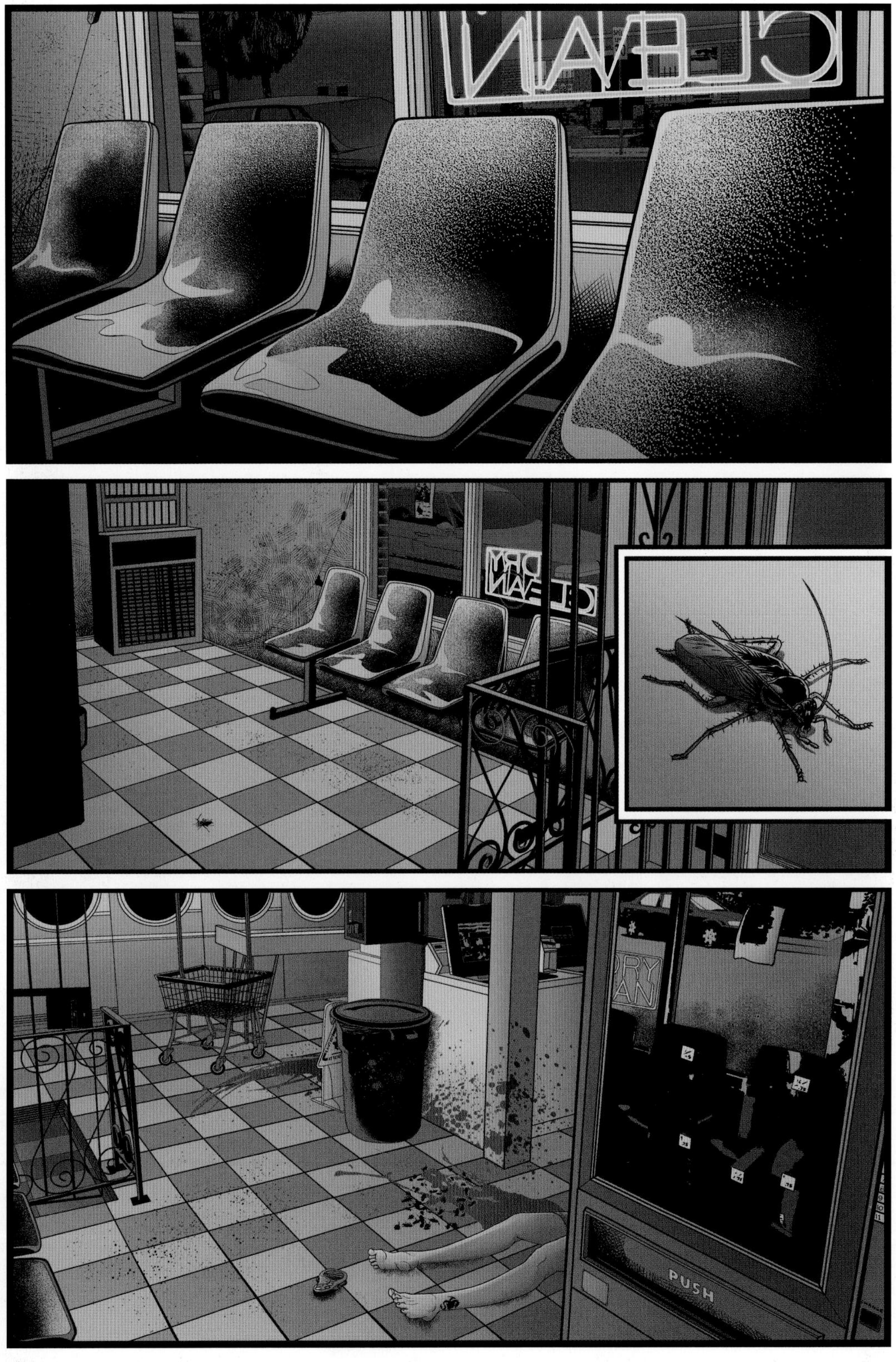
PUSH

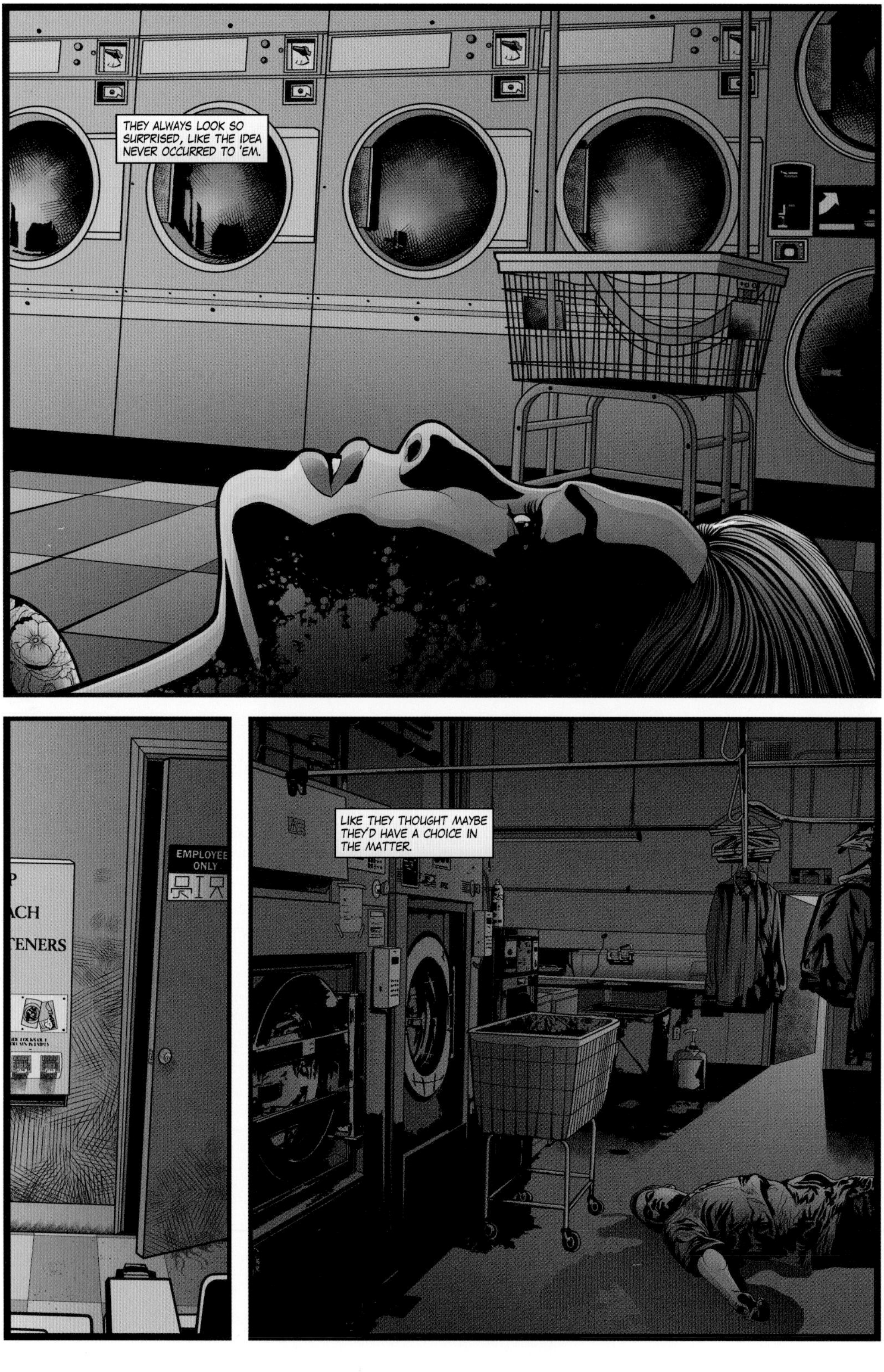
THEY ALWAYS LOOK SO SURPRISED, LIKE THE IDEA NEVER OCCURRED TO 'EM.
EMPLOYEE ONLY
LIKE THEY THOUGHT MAYBE THEY'D HAVE A CHOICE IN THE MATTER.

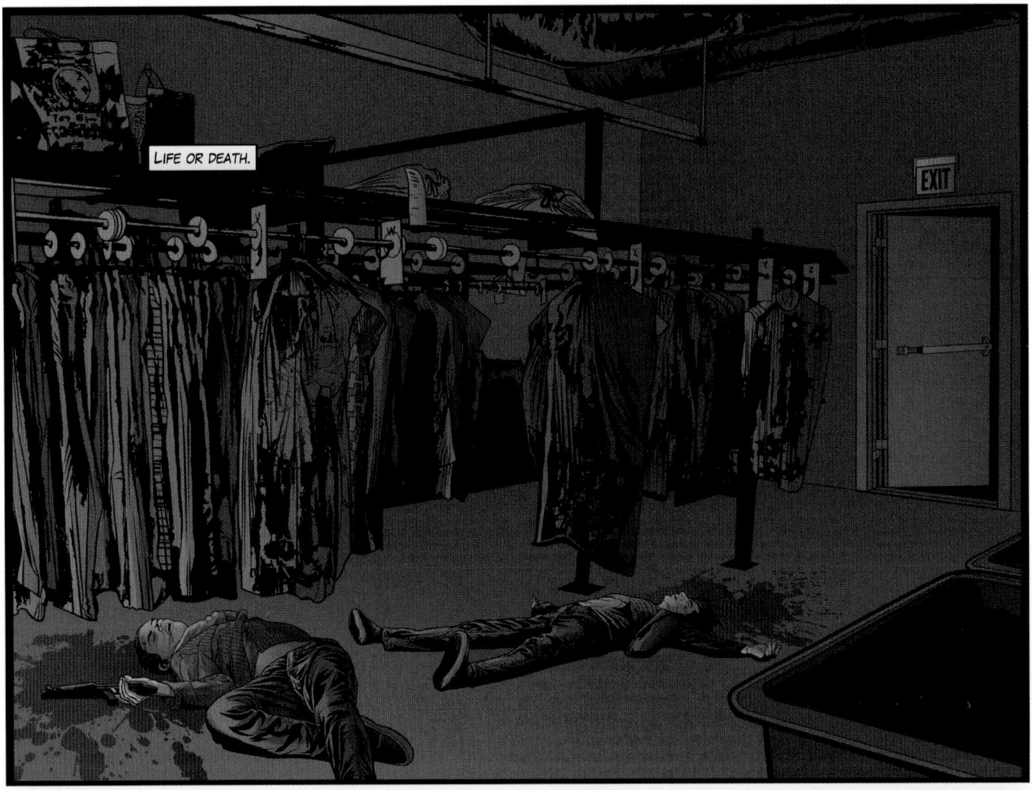
LIFE OR DEATH.
EXIT

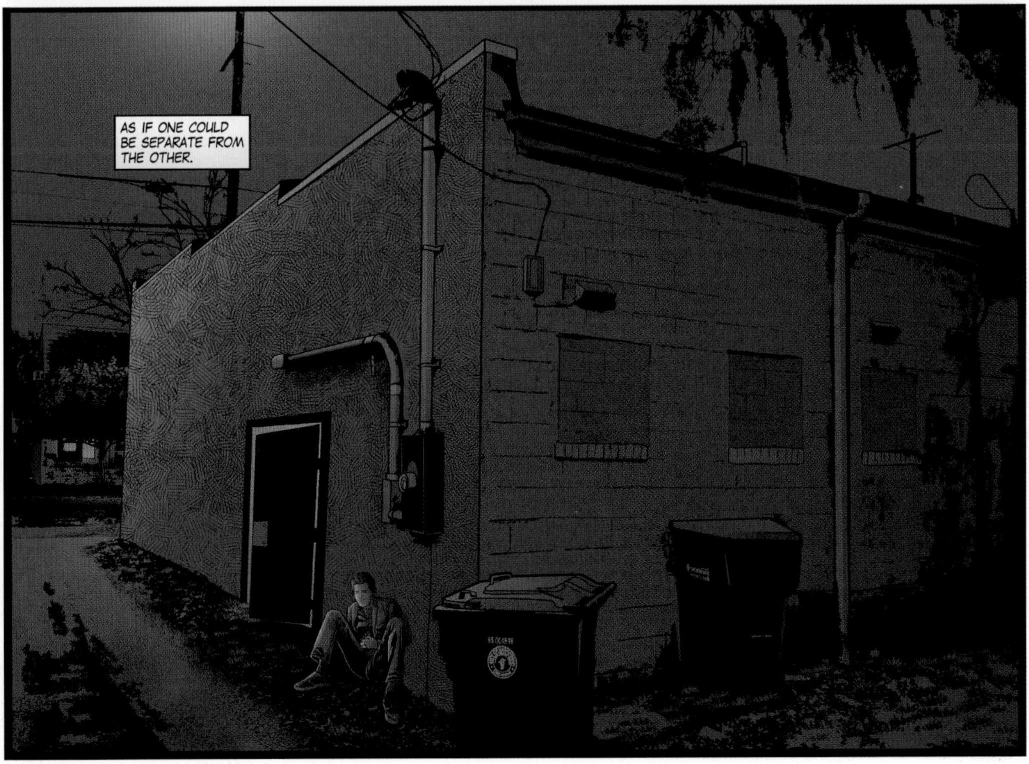
AS IF ONE COULD BE SEPARATE FROM THE OTHER.

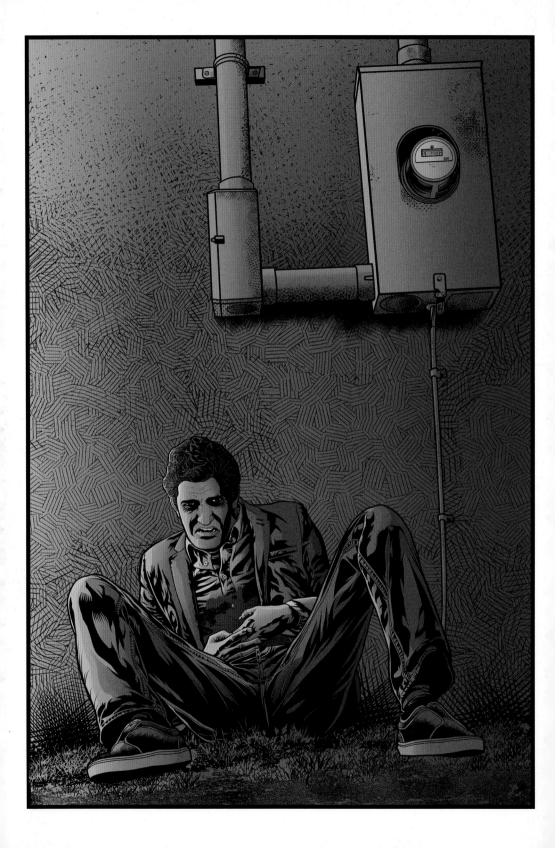

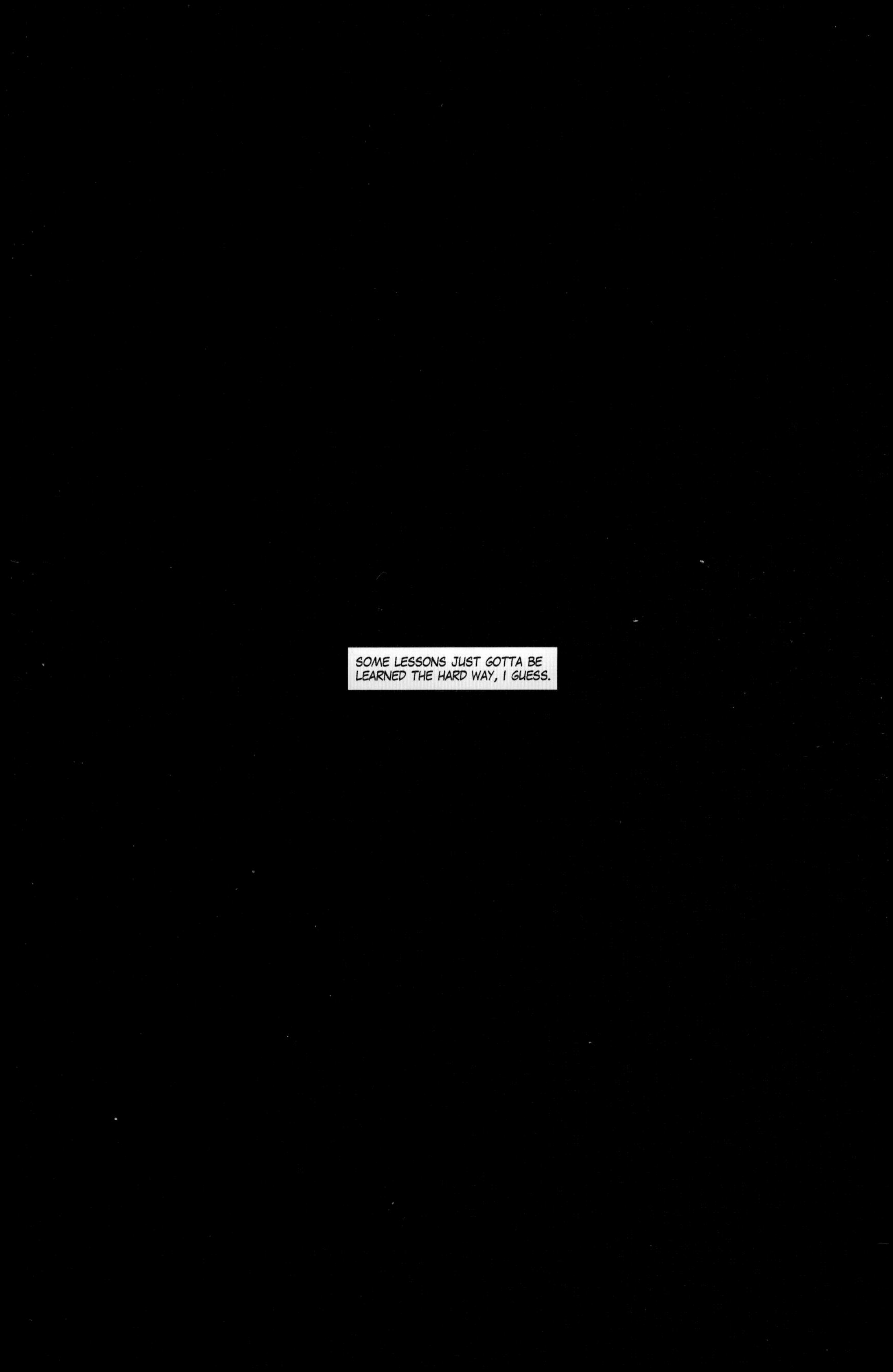
SOME LESSONS JUST GOTTA BE LEARNED THE HARD WAY, I GUESS.

DANIEL WAY   JON

GUN THI

PROCTOR

ORY

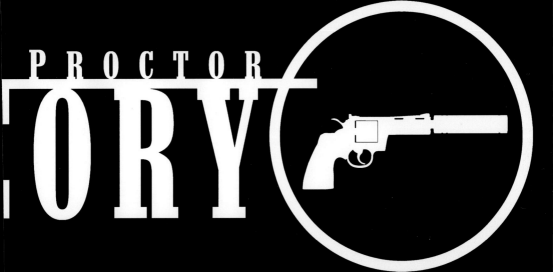

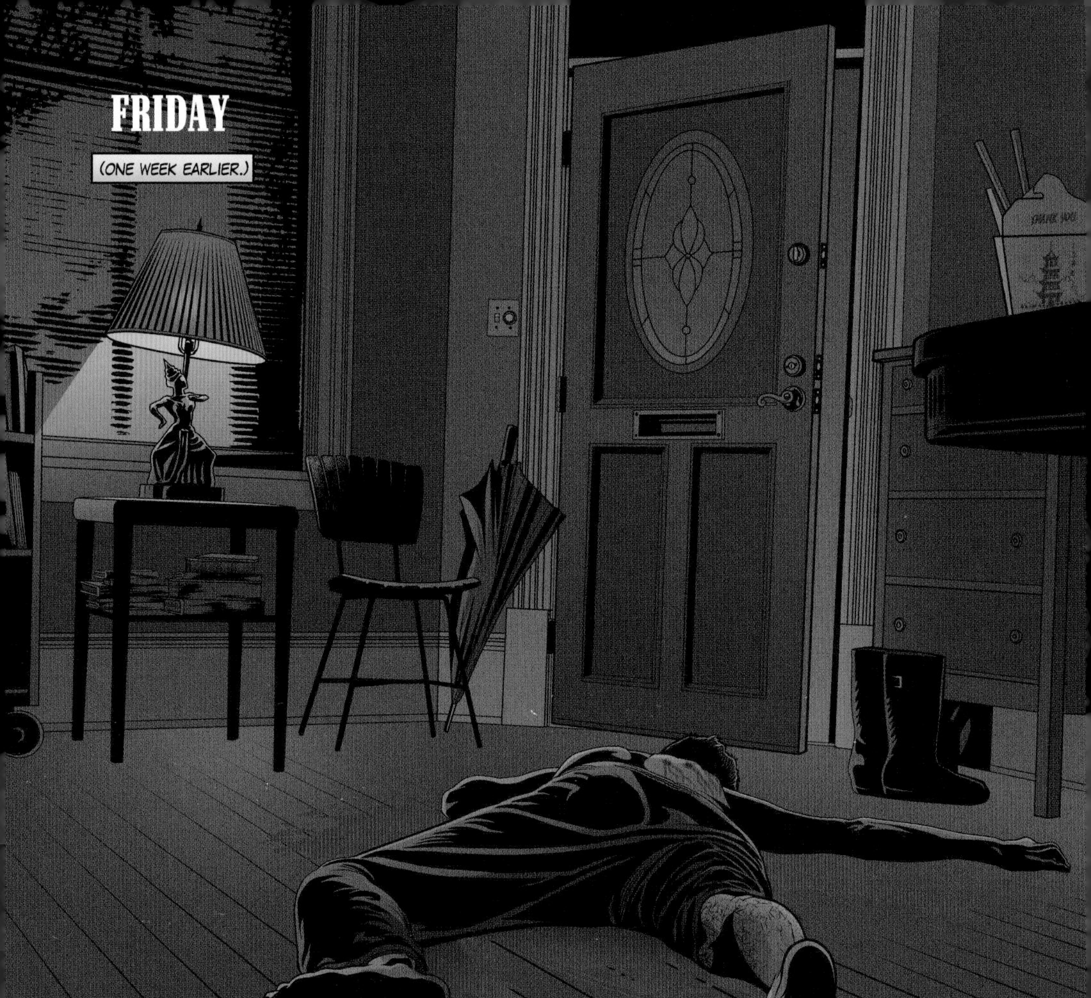
FRIDAY
(ONE WEEK EARLIER.)

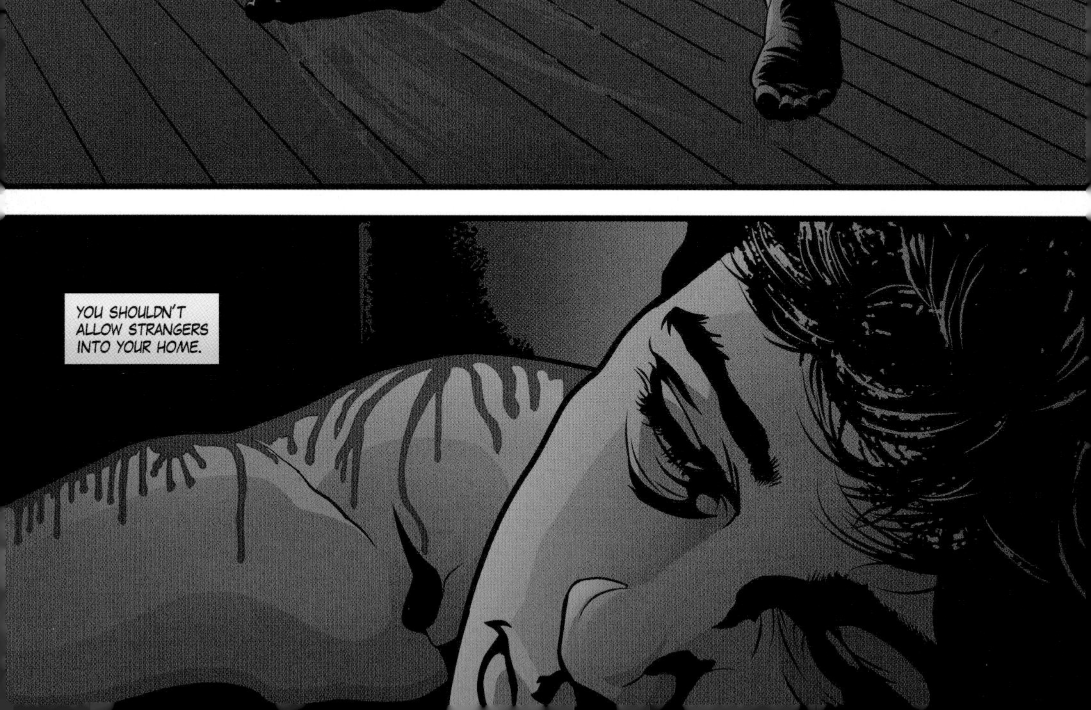
YOU SHOULDN'T ALLOW STRANGERS INTO YOUR HOME.

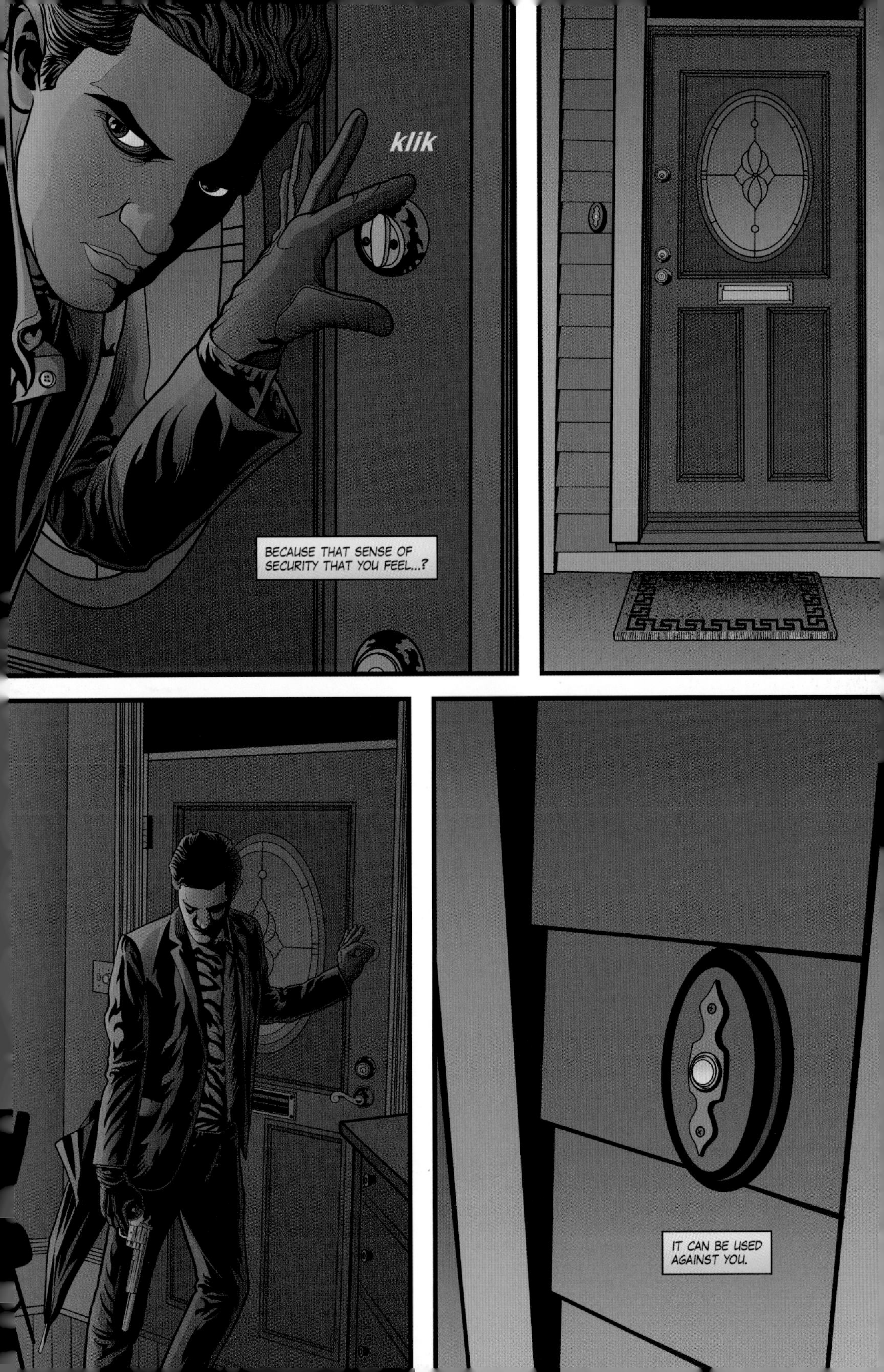
klik
BECAUSE THAT SENSE OF SECURITY THAT YOU FEEL...?
IT CAN BE USED AGAINST YOU.

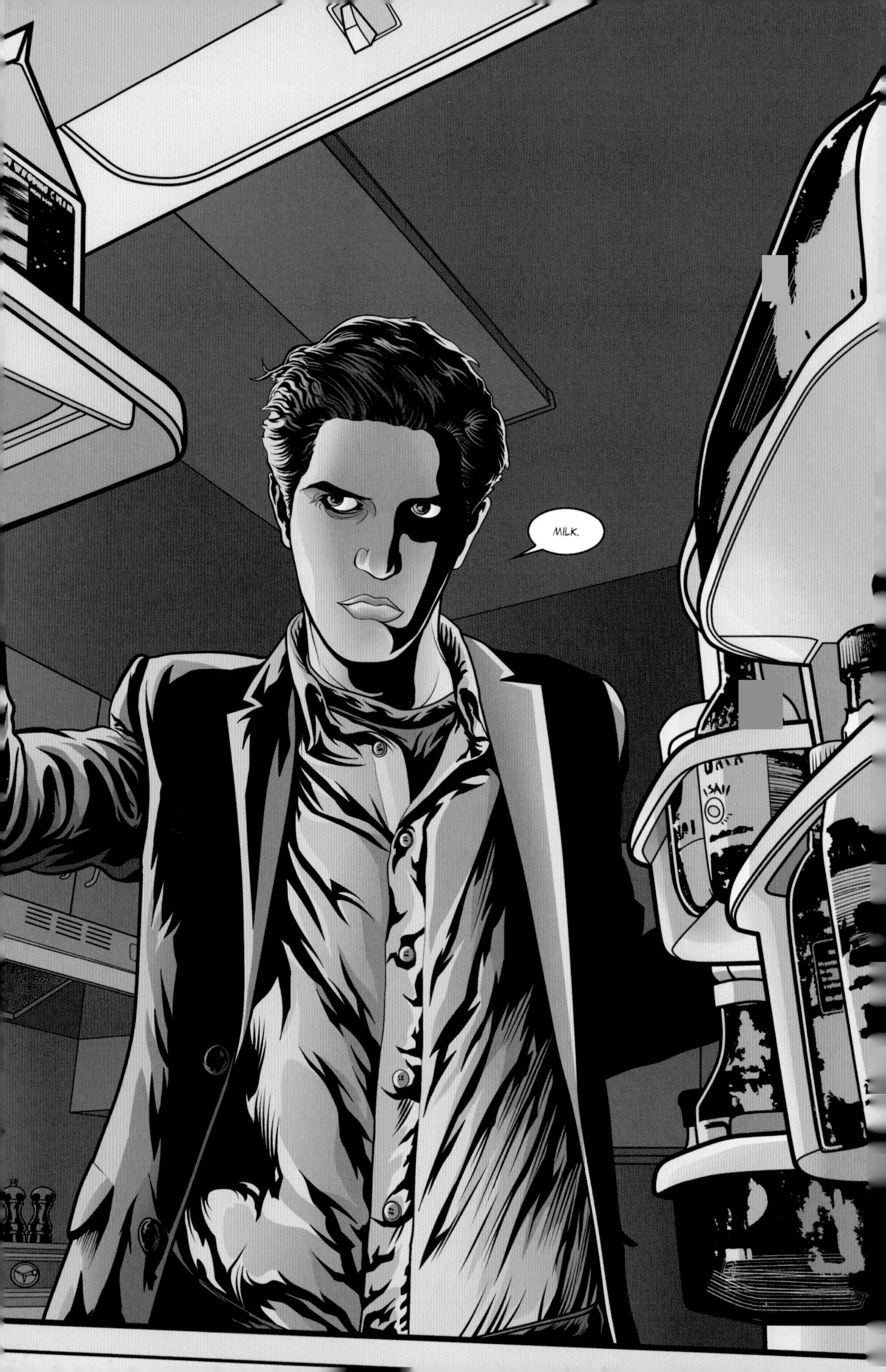
MILK.

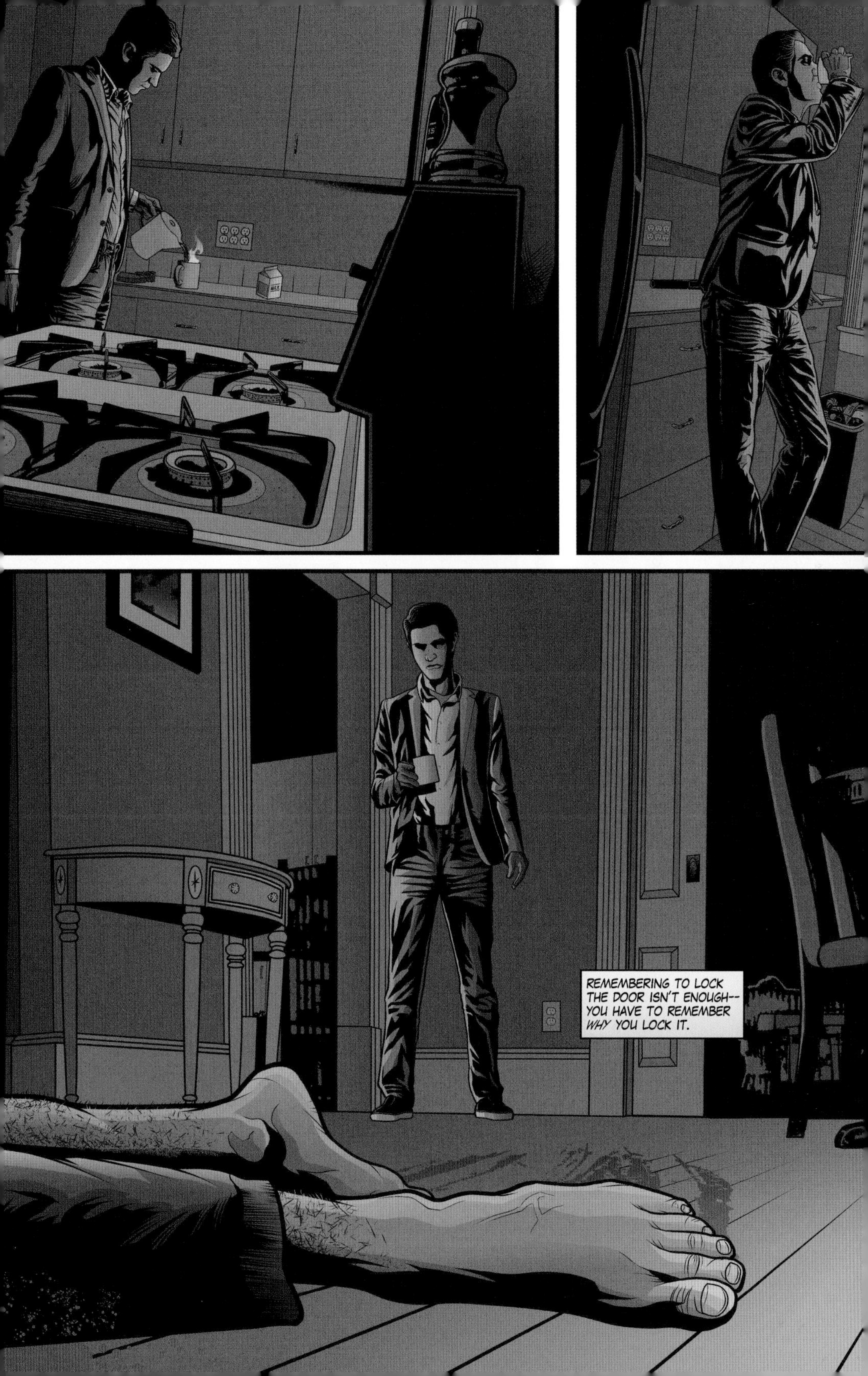
REMEMBERING TO LOCK THE DOOR ISN'T ENOUGH--YOU HAVE TO REMEMBER *WHY* YOU LOCK IT.

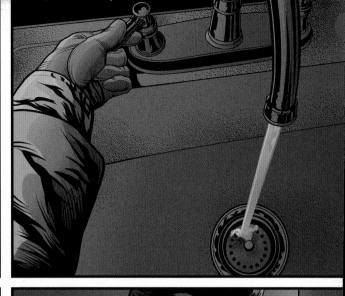

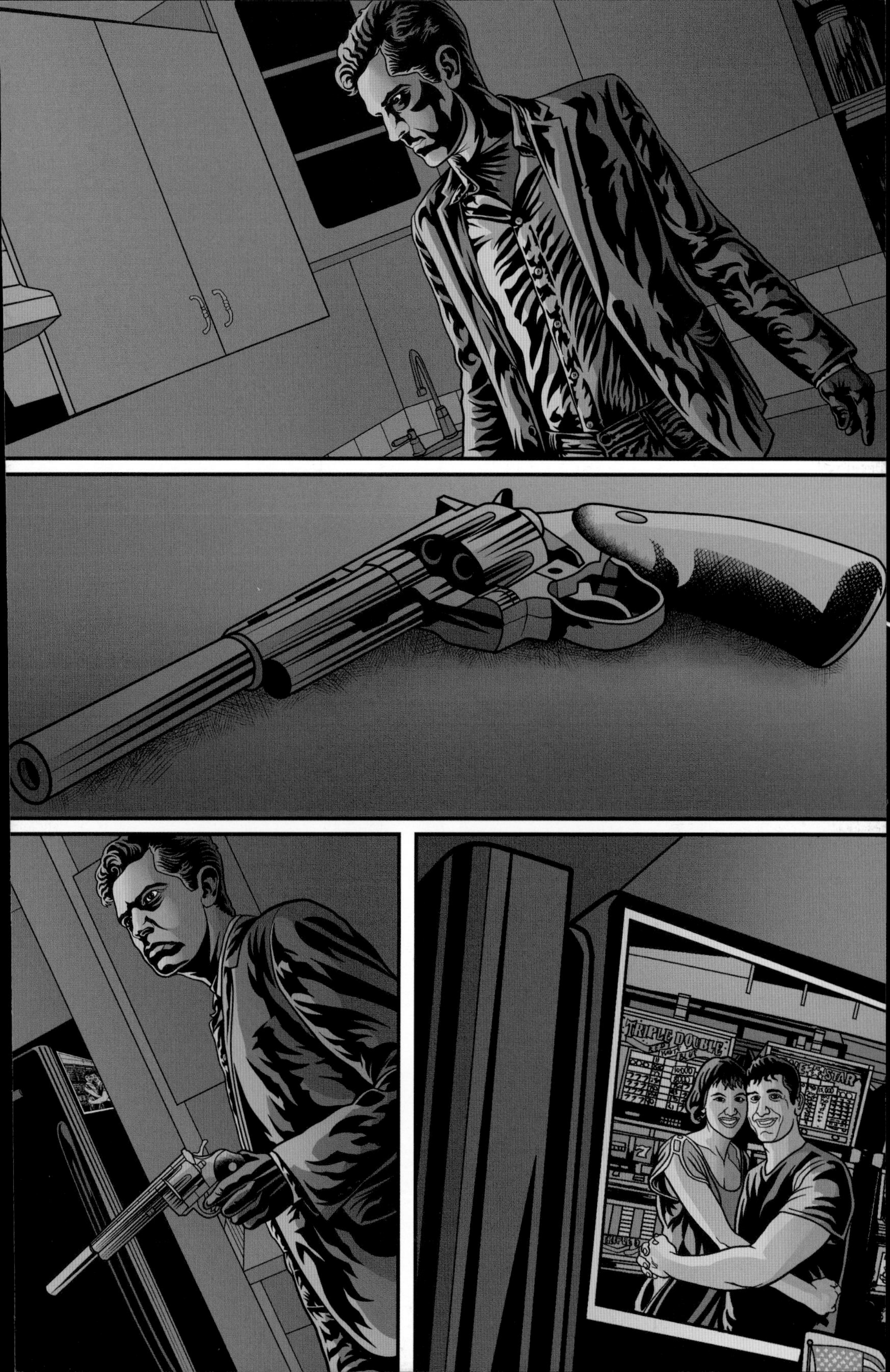
TRIPLE DOUBLE

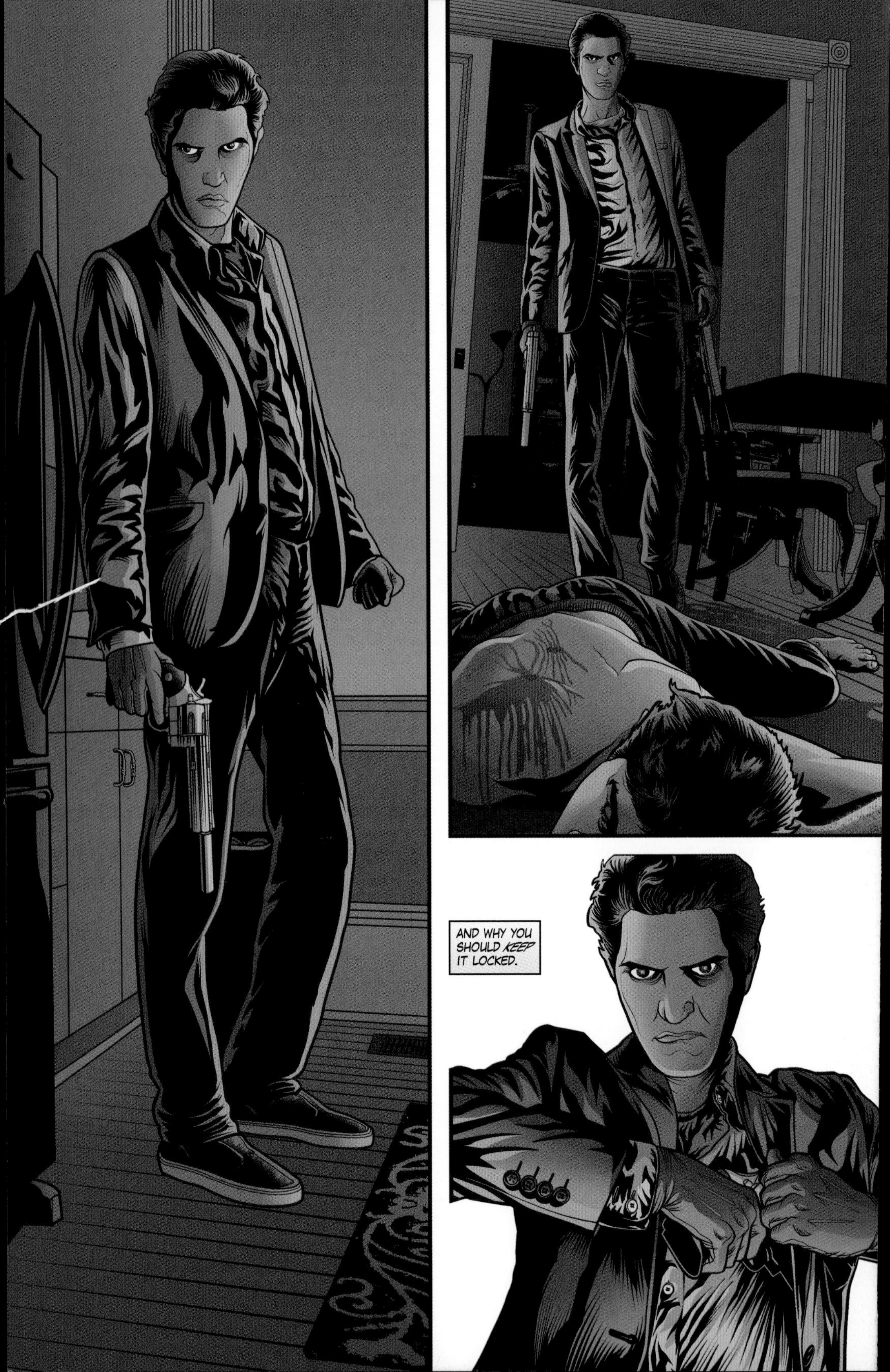
AND WHY YOU SHOULD *KEEP* IT LOCKED.

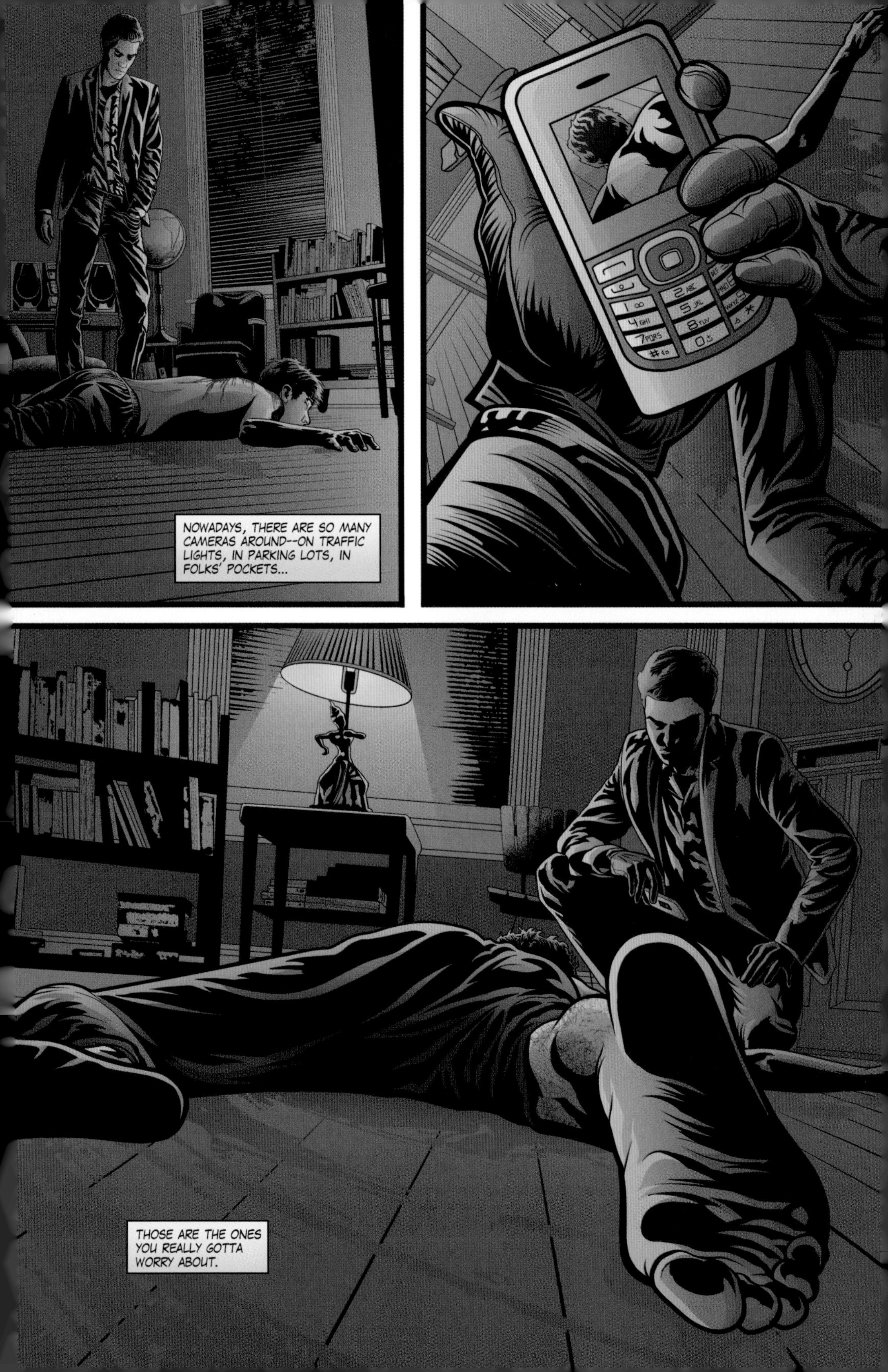
NOWADAYS, THERE ARE SO MANY CAMERAS AROUND--ON TRAFFIC LIGHTS, IN PARKING LOTS, IN FOLKS' POCKETS...
THOSE ARE THE ONES YOU REALLY GOTTA WORRY ABOUT.

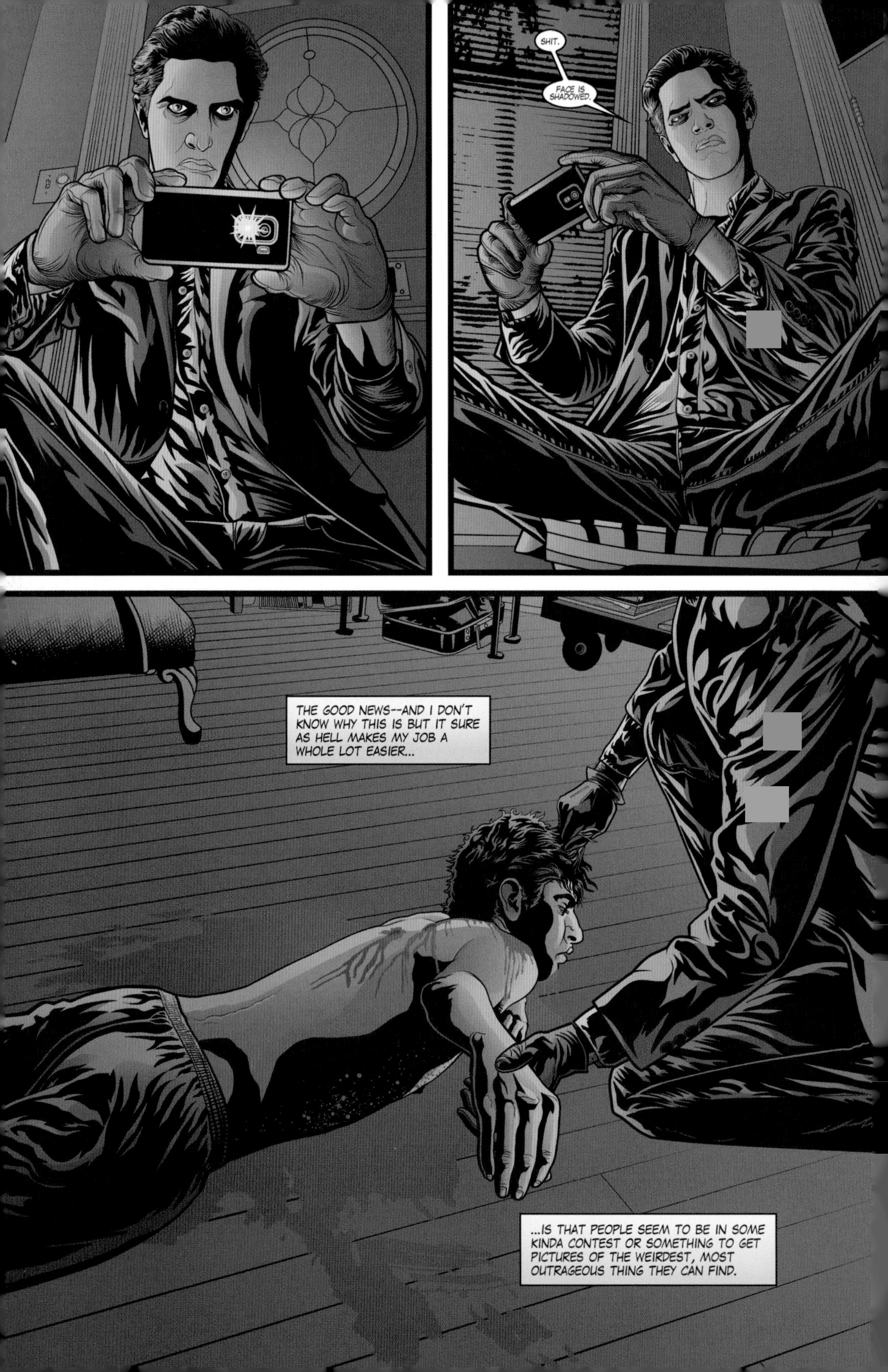
SHIT.
FACE IS SHADOWED.
THE GOOD NEWS--AND I DON'T KNOW WHY THIS IS BUT IT SURE AS HELL MAKES MY JOB A WHOLE LOT EASIER...
...IS THAT PEOPLE SEEM TO BE IN SOME KINDA CONTEST OR SOMETHING TO GET PICTURES OF THE WEIRDEST, MOST OUTRAGEOUS THING THEY CAN FIND.

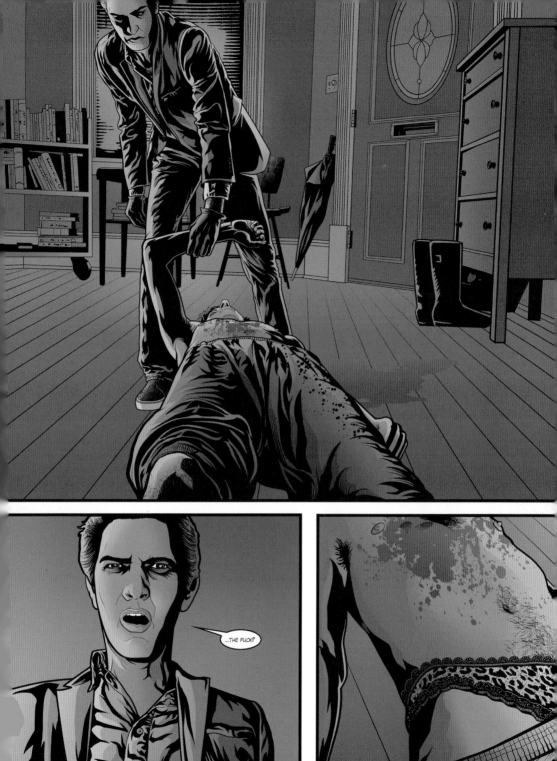

...THE FUCK?

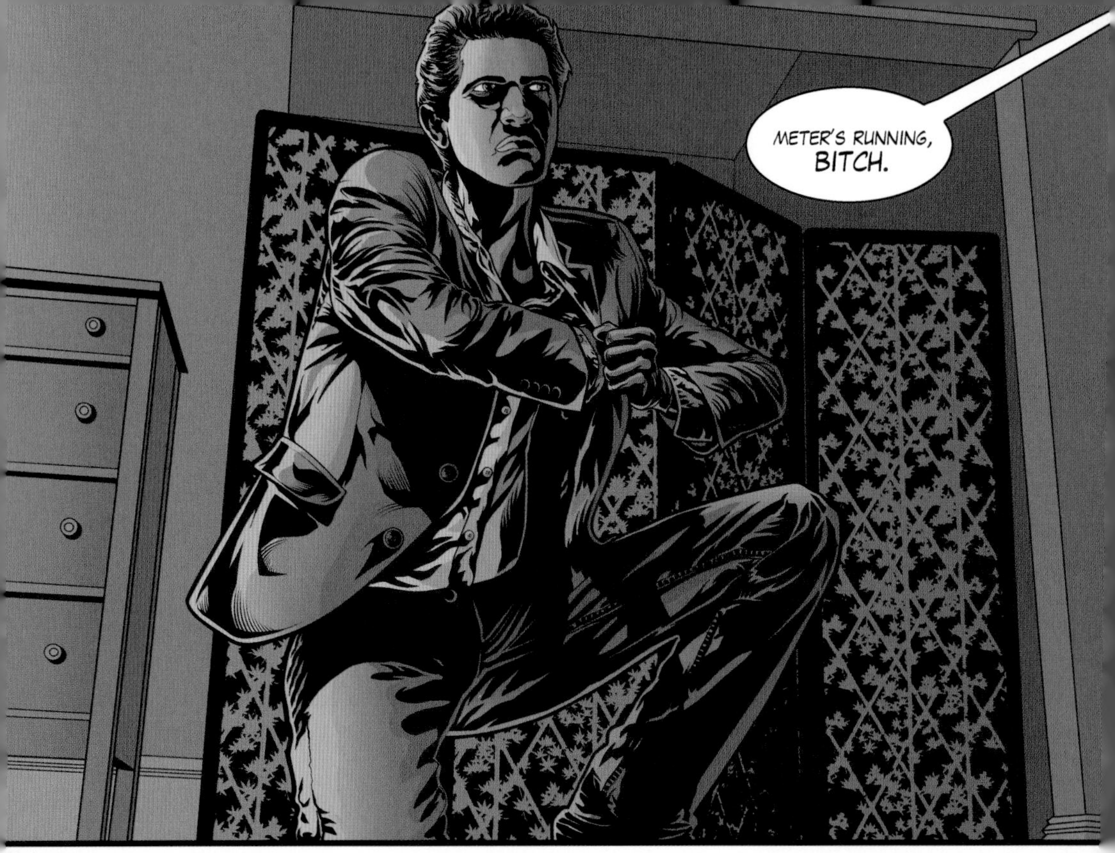
METER'S RUNNING,
BITCH.

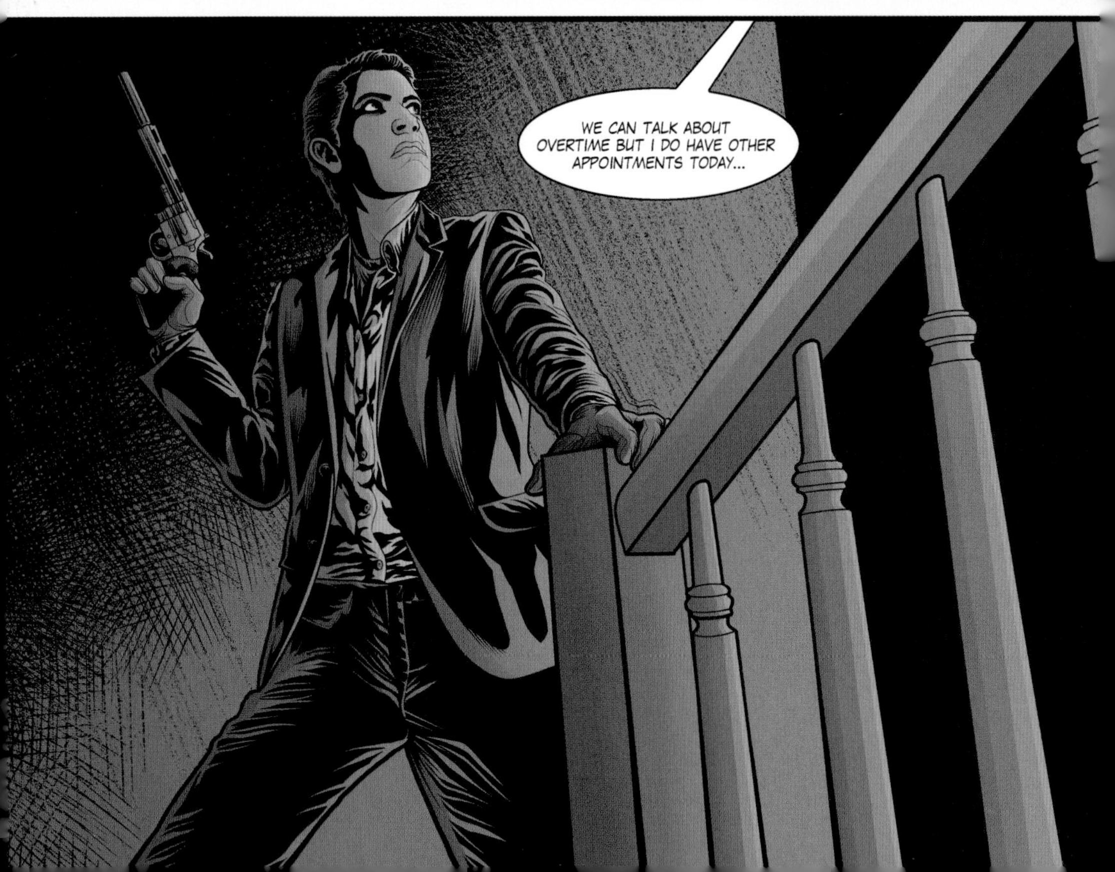
WE CAN TALK ABOUT
OVERTIME BUT I DO HAVE OTHER
APPOINTMENTS TODAY...

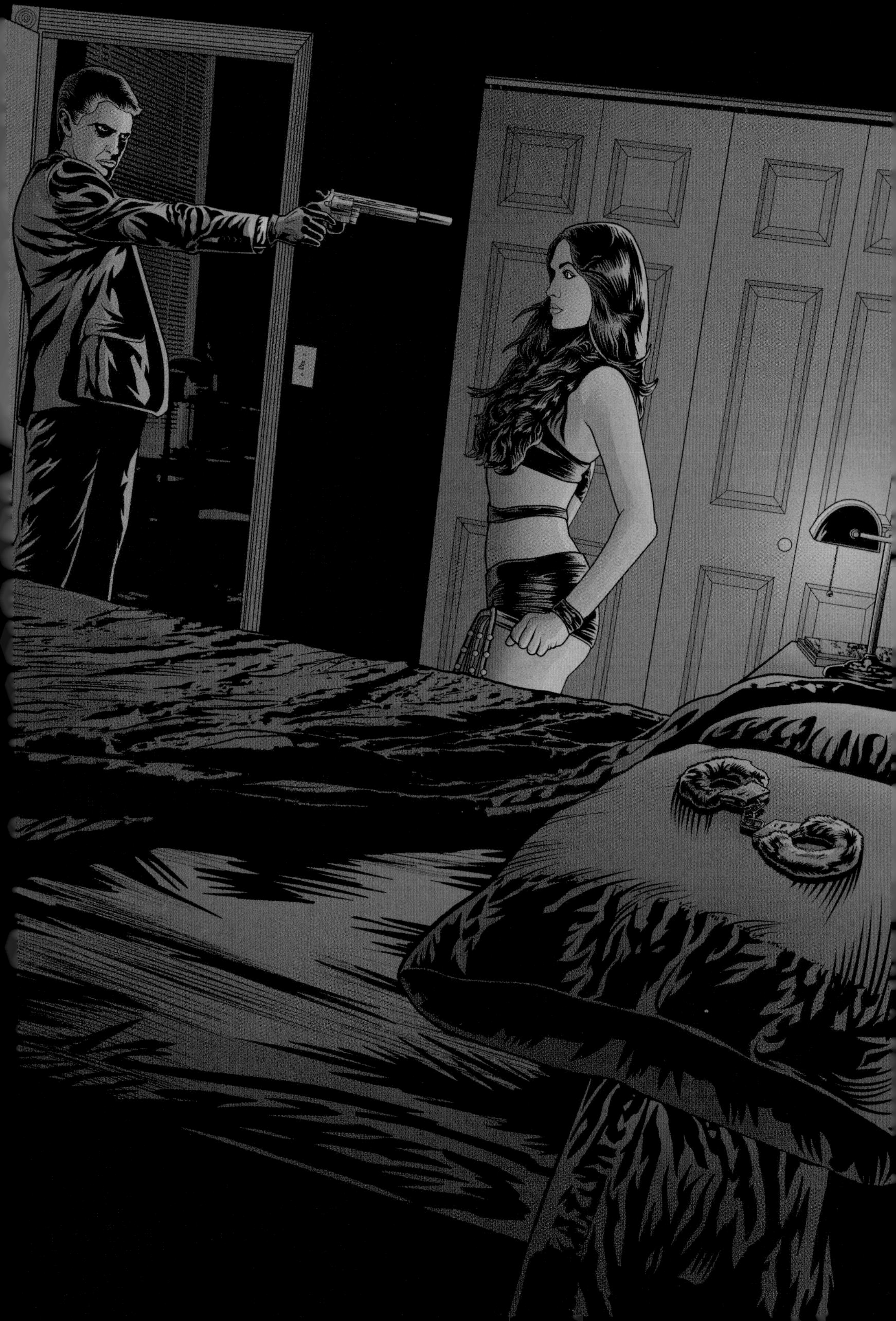

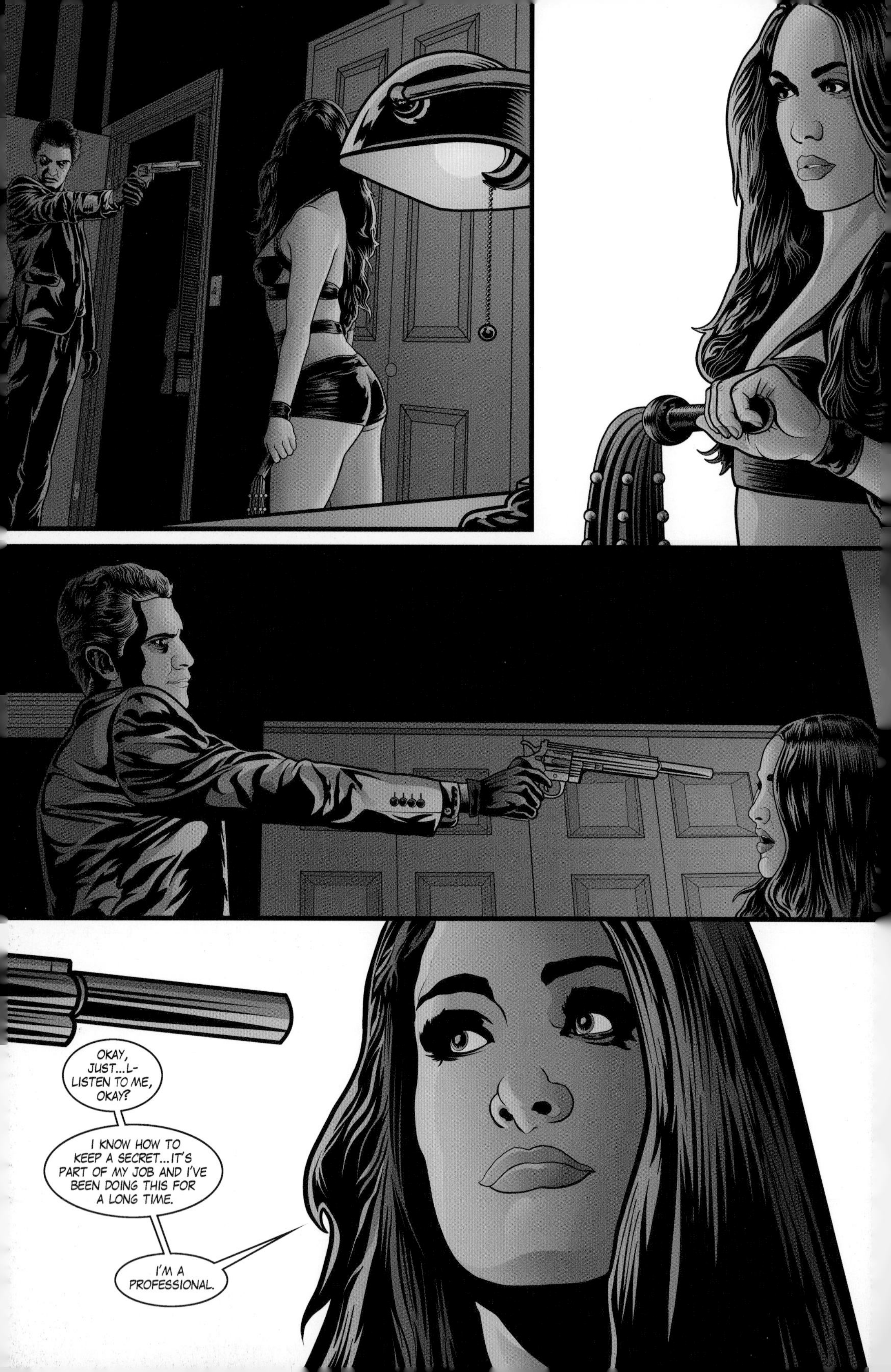
OKAY, JUST...L-LISTEN TO ME, OKAY?
I KNOW HOW TO KEEP A SECRET...IT'S PART OF MY JOB AND I'VE BEEN DOING THIS FOR A LONG TIME.
I'M A PROFESSIONAL.

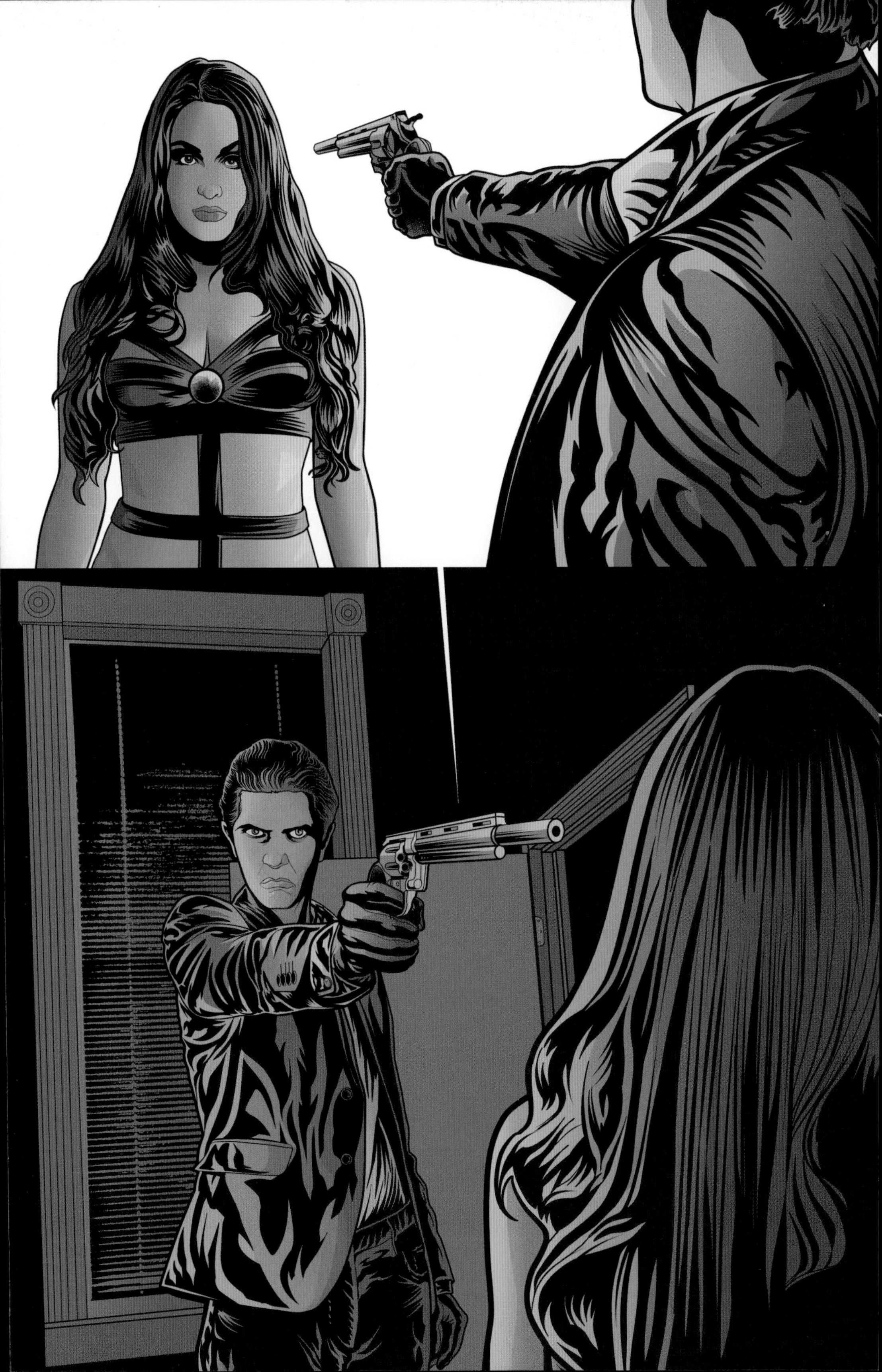

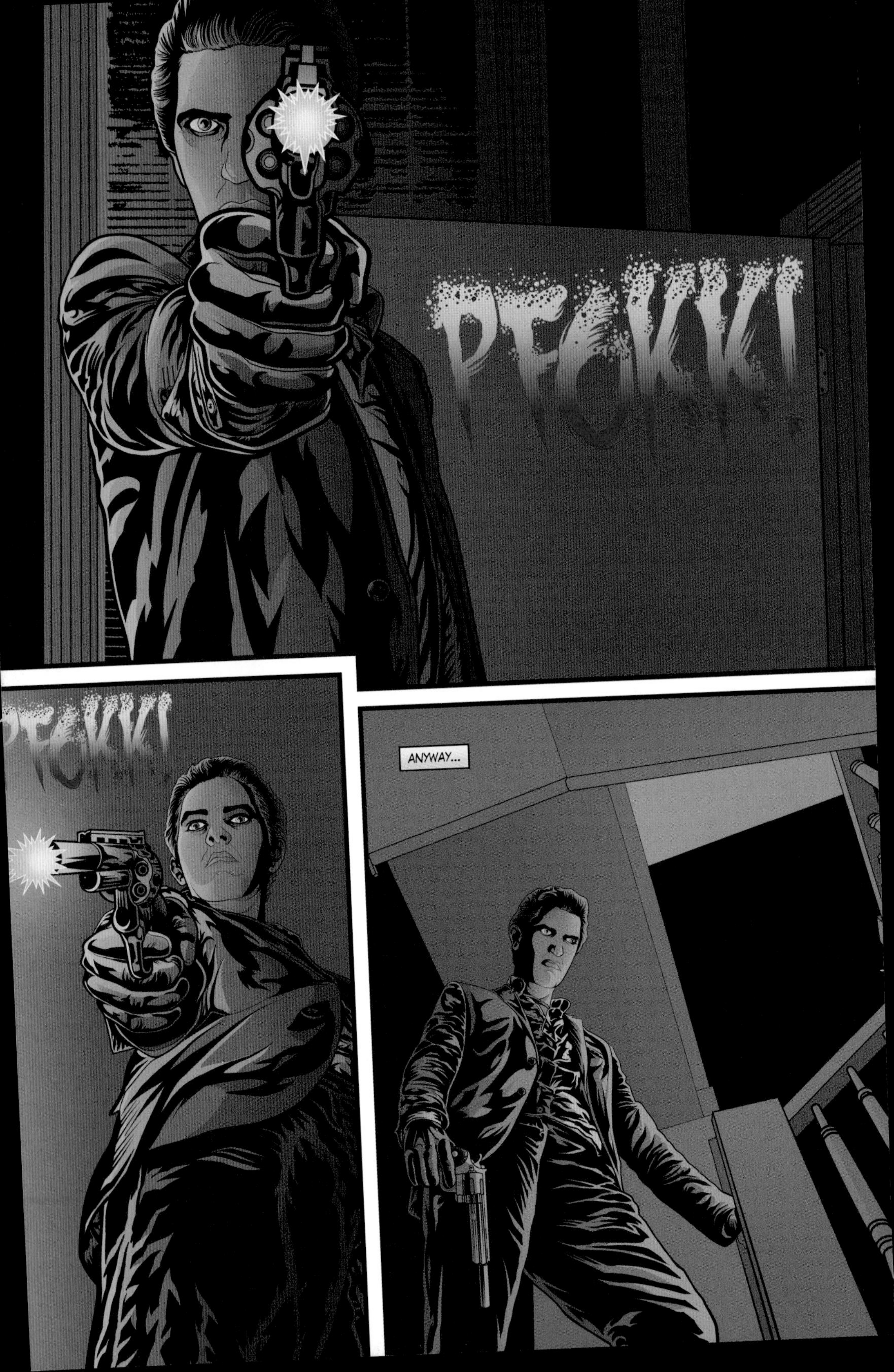
PFOKK!
PFOKK!
ANYWAY...

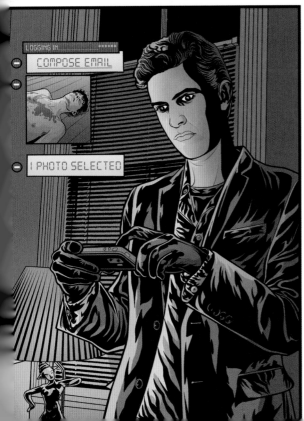

LOGGING IN......

COMPOSE EMAIL

1 PHOTO SELECTED

CANCEL

DELETE DRAFT? SAVE DRAFT?

DRAFT SAVED

THE NORMAL, EVERYDAY STUFF?
NOBODY'S INTERESTED IN THAT.

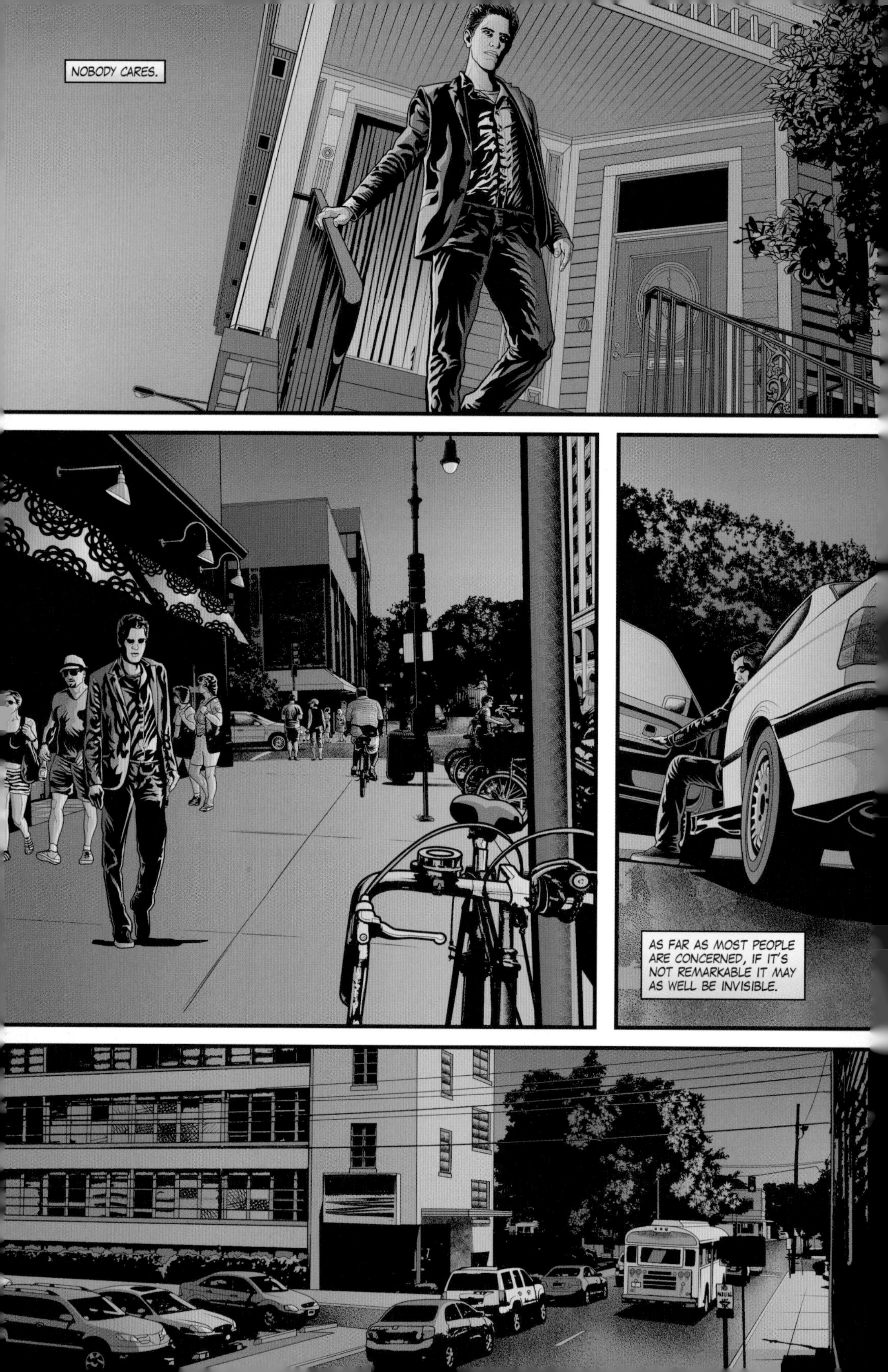
NOBODY CARES.
AS FAR AS MOST PEOPLE ARE CONCERNED, IF IT'S NOT REMARKABLE IT MAY AS WELL BE INVISIBLE.

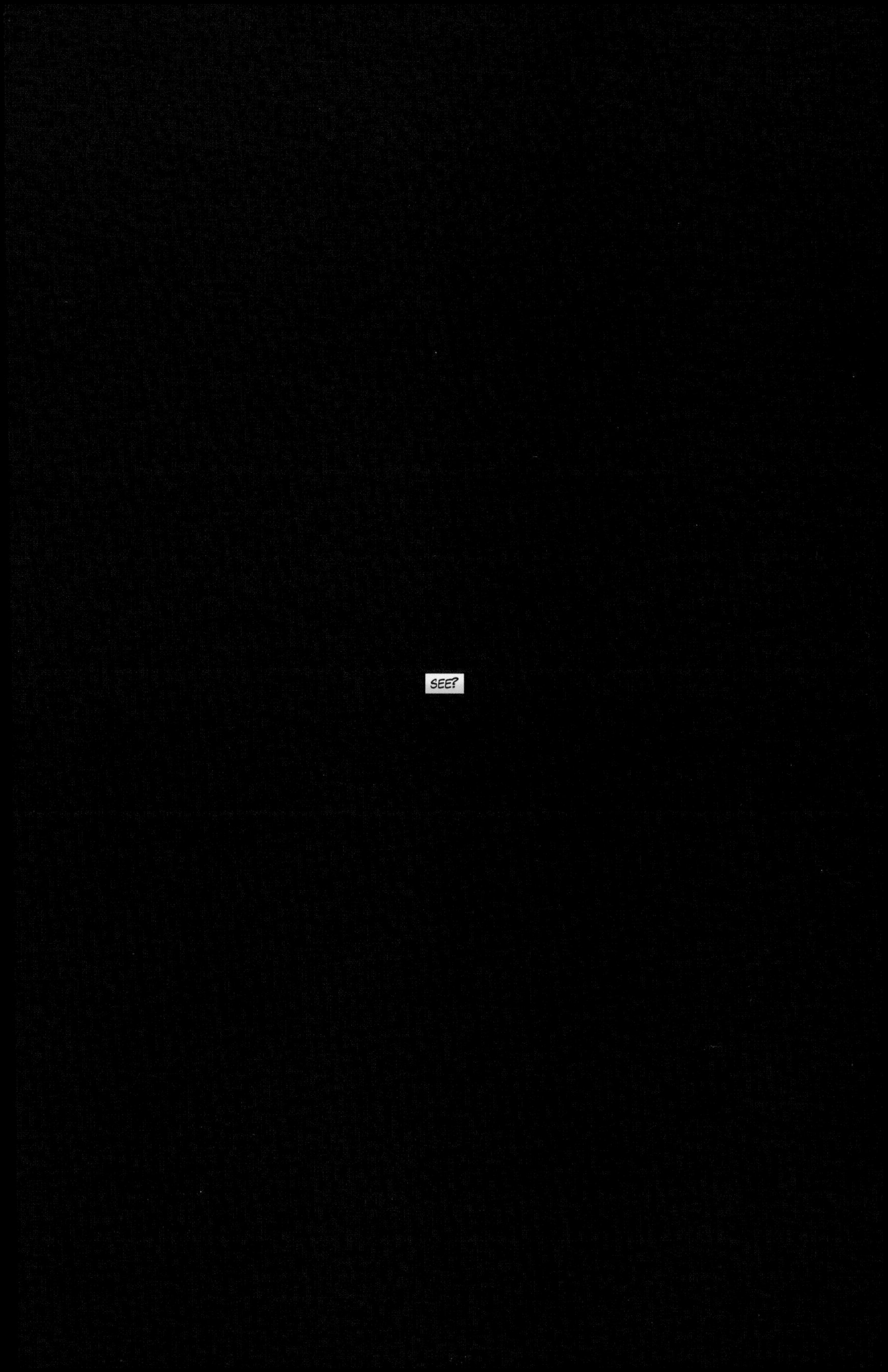
SEE?

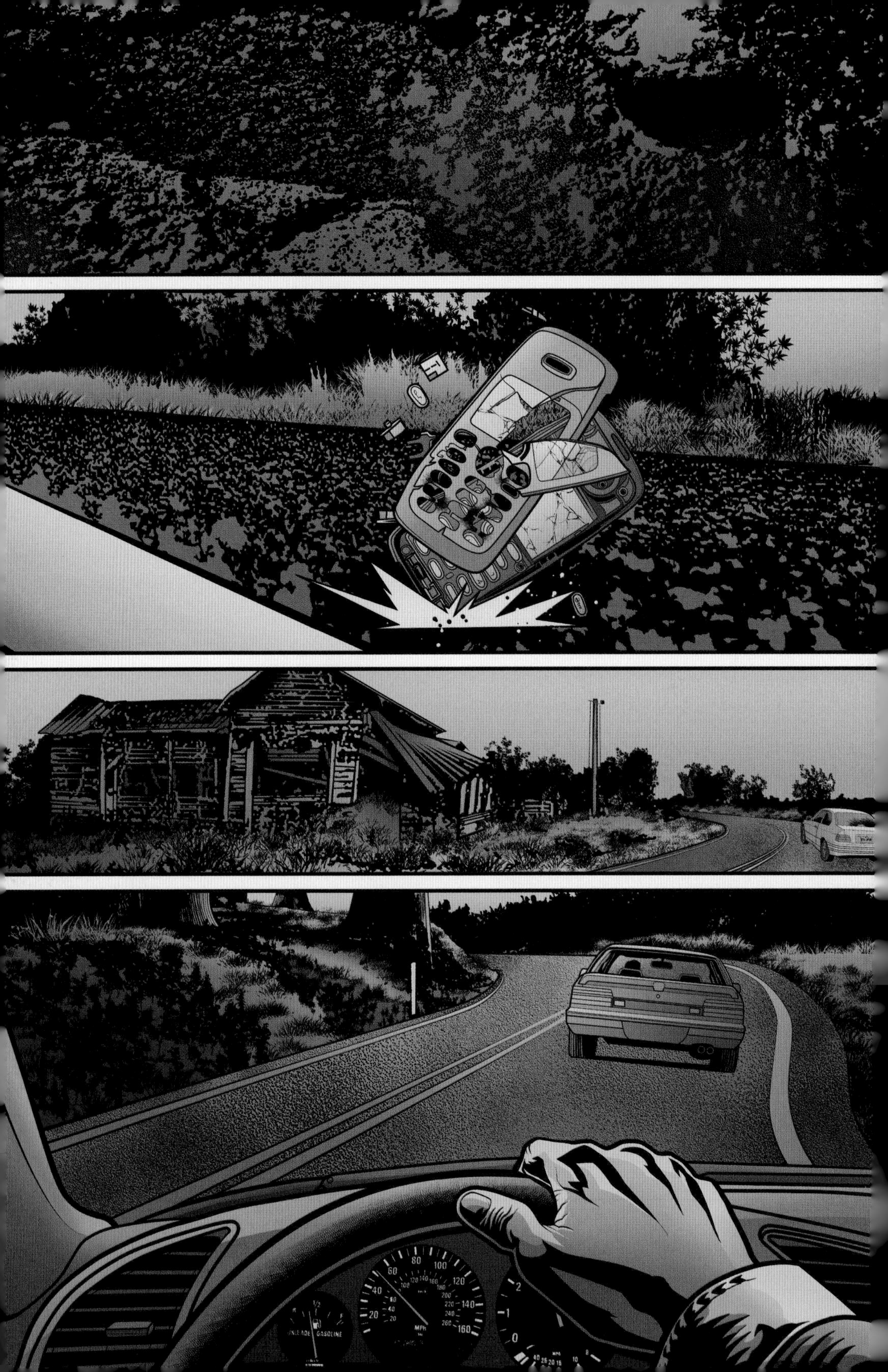

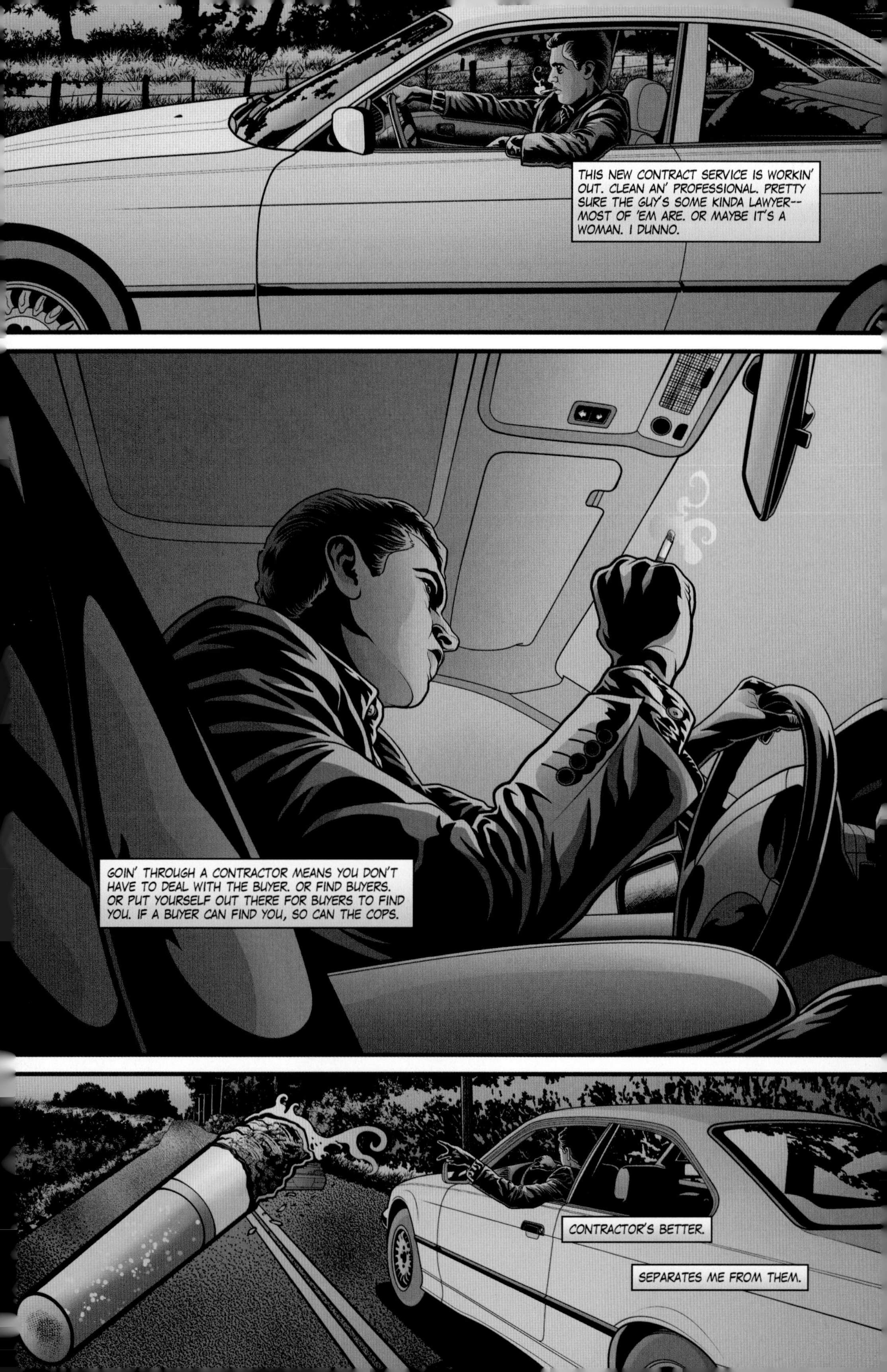
THIS NEW CONTRACT SERVICE IS WORKIN' OUT. CLEAN AN' PROFESSIONAL. PRETTY SURE THE GUY'S SOME KINDA LAWYER-- MOST OF 'EM ARE. OR MAYBE IT'S A WOMAN. I DUNNO.
GOIN' THROUGH A CONTRACTOR MEANS YOU DON'T HAVE TO DEAL WITH THE BUYER. OR FIND BUYERS. OR PUT YOURSELF OUT THERE FOR BUYERS TO FIND YOU. IF A BUYER CAN FIND YOU, SO CAN THE COPS.
CONTRACTOR'S BETTER.
SEPARATES ME FROM THEM.

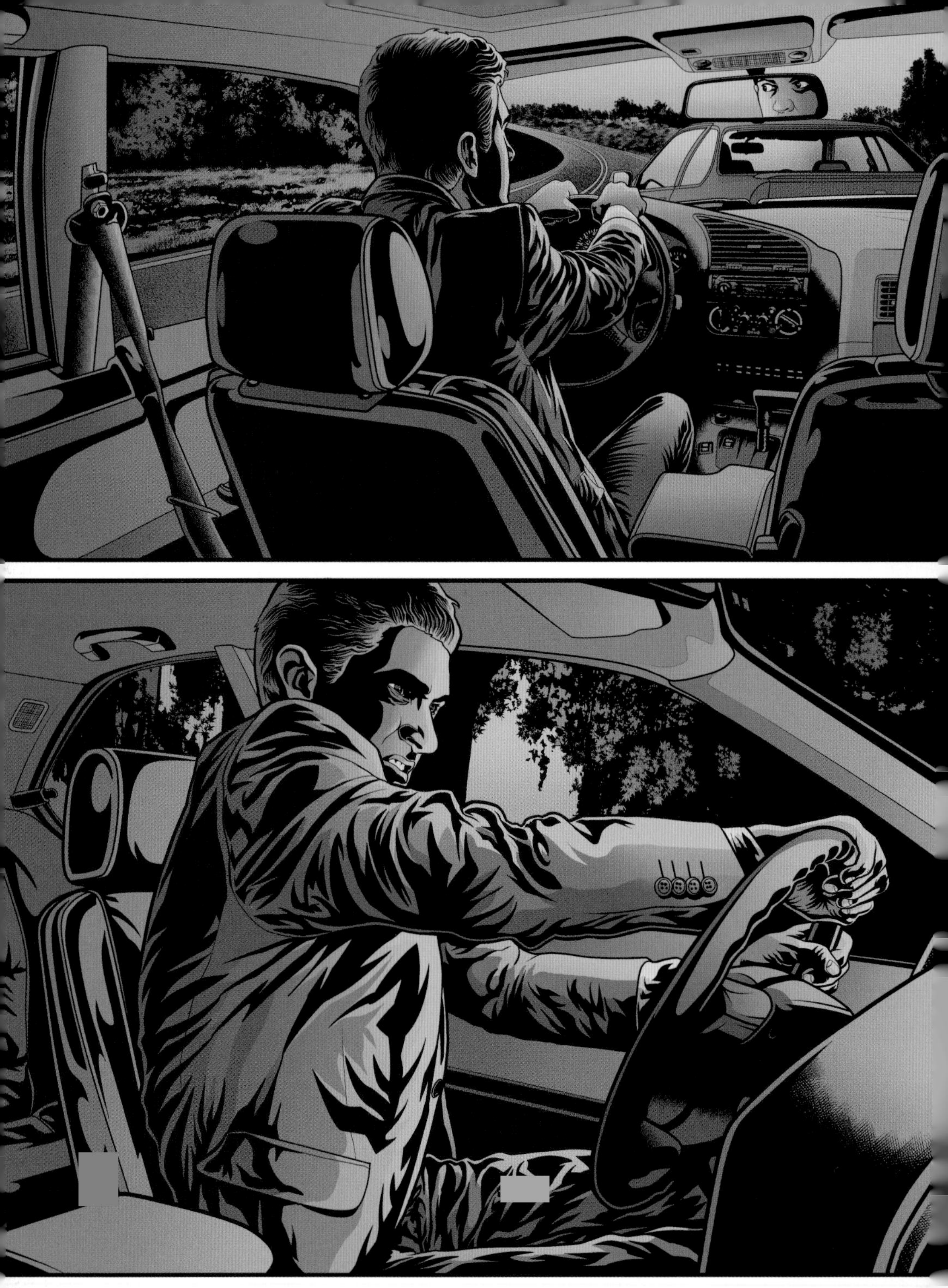

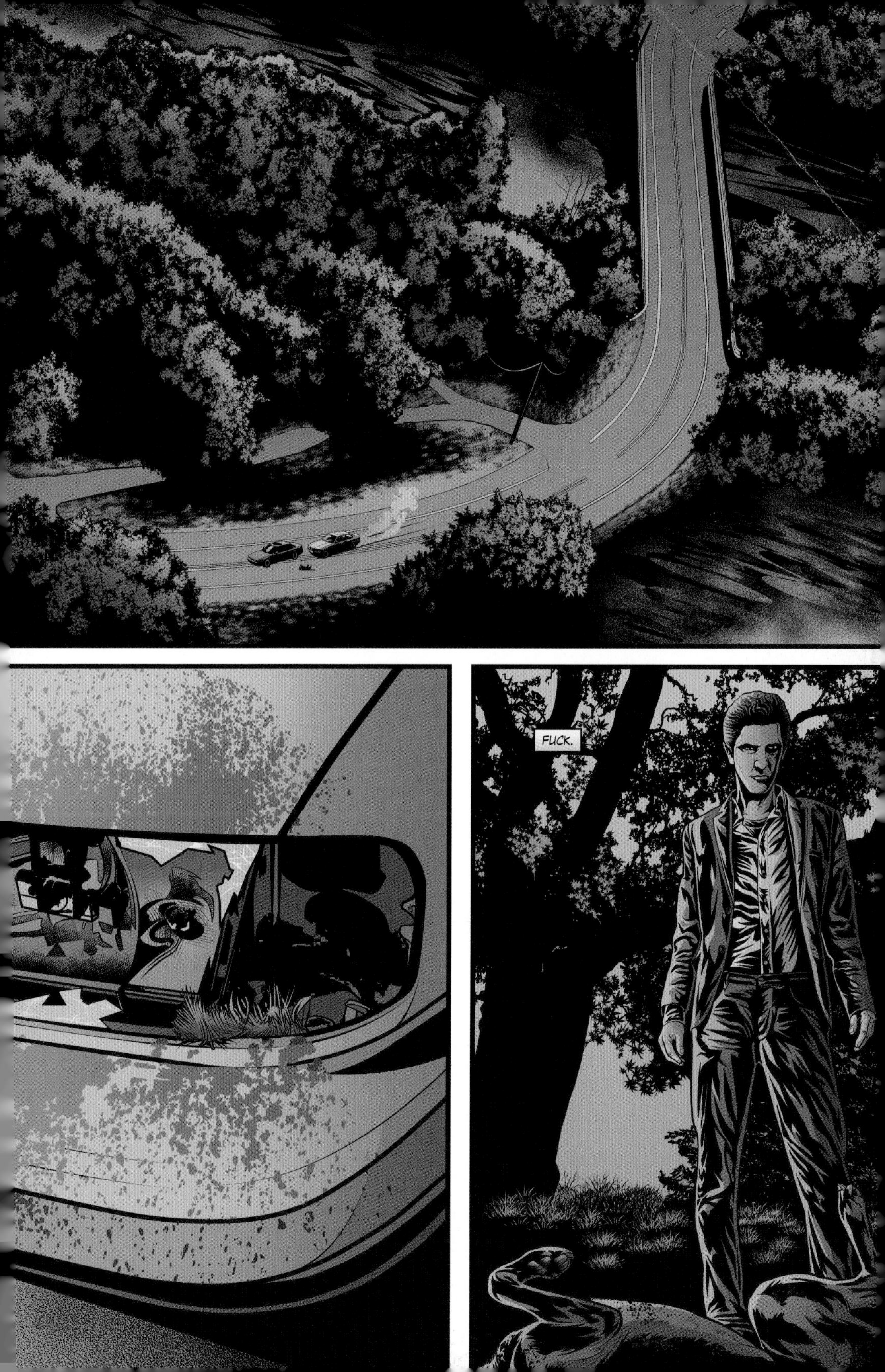
FUCK.

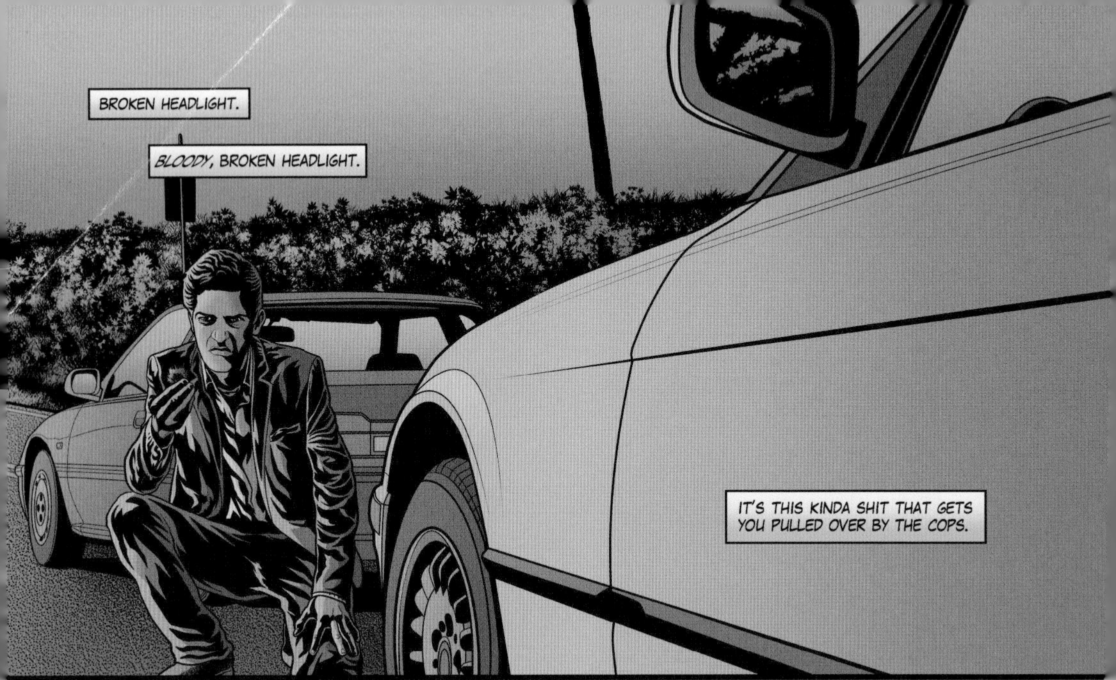
BROKEN HEADLIGHT.
BLOODY, BROKEN HEADLIGHT.
IT'S THIS KINDA SHIT THAT GETS YOU PULLED OVER BY THE COPS.
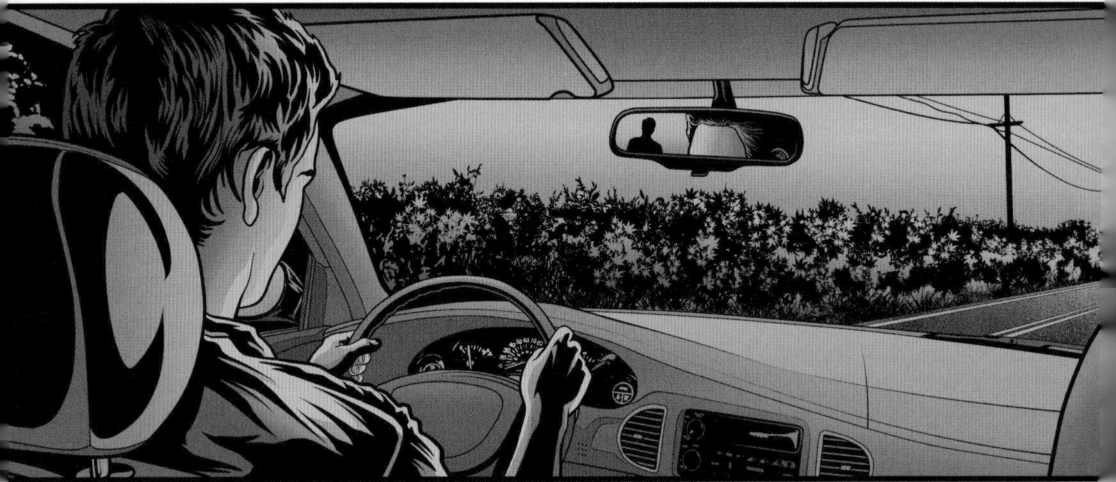
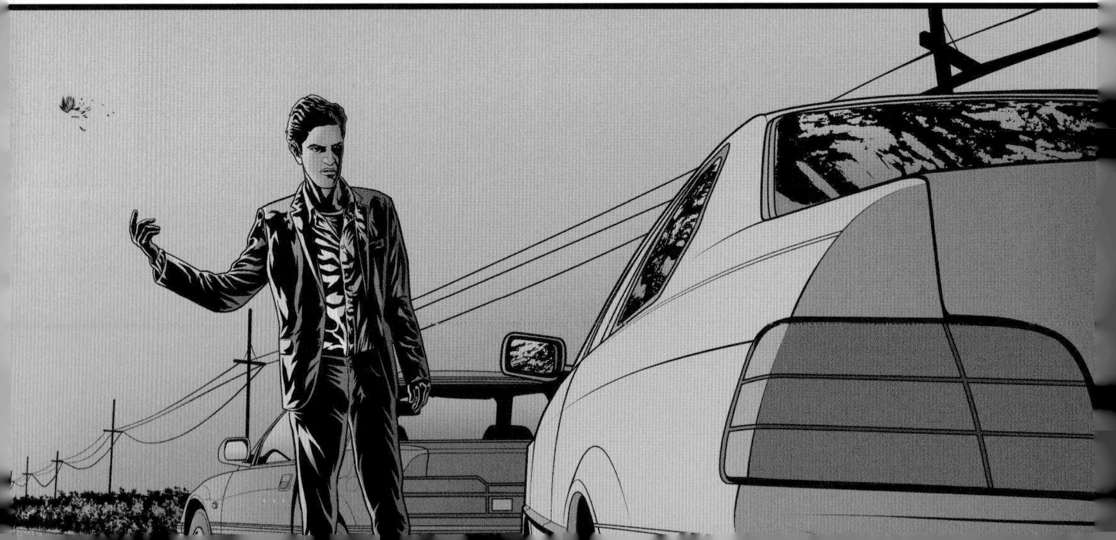

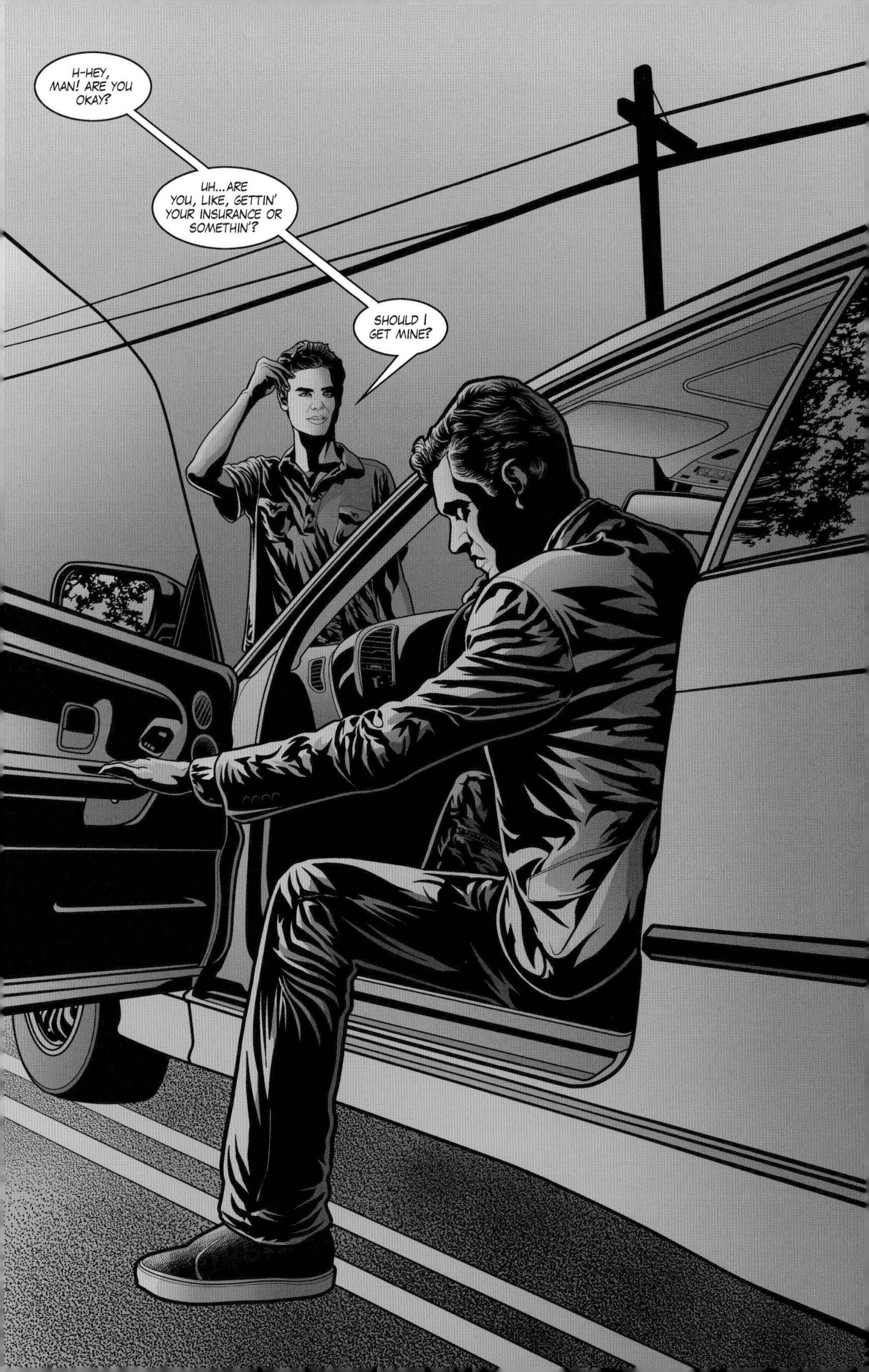
H-HEY, MAN! ARE YOU OKAY?
UH...ARE YOU, LIKE, GETTIN' YOUR INSURANCE OR SOMETHIN'?
SHOULD I GET MINE?

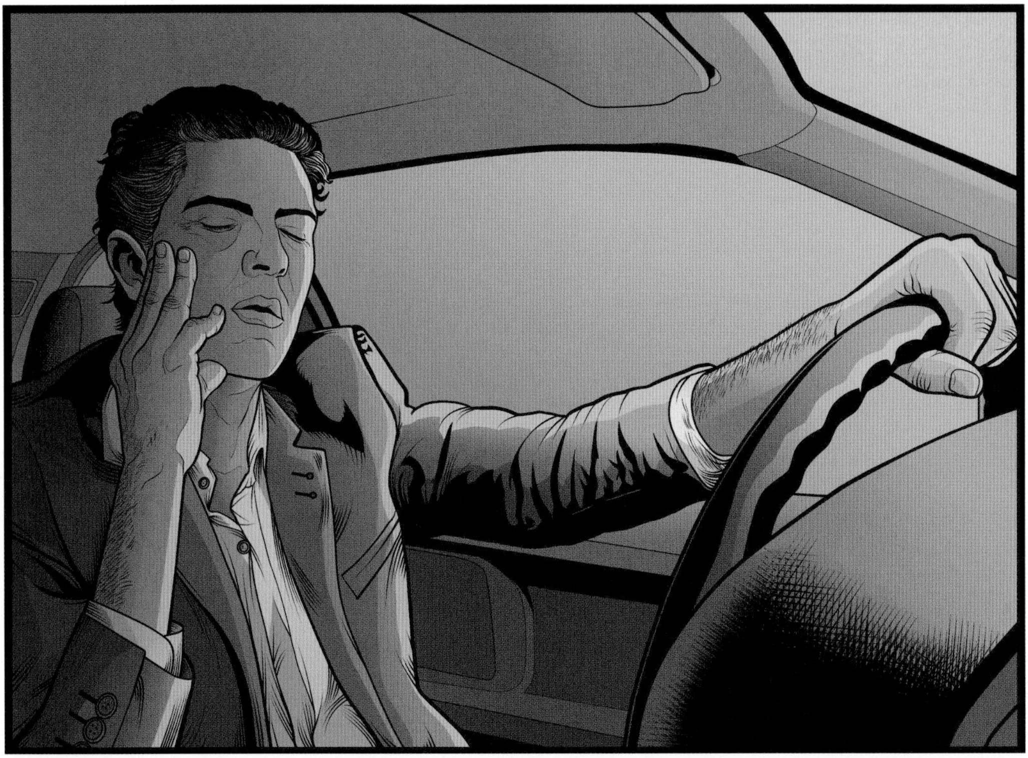

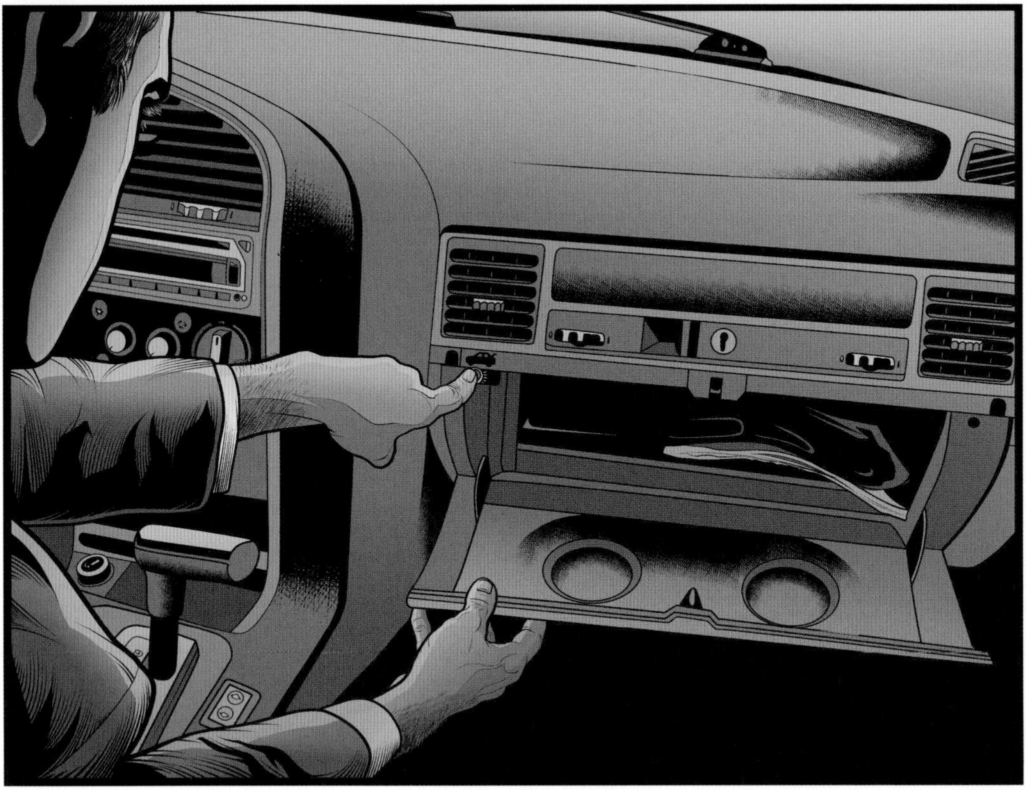

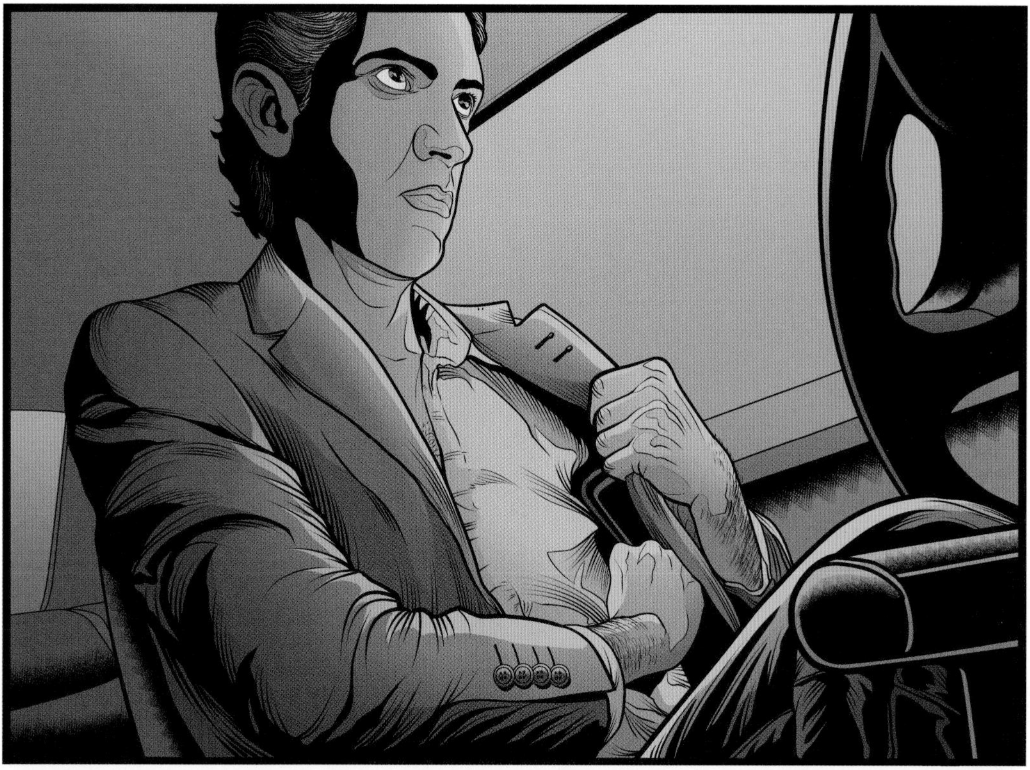

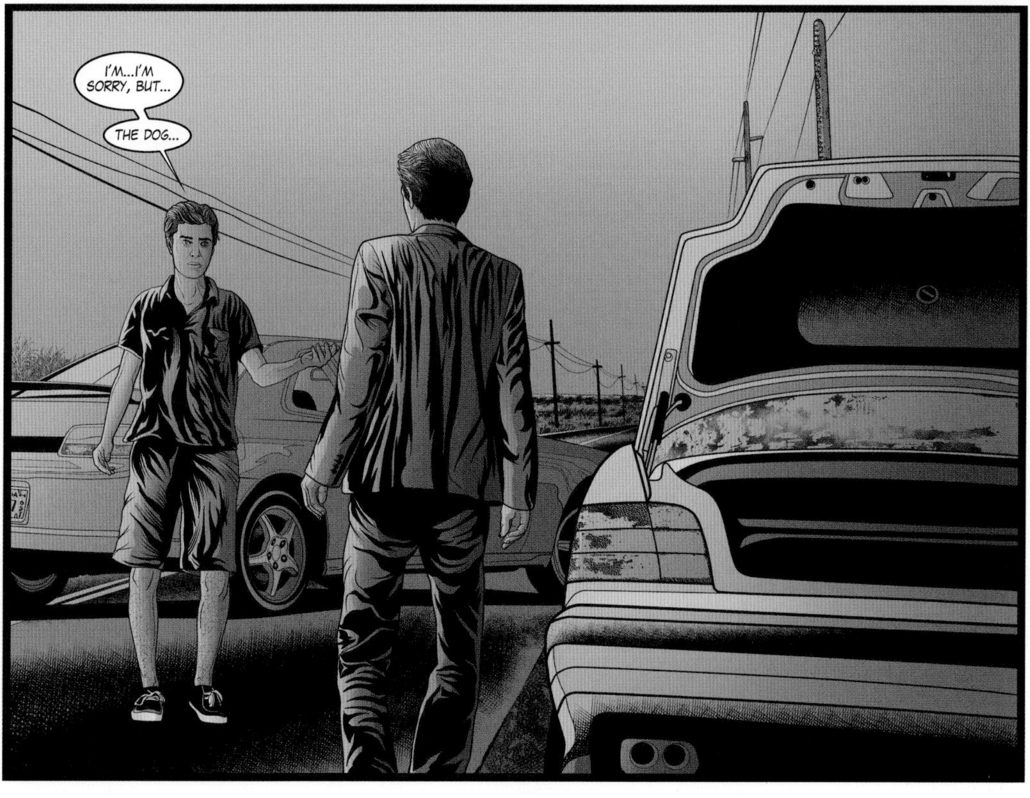
I'M...I'M SORRY, BUT...
THE DOG...

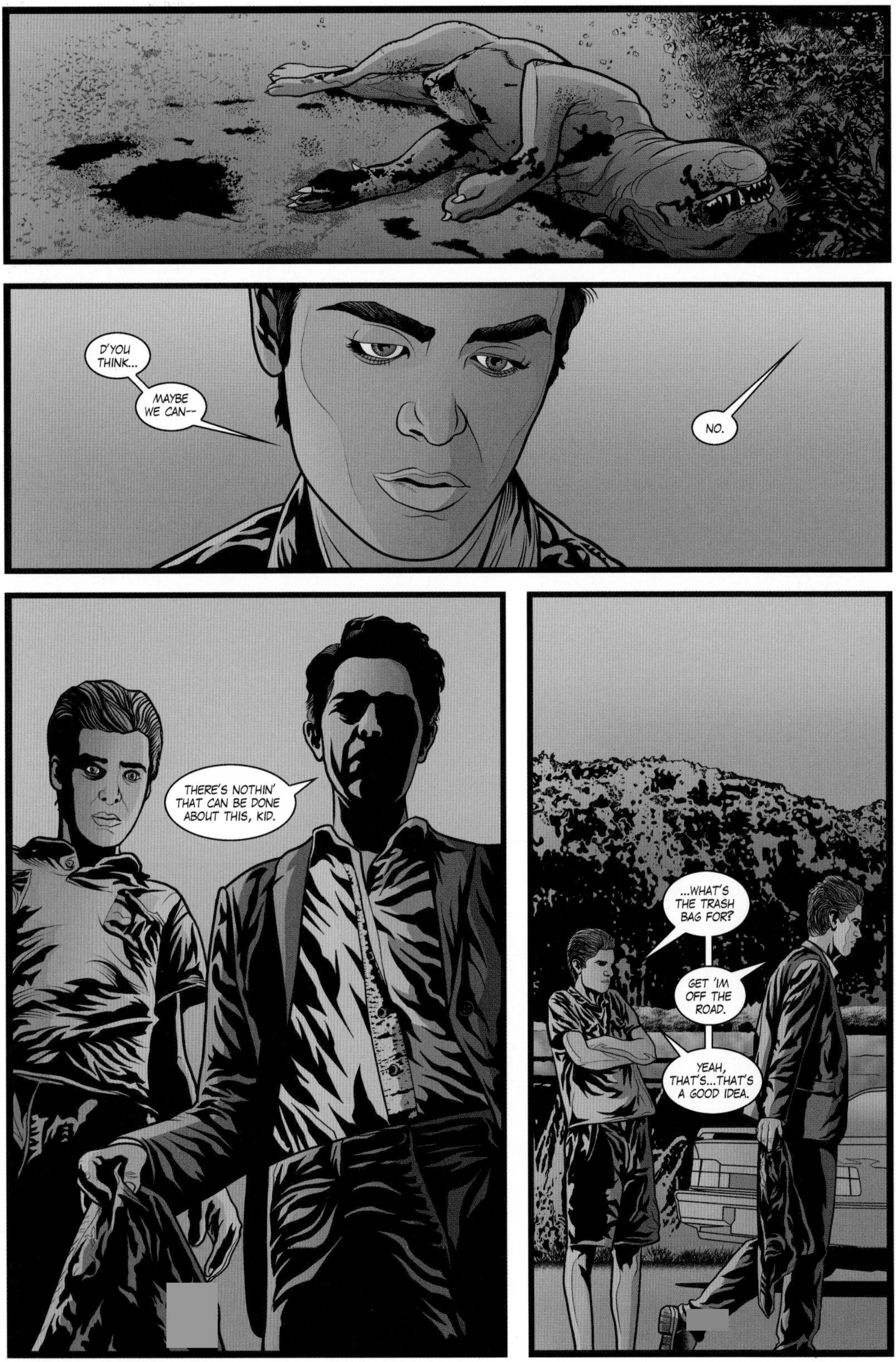
D'YOU THINK...
MAYBE WE CAN--
NO.
THERE'S NOTHIN' THAT CAN BE DONE ABOUT THIS, KID.
...WHAT'S THE TRASH BAG FOR?
GET 'IM OFF THE ROAD.
YEAH, THAT'S...THAT'S A GOOD IDEA.

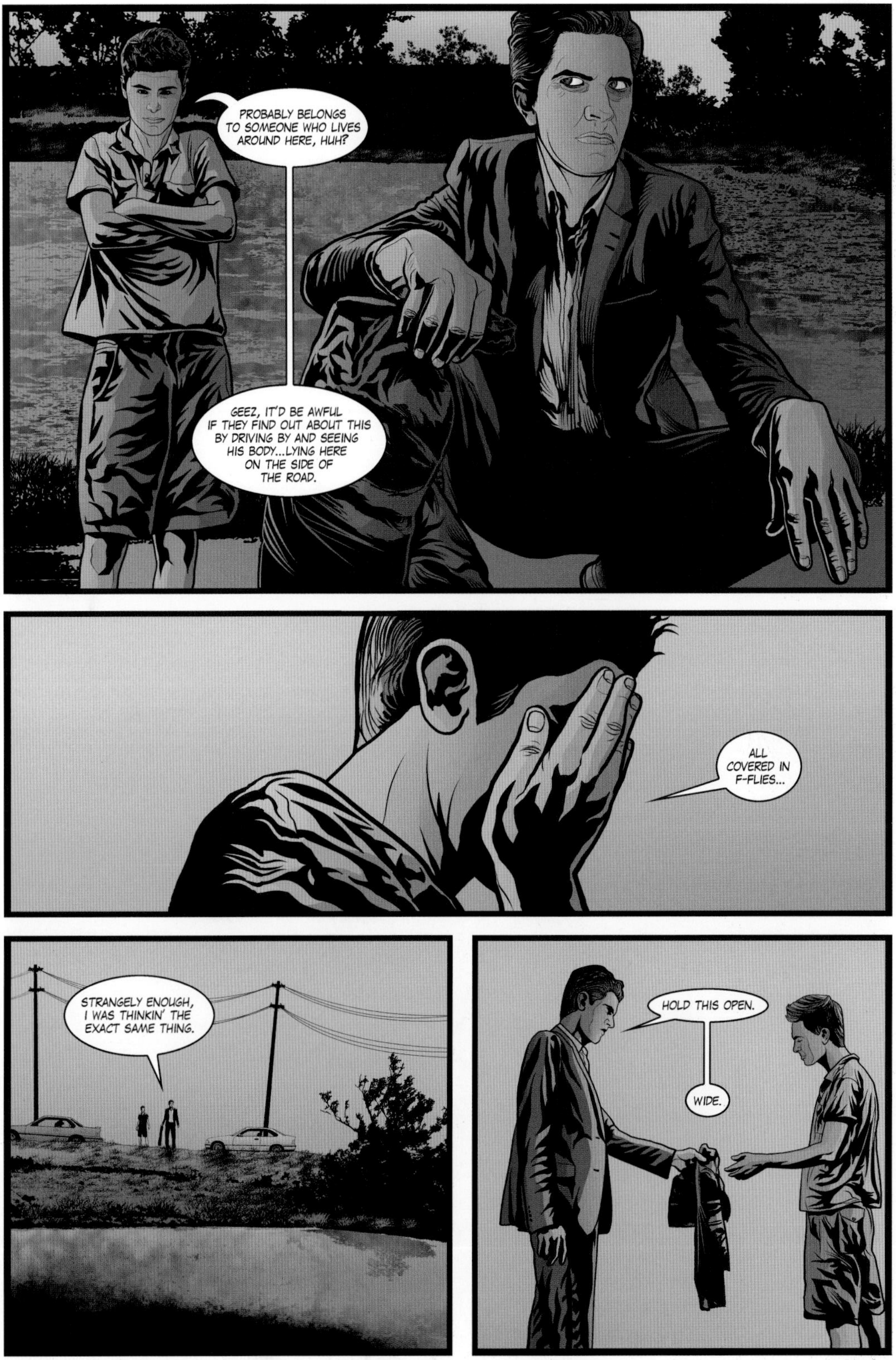
PROBABLY BELONGS TO SOMEONE WHO LIVES AROUND HERE, HUH?
GEEZ, IT'D BE AWFUL IF THEY FIND OUT ABOUT THIS BY DRIVING BY AND SEEING HIS BODY...LYING HERE ON THE SIDE OF THE ROAD.
ALL COVERED IN F-FLIES...
STRANGELY ENOUGH, I WAS THINKIN' THE EXACT SAME THING.
HOLD THIS OPEN.
WIDE.

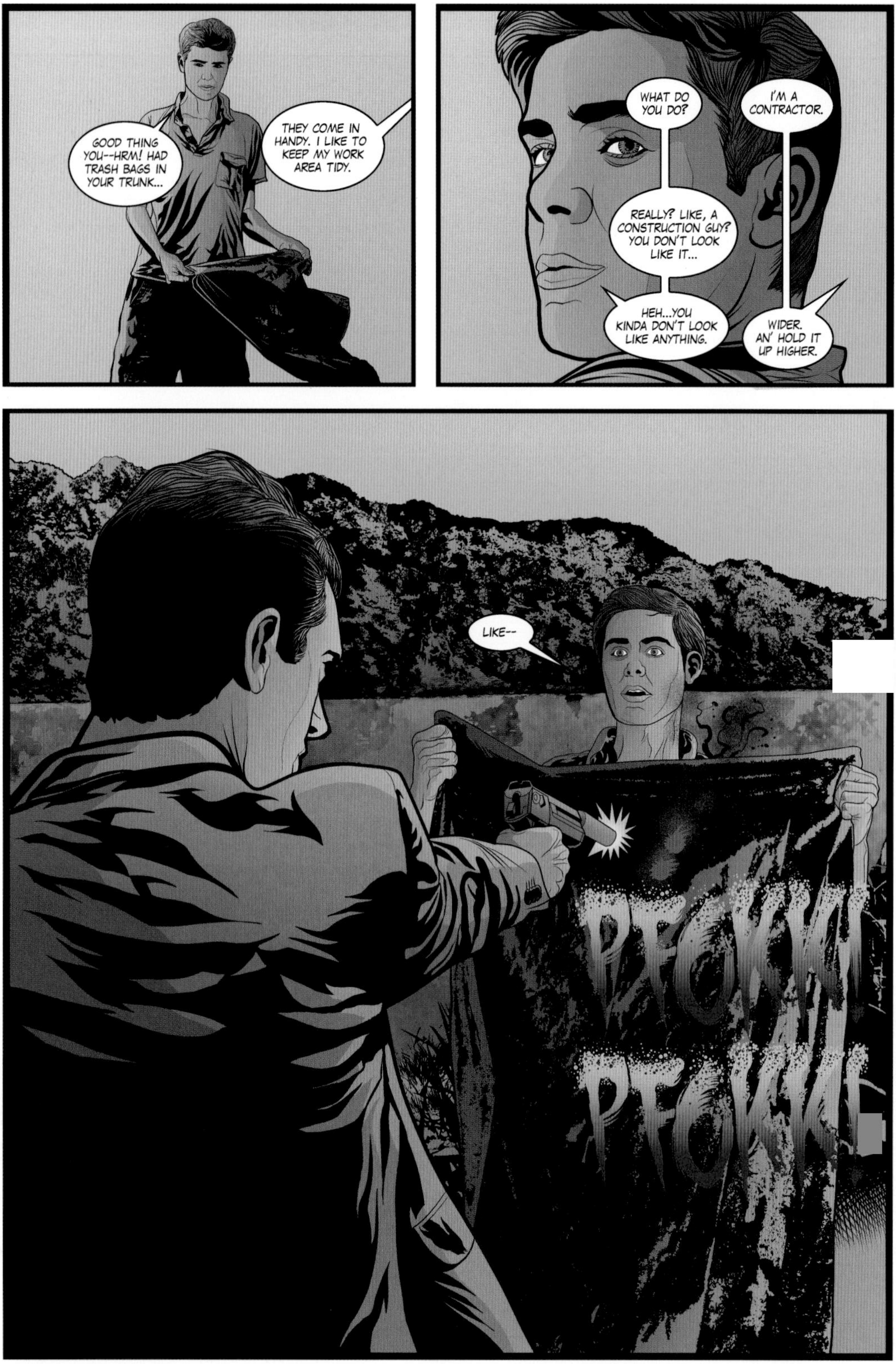
GOOD THING YOU--HRM! HAD TRASH BAGS IN YOUR TRUNK...
THEY COME IN HANDY. I LIKE TO KEEP MY WORK AREA TIDY.
WHAT DO YOU DO?
I'M A CONTRACTOR.
REALLY? LIKE, A CONSTRUCTION GUY? YOU DON'T LOOK LIKE IT...
HEH...YOU KINDA DON'T LOOK LIKE ANYTHING.
WIDER. AN' HOLD IT UP HIGHER.
LIKE--
PFOKK! PFOKK!

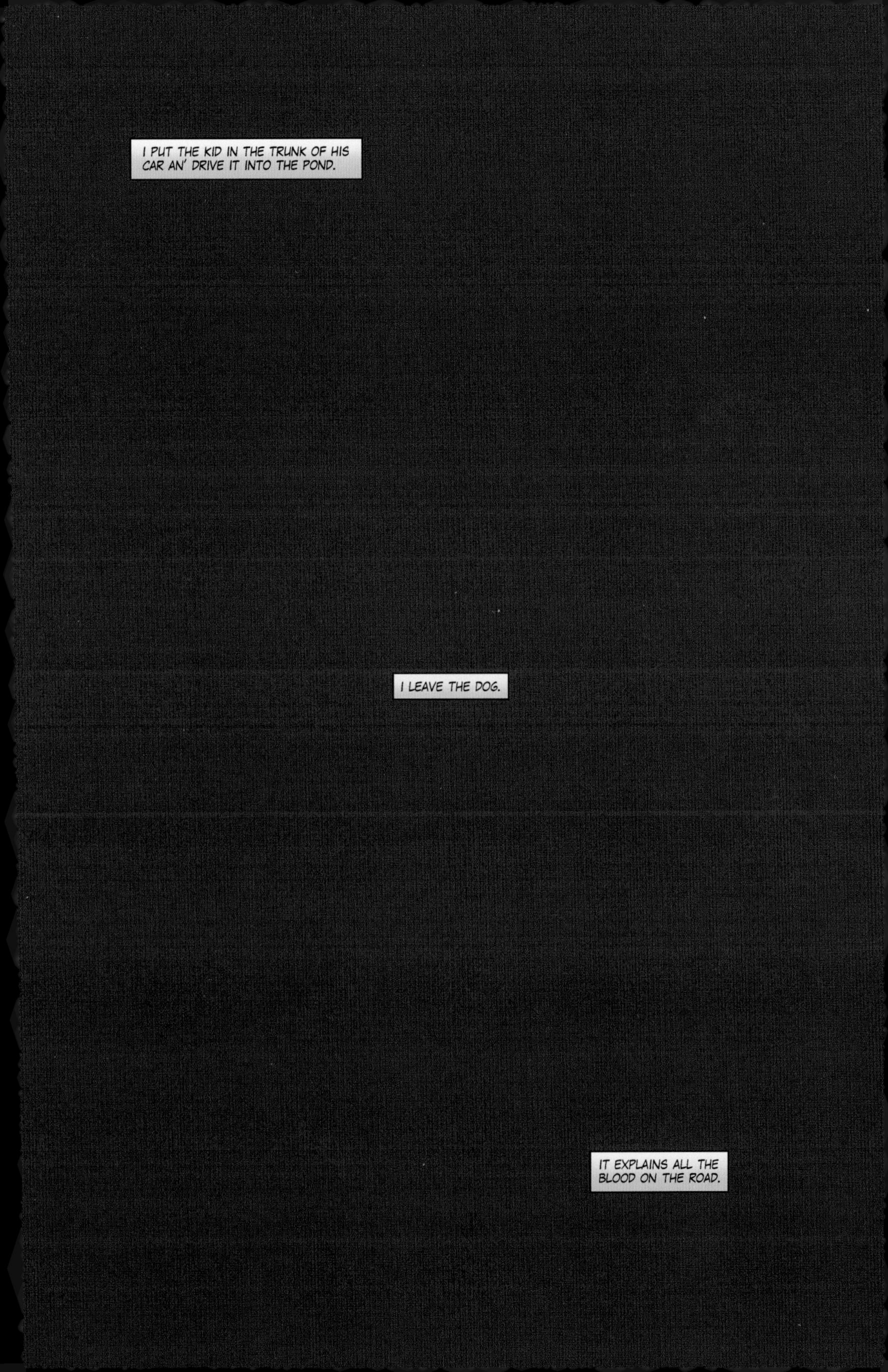
I PUT THE KID IN THE TRUNK OF HIS CAR AN' DRIVE IT INTO THE POND.
I LEAVE THE DOG.
IT EXPLAINS ALL THE BLOOD ON THE ROAD.

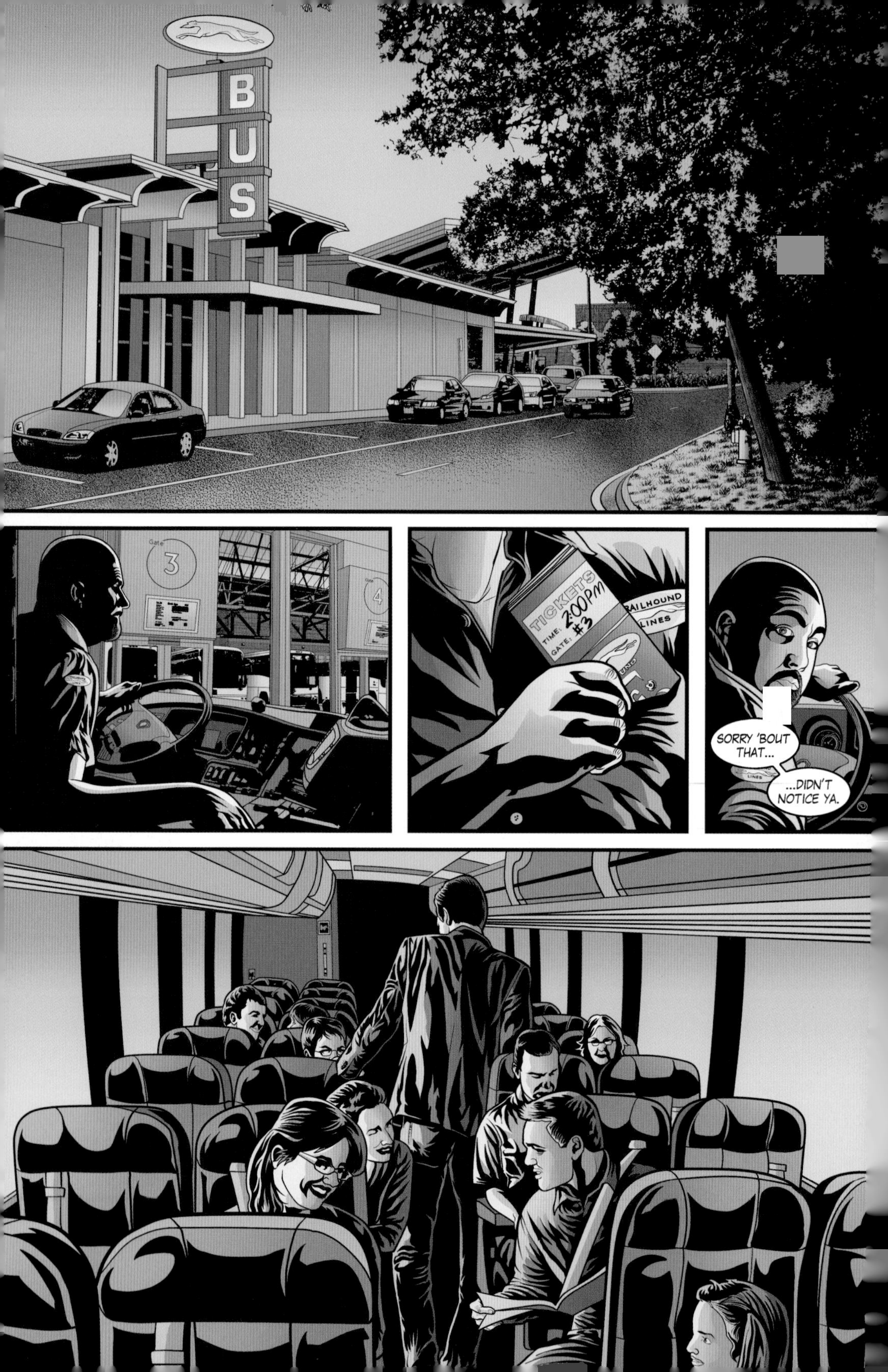
BUS
Gate 3
Gate 4
RAILHOUND LINES
TICKETS
TIME: 2:00PM
GATE: #3
SORRY 'BOUT THAT...
...DIDN'T NOTICE YA.

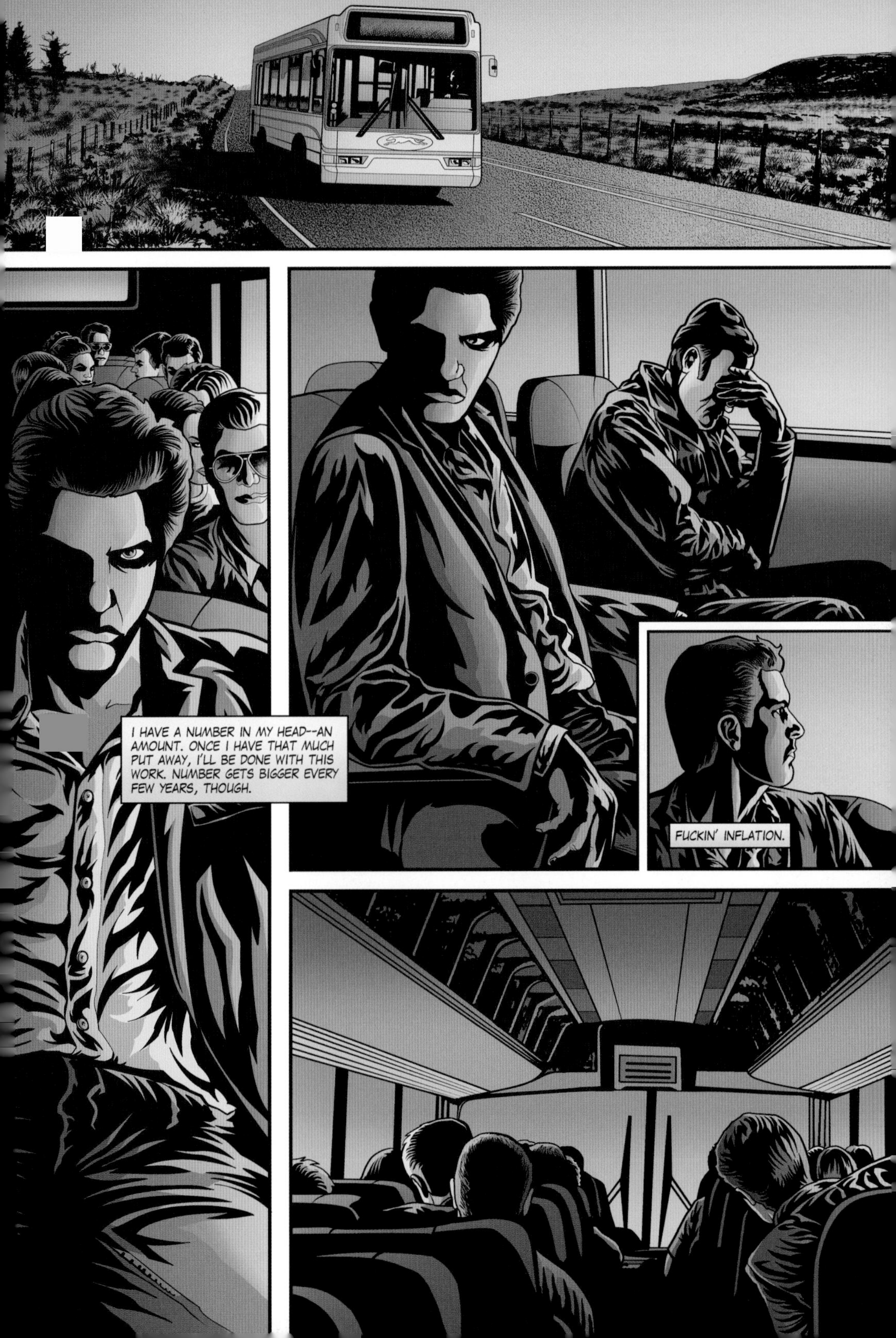
I HAVE A NUMBER IN MY HEAD--AN AMOUNT. ONCE I HAVE THAT MUCH PUT AWAY, I'LL BE DONE WITH THIS WORK. NUMBER GETS BIGGER EVERY FEW YEARS, THOUGH.
FUCKIN' INFLATION.

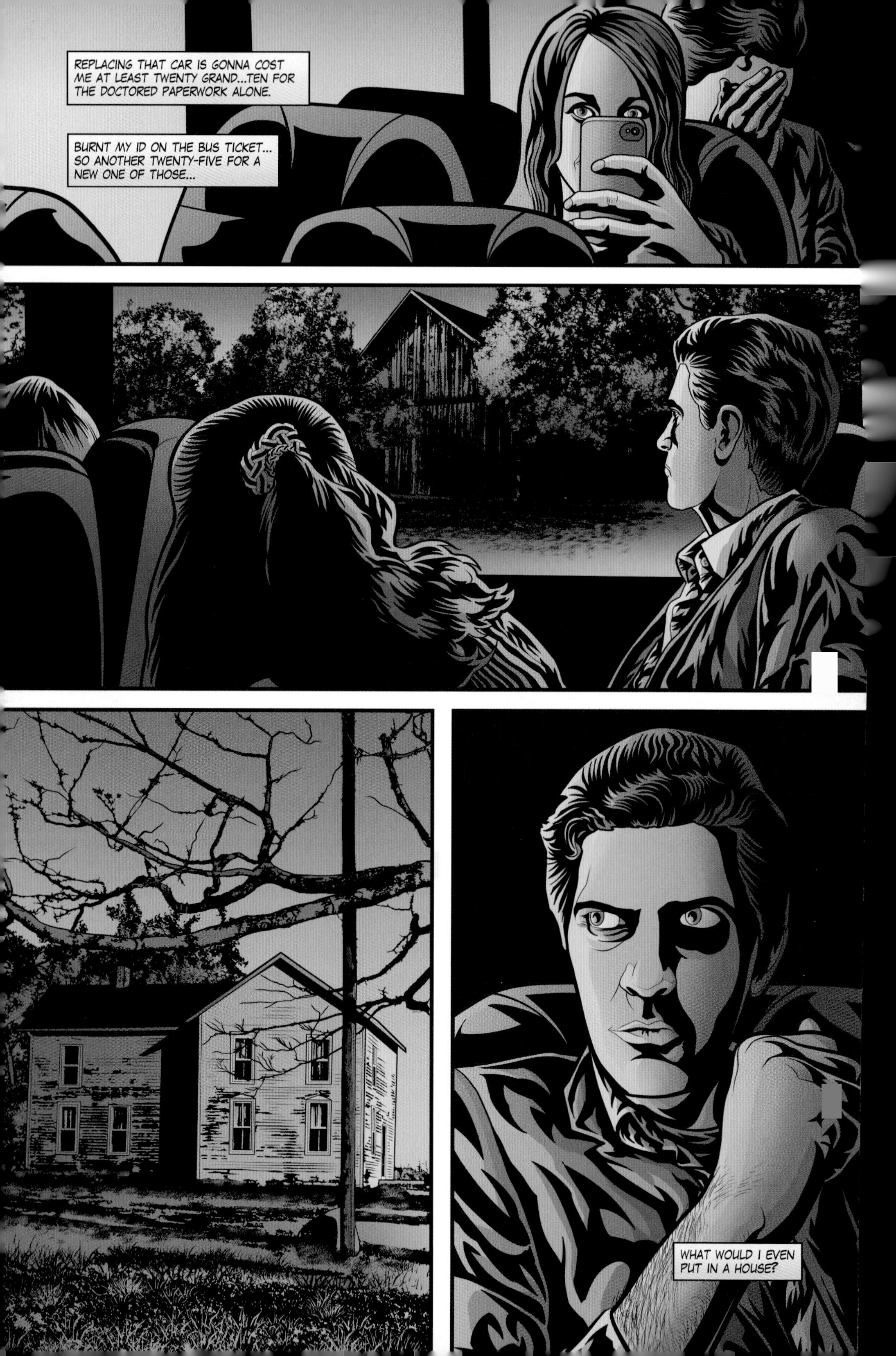
REPLACING THAT CAR IS GONNA COST ME AT LEAST TWENTY GRAND...TEN FOR THE DOCTORED PAPERWORK ALONE.
BURNT MY ID ON THE BUS TICKET... SO ANOTHER TWENTY-FIVE FOR A NEW ONE OF THOSE...
WHAT WOULD I EVEN PUT IN A HOUSE?

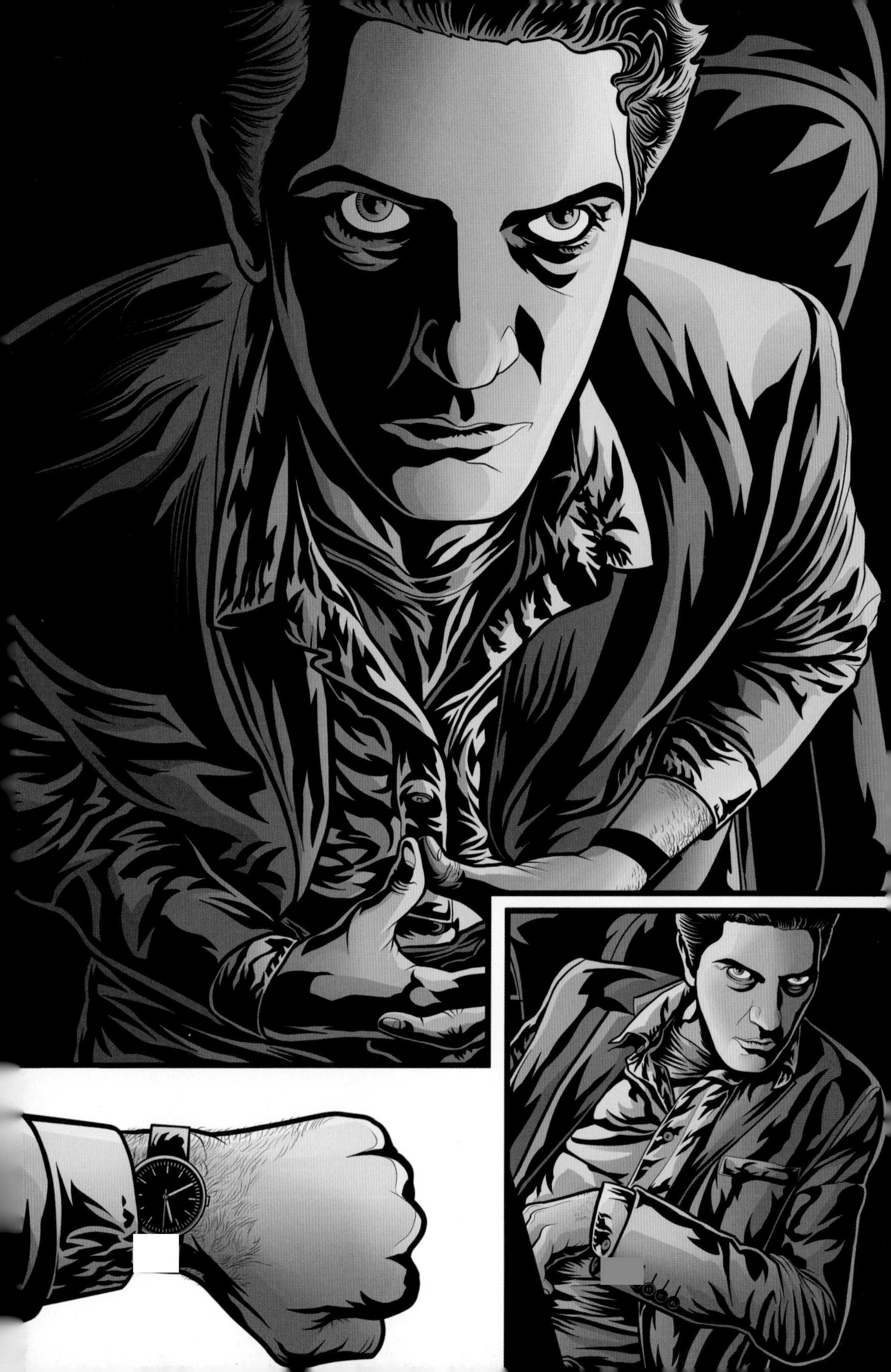

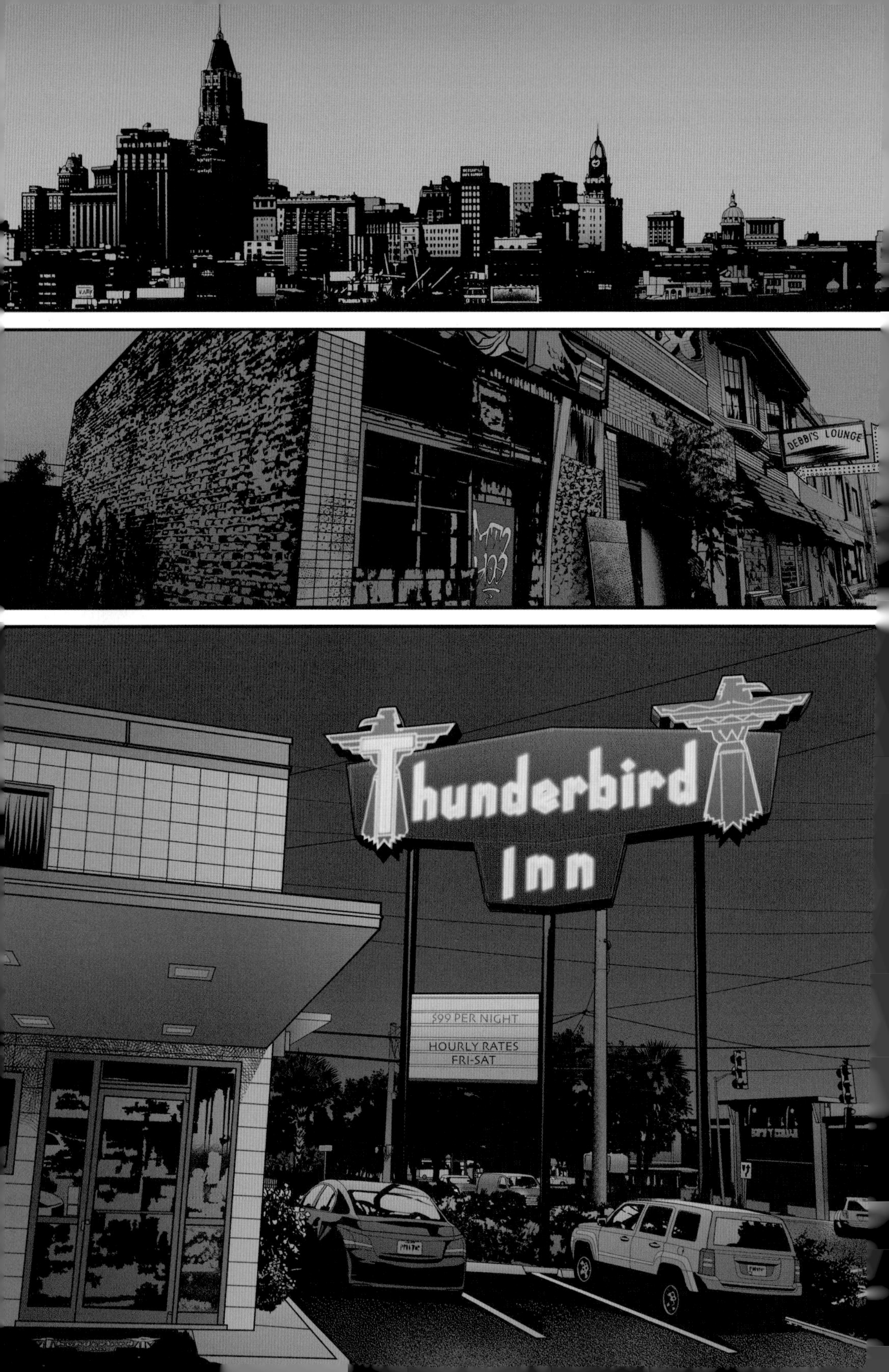
DEBBI'S LOUNGE
Thunderbird Inn
$99 PER NIGHT
HOURLY RATES
FRI-SAT

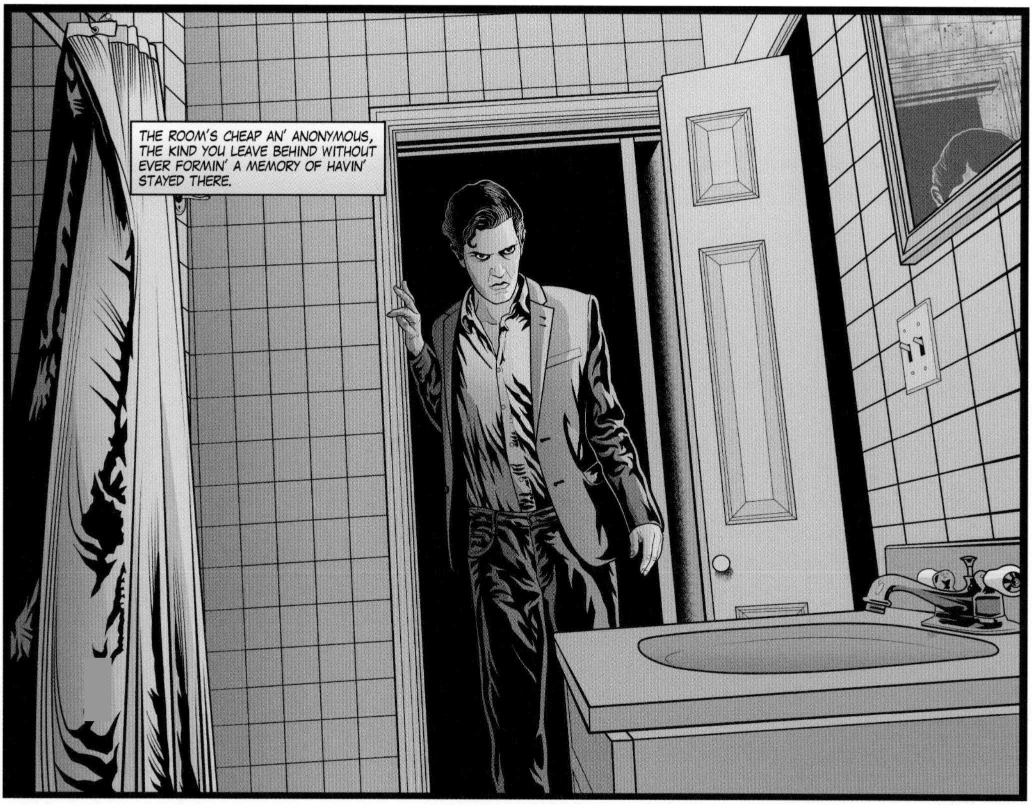
THE ROOM'S CHEAP AN' ANONYMOUS, THE KIND YOU LEAVE BEHIND WITHOUT EVER FORMIN' A MEMORY OF HAVIN' STAYED THERE.

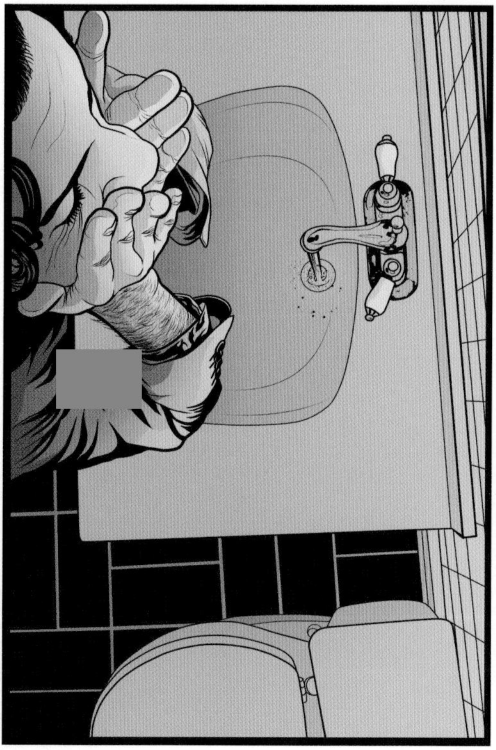

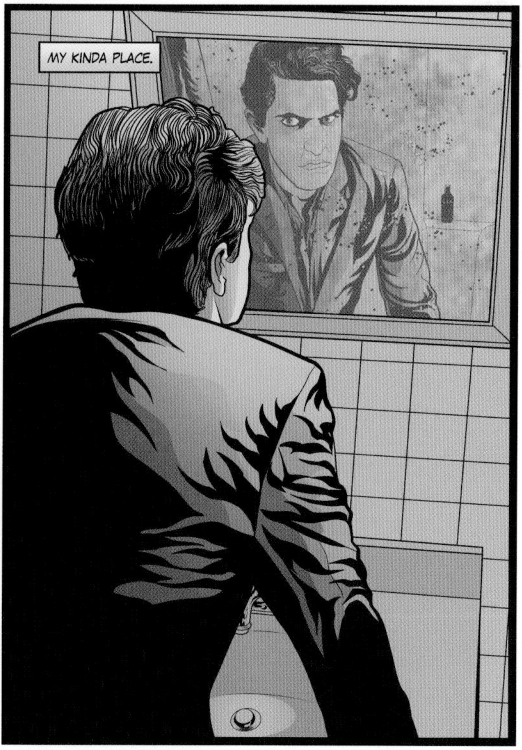
MY KINDA PLACE.

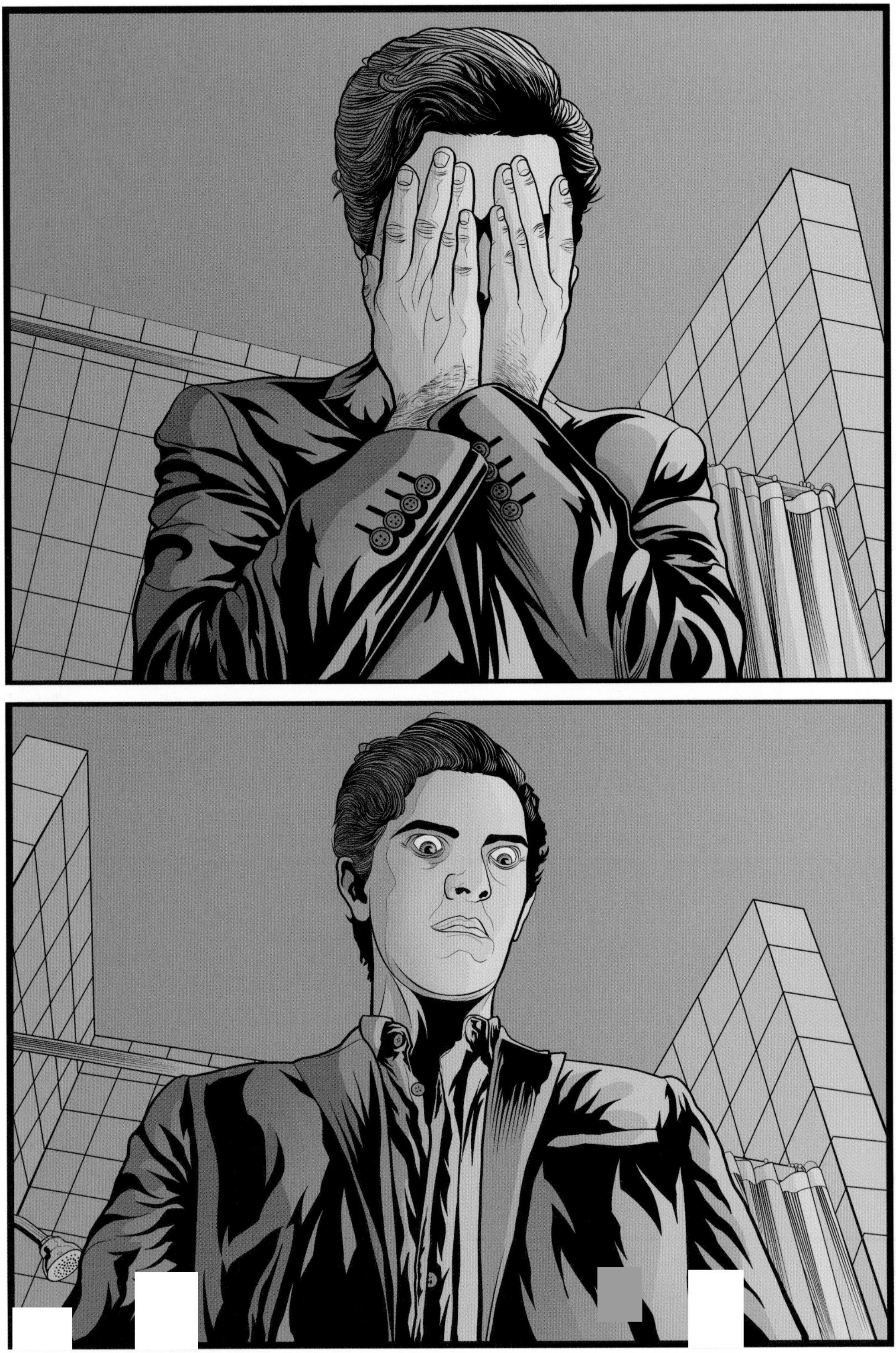

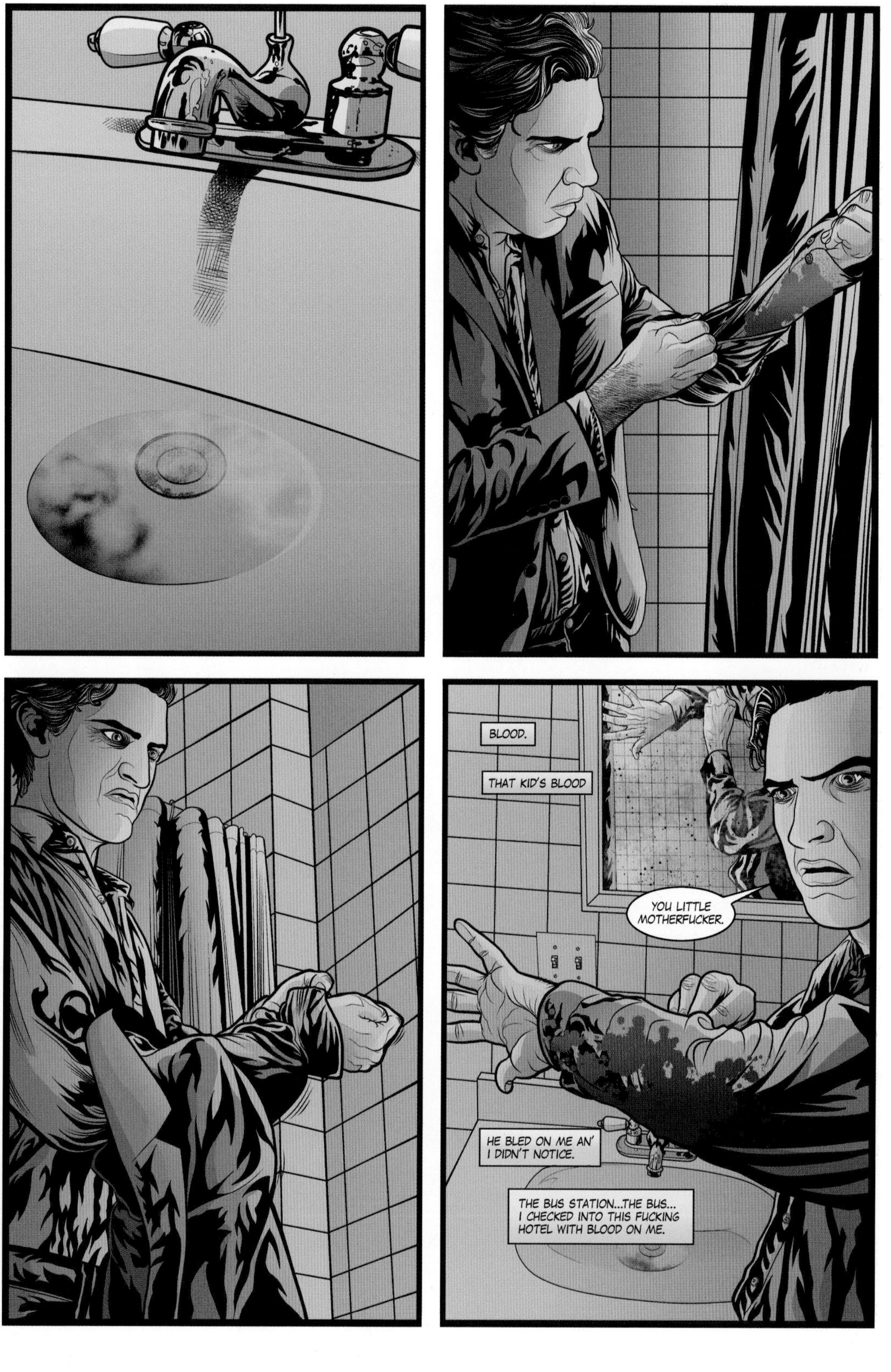
BLOOD.
THAT KID'S BLOOD
YOU LITTLE MOTHERFUCKER.
HE BLED ON ME AN' I DIDN'T NOTICE.
THE BUS STATION...THE BUS... I CHECKED INTO THIS FUCKING HOTEL WITH BLOOD ON ME.

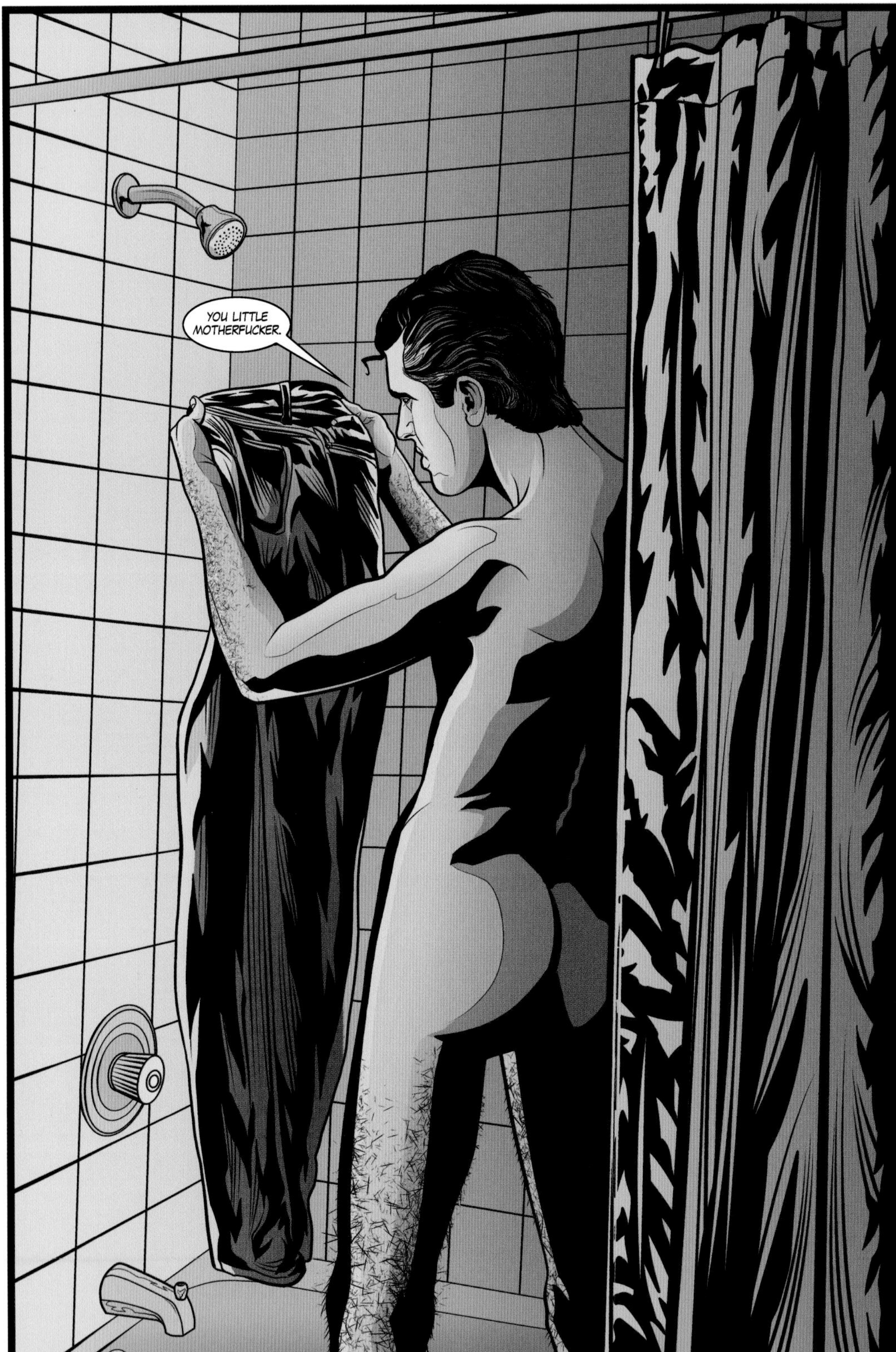
YOU LITTLE MOTHERFUCKER.

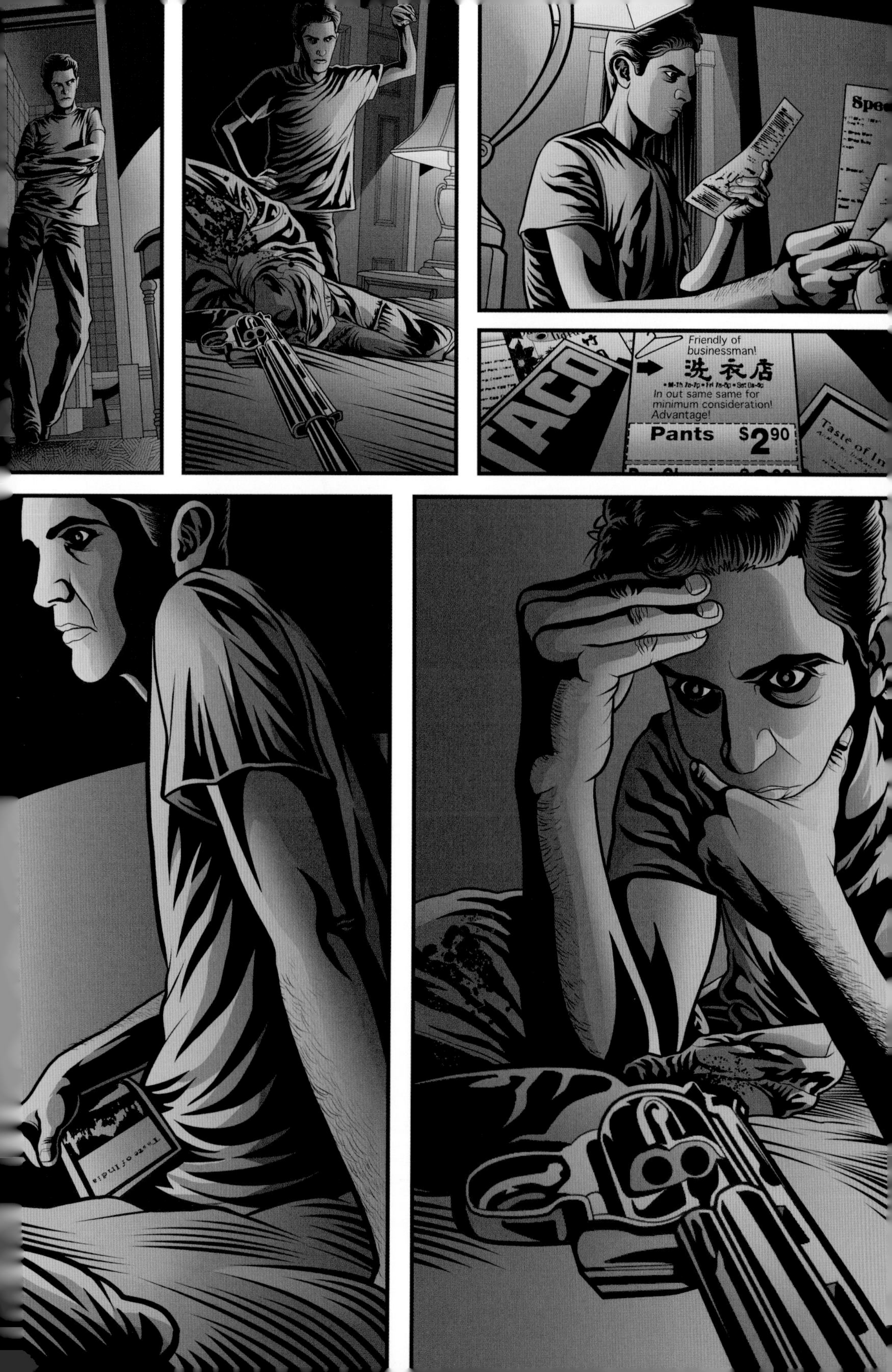
ACO
Friendly of businessman!
洗衣店
In out same same for minimum consideration! Advantage!
Pants $2.90
Taste of India

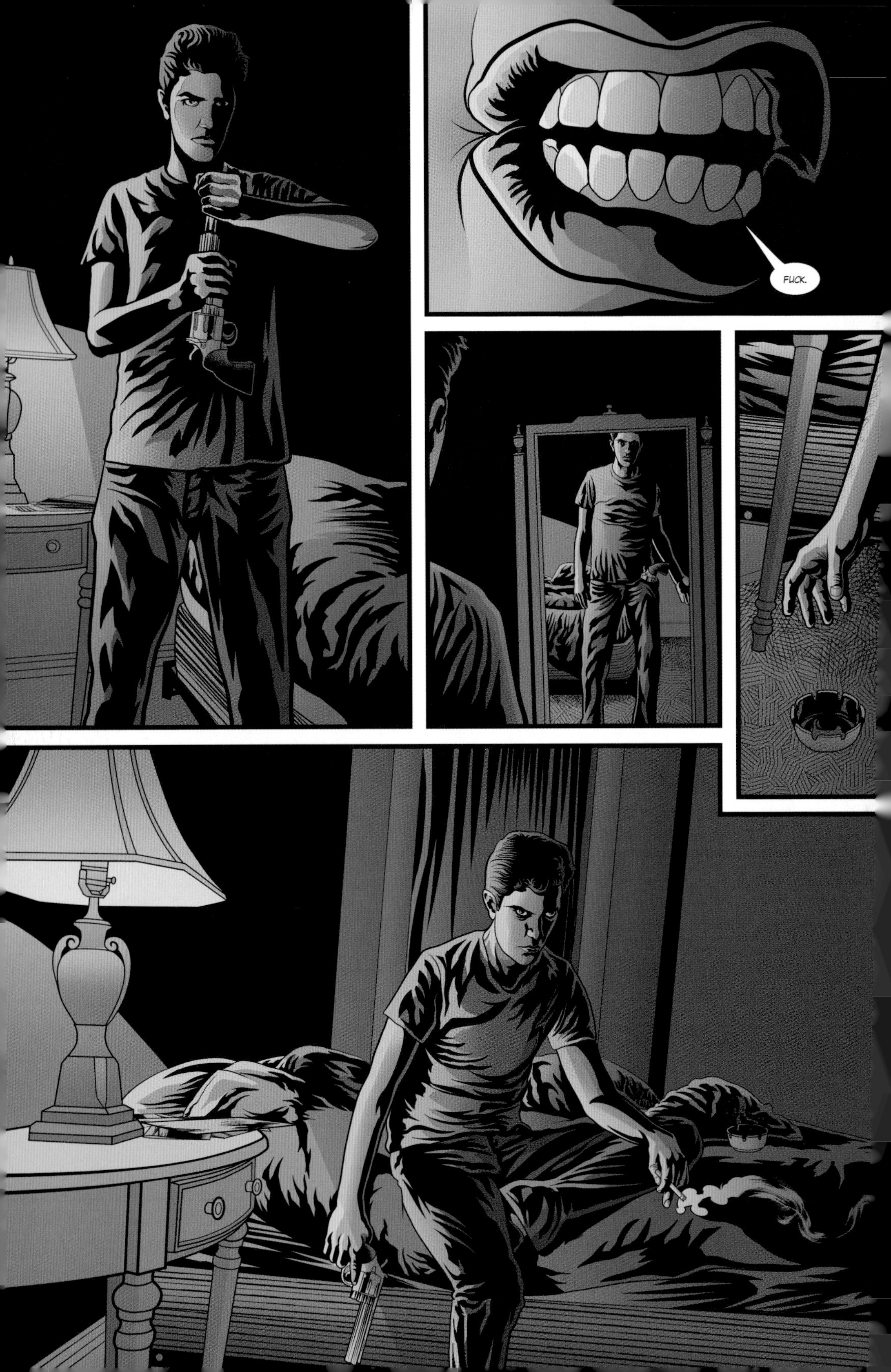
FUCK.

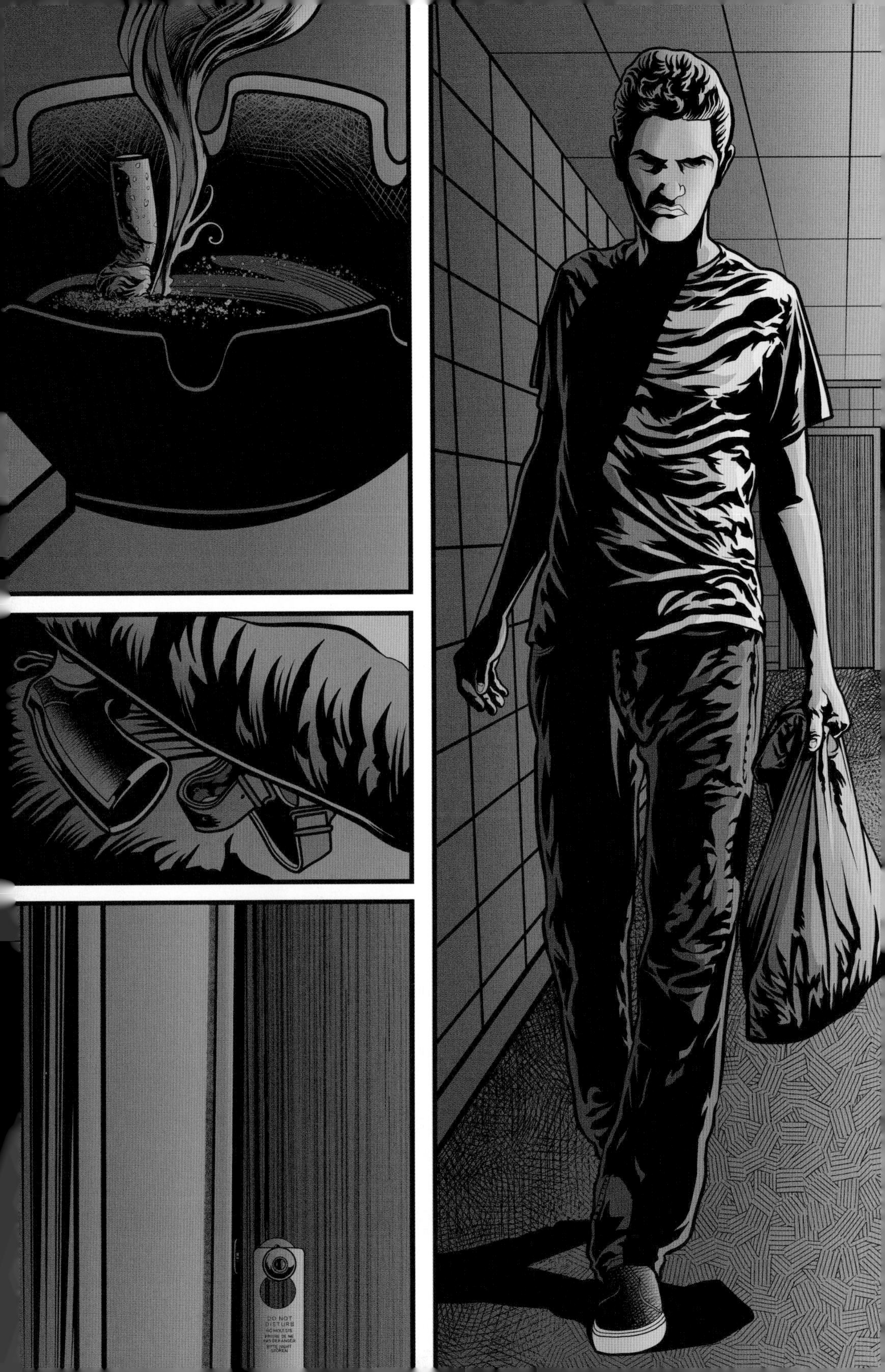
DO NOT
DISTURB

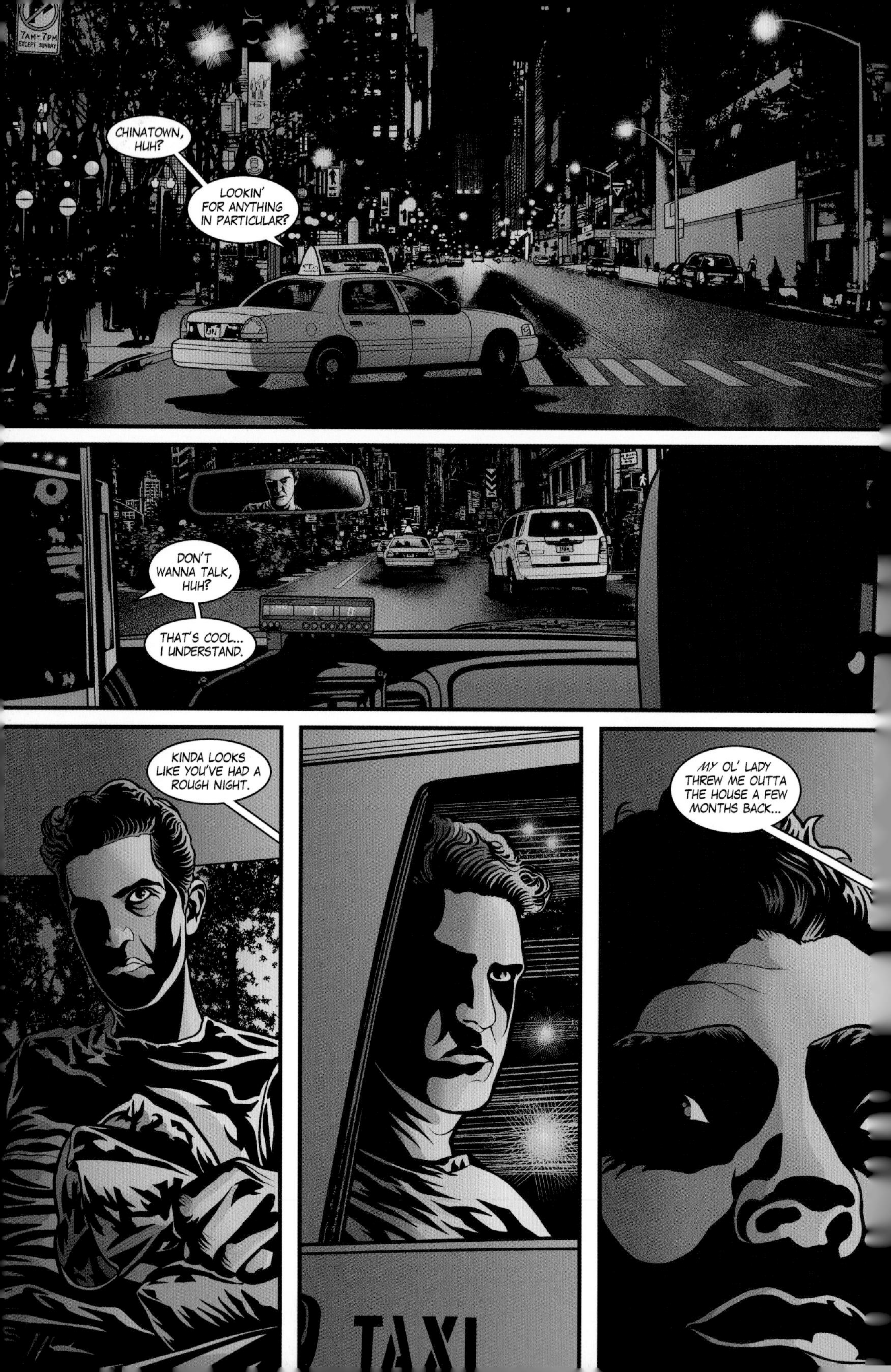
7AM-7PM
EXCEPT SUNDAY
CHINATOWN, HUH?
LOOKIN' FOR ANYTHING IN PARTICULAR?
DON'T WANNA TALK, HUH?
THAT'S COOL... I UNDERSTAND.
KINDA LOOKS LIKE YOU'VE HAD A ROUGH NIGHT.
MY OL' LADY THREW ME OUTTA THE HOUSE A FEW MONTHS BACK...
TAXI

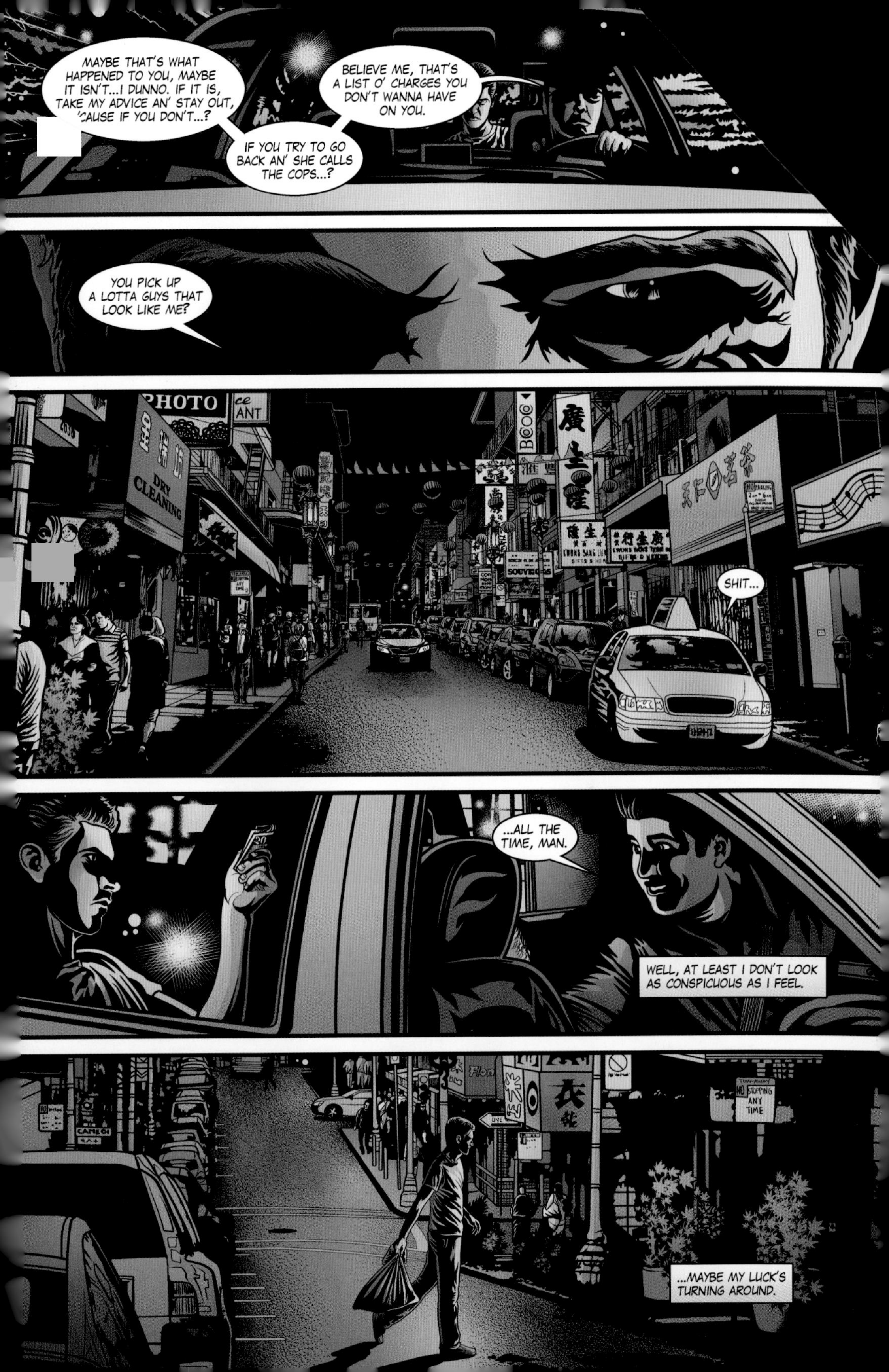

MAYBE THAT'S WHAT HAPPENED TO YOU, MAYBE IT ISN'T...I DUNNO. IF IT IS, TAKE MY ADVICE AN' STAY OUT, 'CAUSE IF YOU DON'T...?
IF YOU TRY TO GO BACK AN' SHE CALLS THE COPS...?
BELIEVE ME, THAT'S A LIST O' CHARGES YOU DON'T WANNA HAVE ON YOU.
YOU PICK UP A LOTTA GUYS THAT LOOK LIKE ME?
PHOTO
DRY CLEANING
SHIT...
...ALL THE TIME, MAN.
WELL, AT LEAST I DON'T LOOK AS CONSPICUOUS AS I FEEL.
NO STOPPING ANY TIME
...MAYBE MY LUCK'S TURNING AROUND.

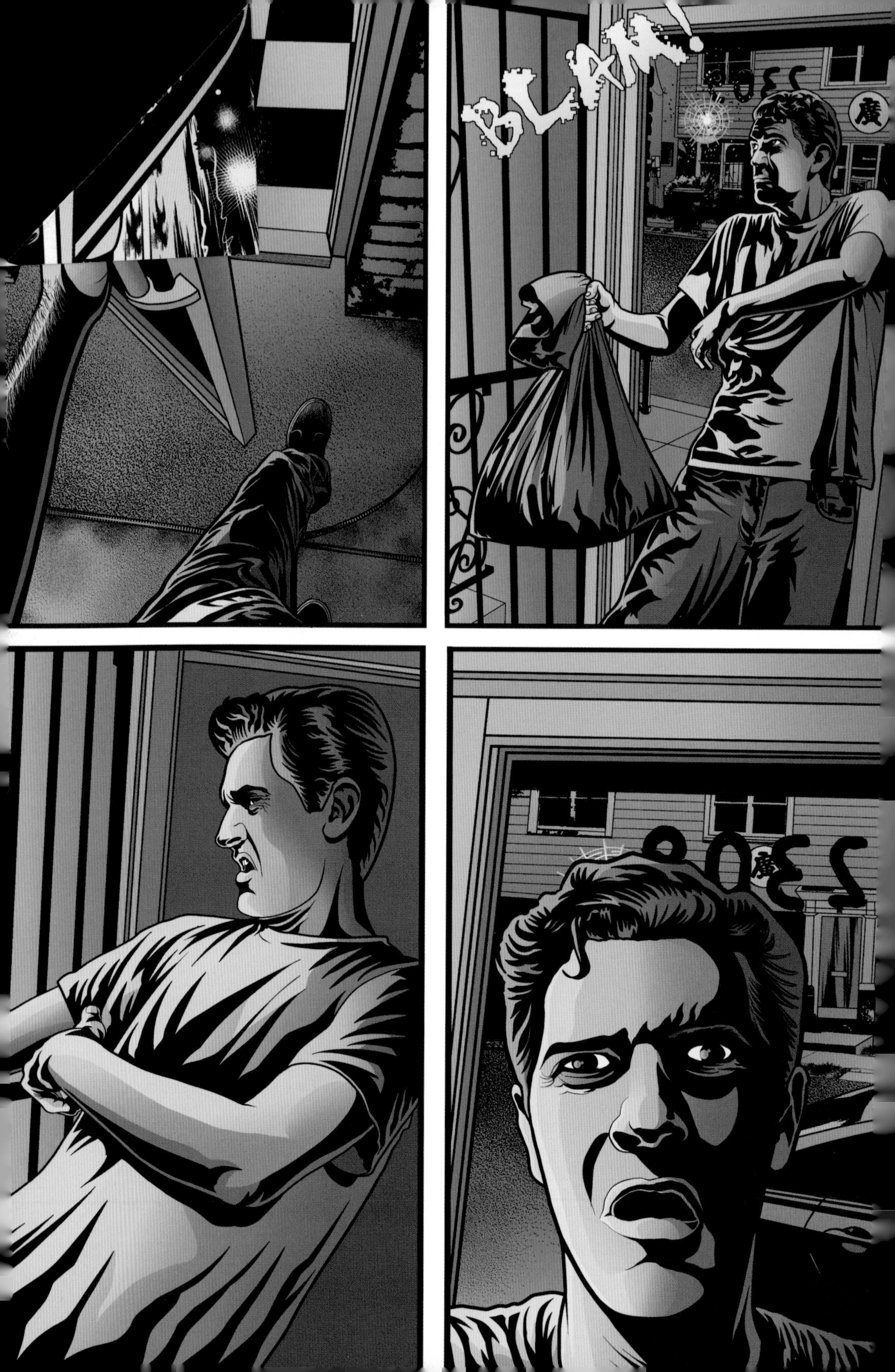
BLAM!

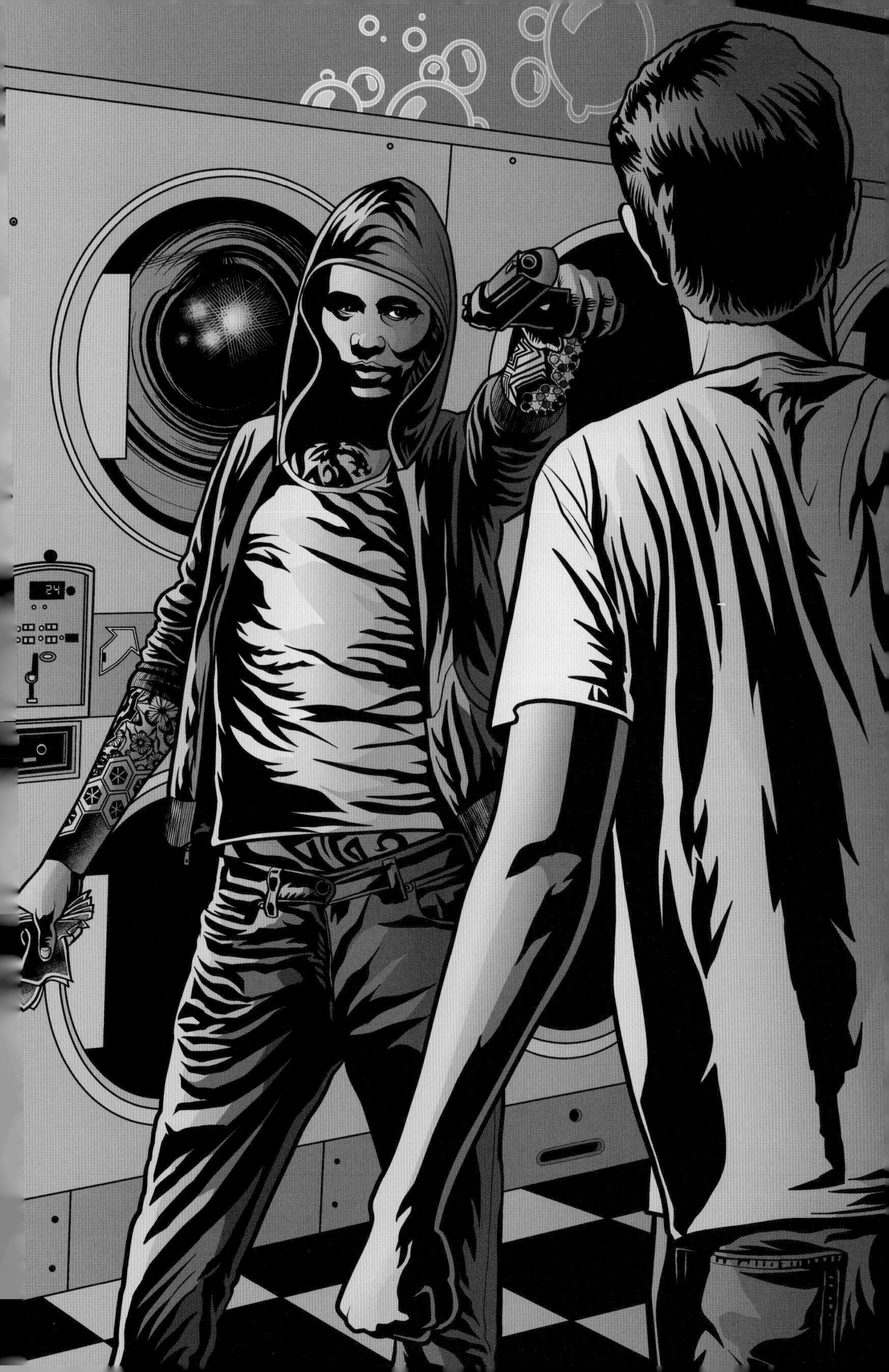
24

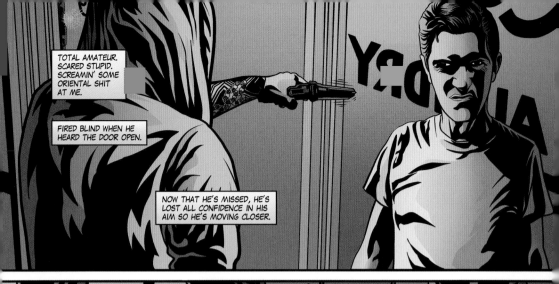

TOTAL AMATEUR. SCARED STUPID. SCREAMIN' SOME ORIENTAL SHIT AT ME.

FIRED BLIND WHEN HE HEARD THE DOOR OPEN.

NOW THAT HE'S MISSED, HE'S LOST ALL CONFIDENCE IN HIS AIM SO HE'S MOVING CLOSER.

I DO THE SAME.

BECAUSE I'VE YET TO SEE A PISTOL THAT FIRES BACKWARD.

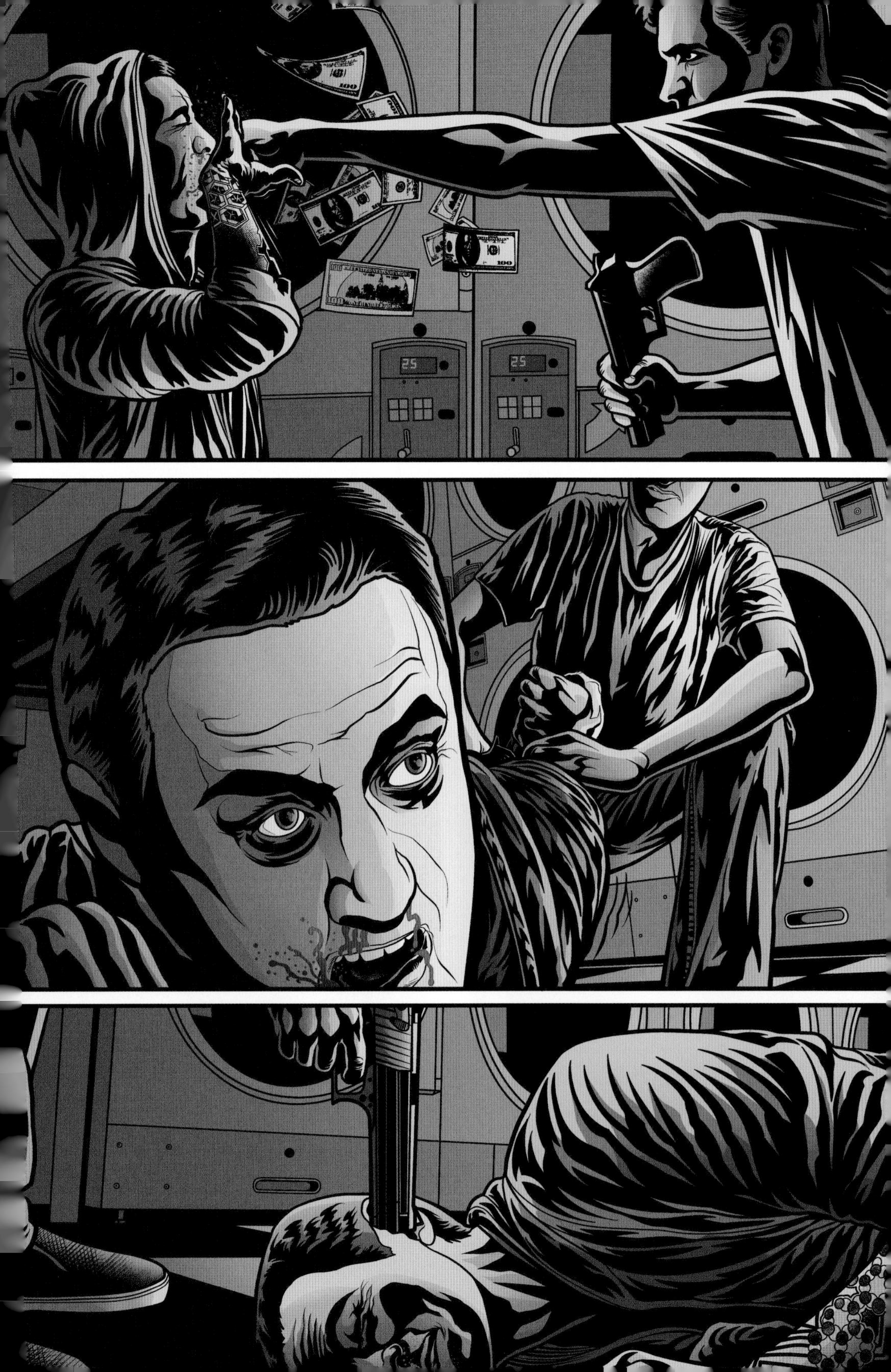
25
25

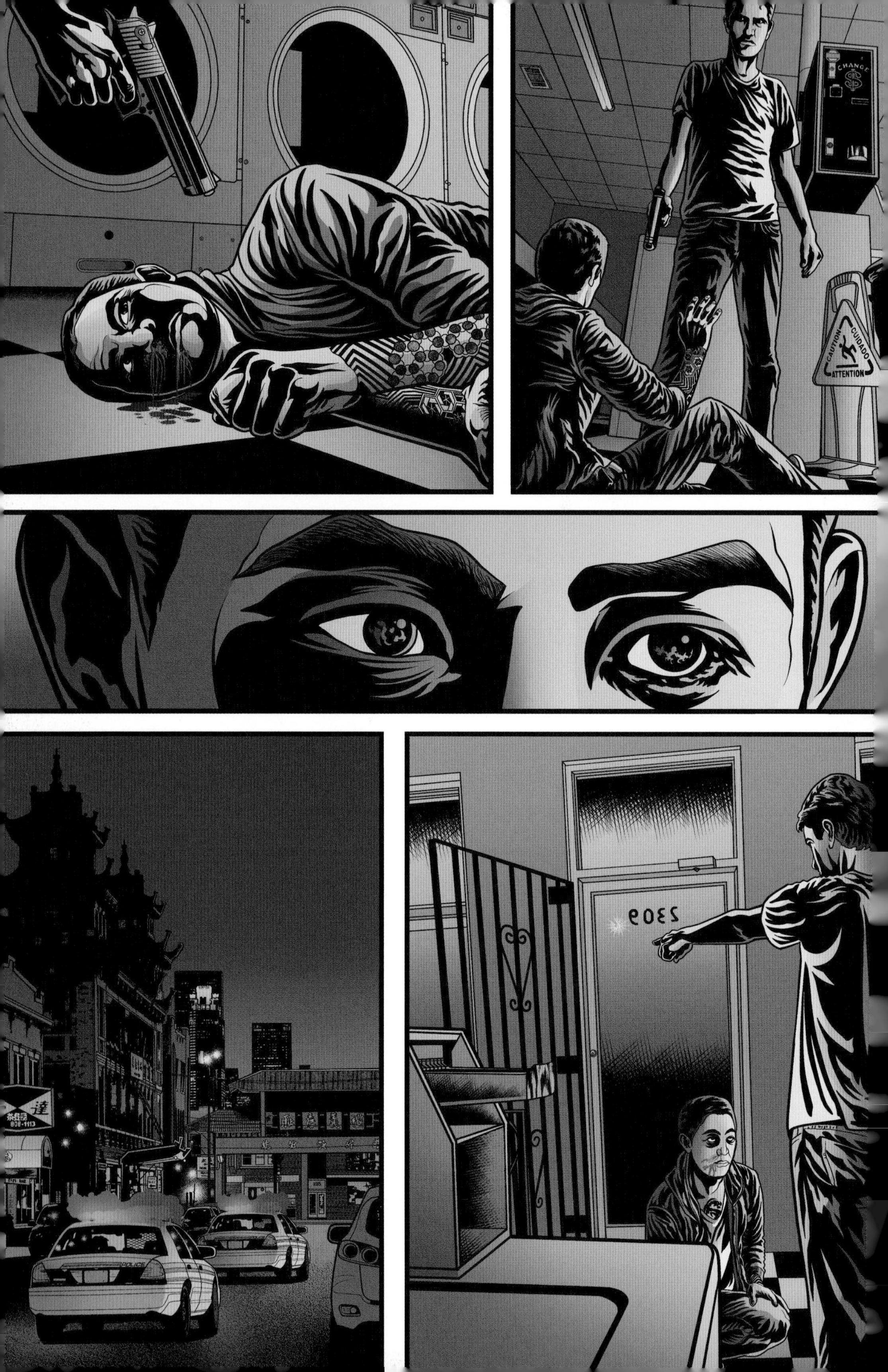
CHANGE
CAUTION
CUIDADO
ATTENTION
808-1113
POLICE
2309

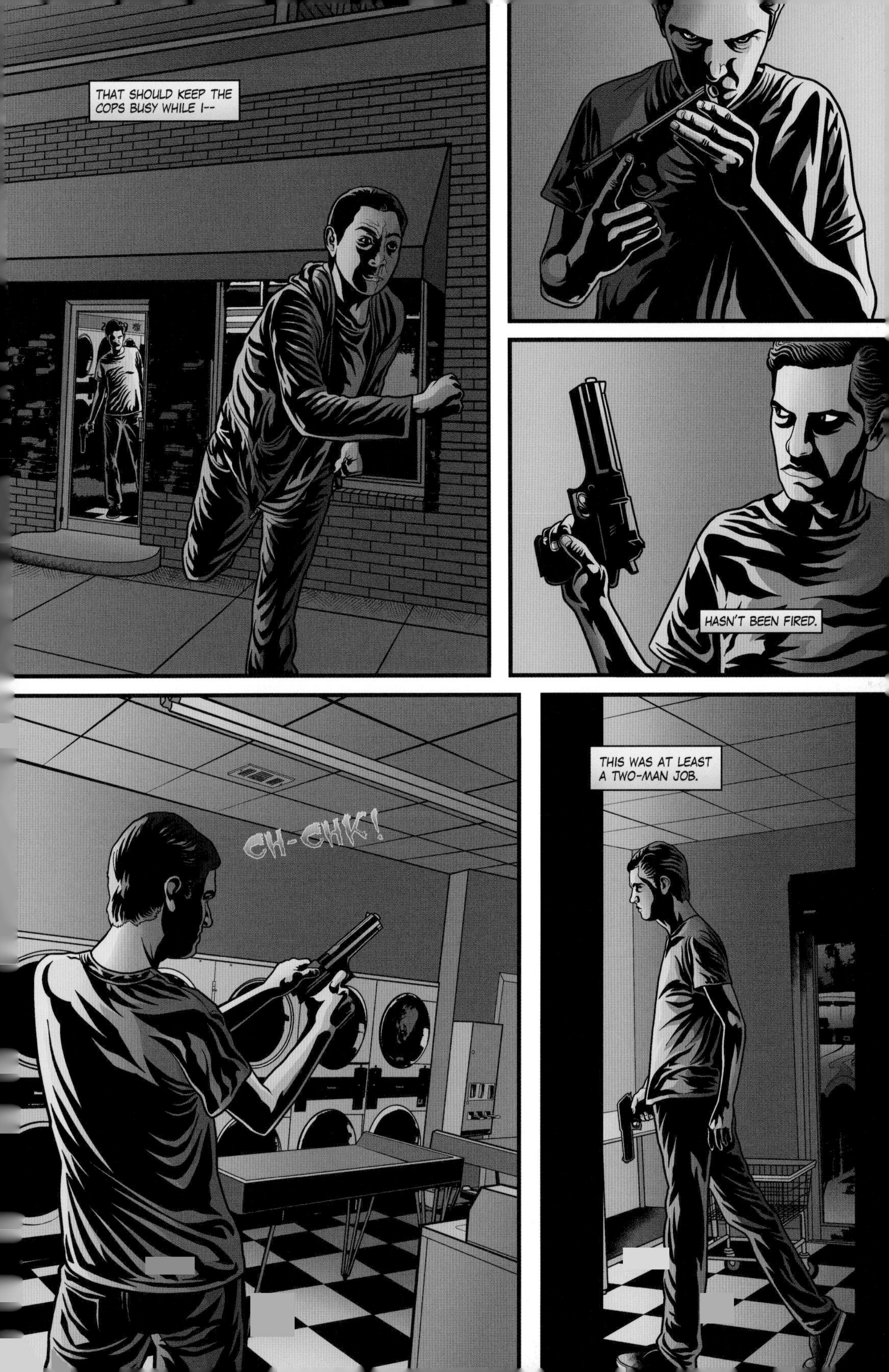
THAT SHOULD KEEP THE COPS BUSY WHILE I--
HASN'T BEEN FIRED.
CH-CHK!
THIS WAS AT LEAST A TWO-MAN JOB.

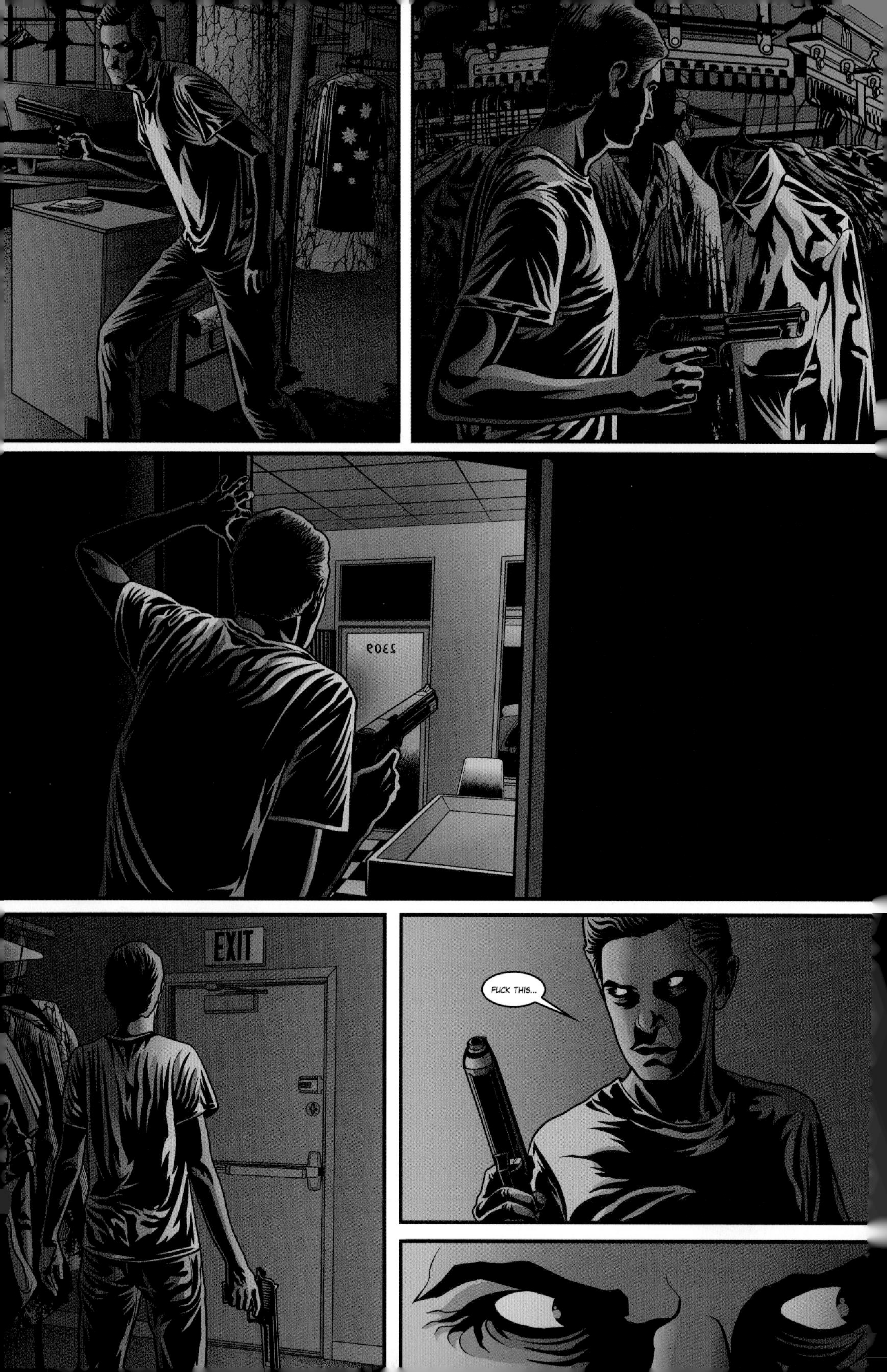
EXIT
FUCK THIS...

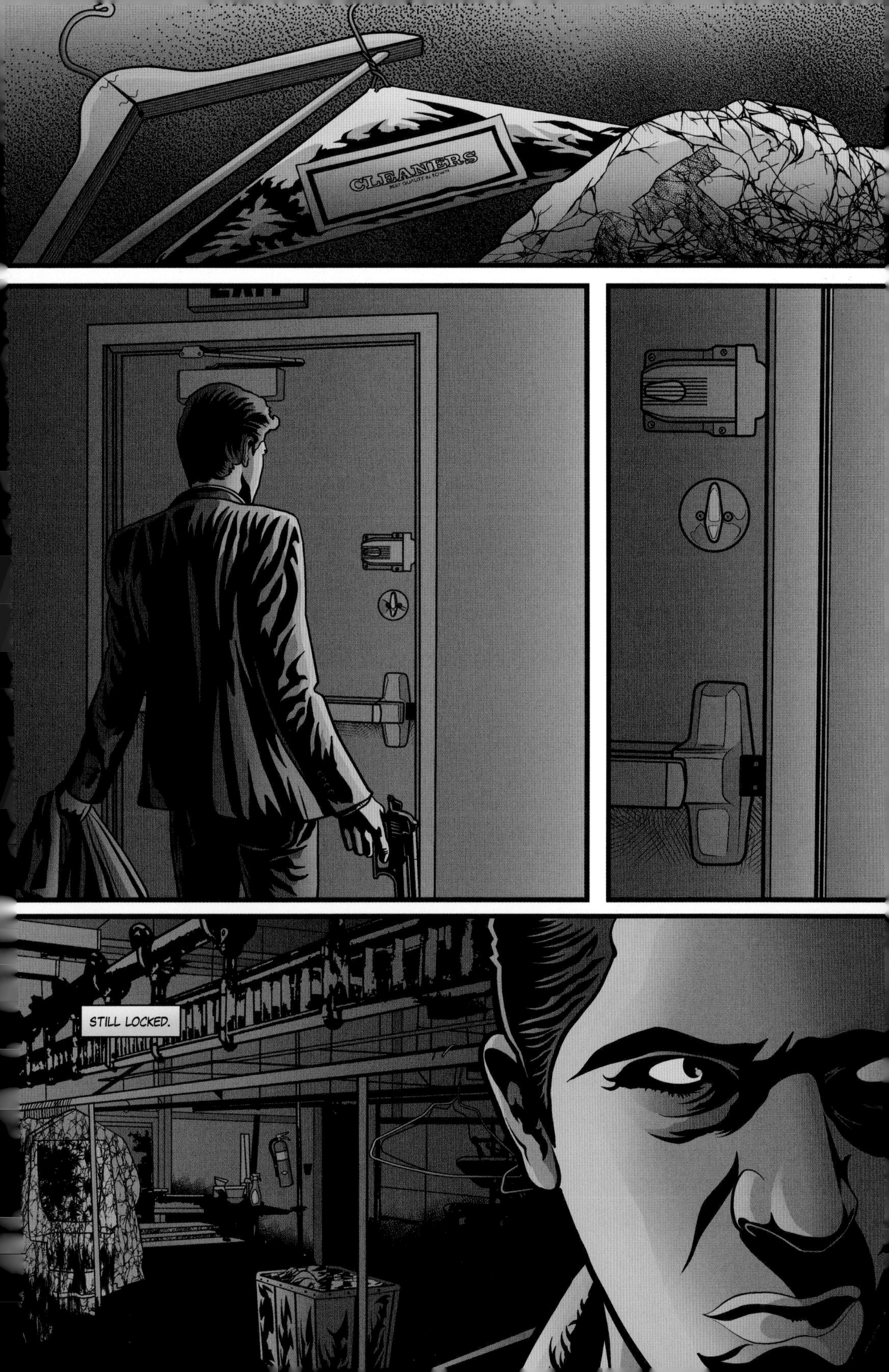
CLEANERS
BEST QUALITY IN TOWN
STILL LOCKED.

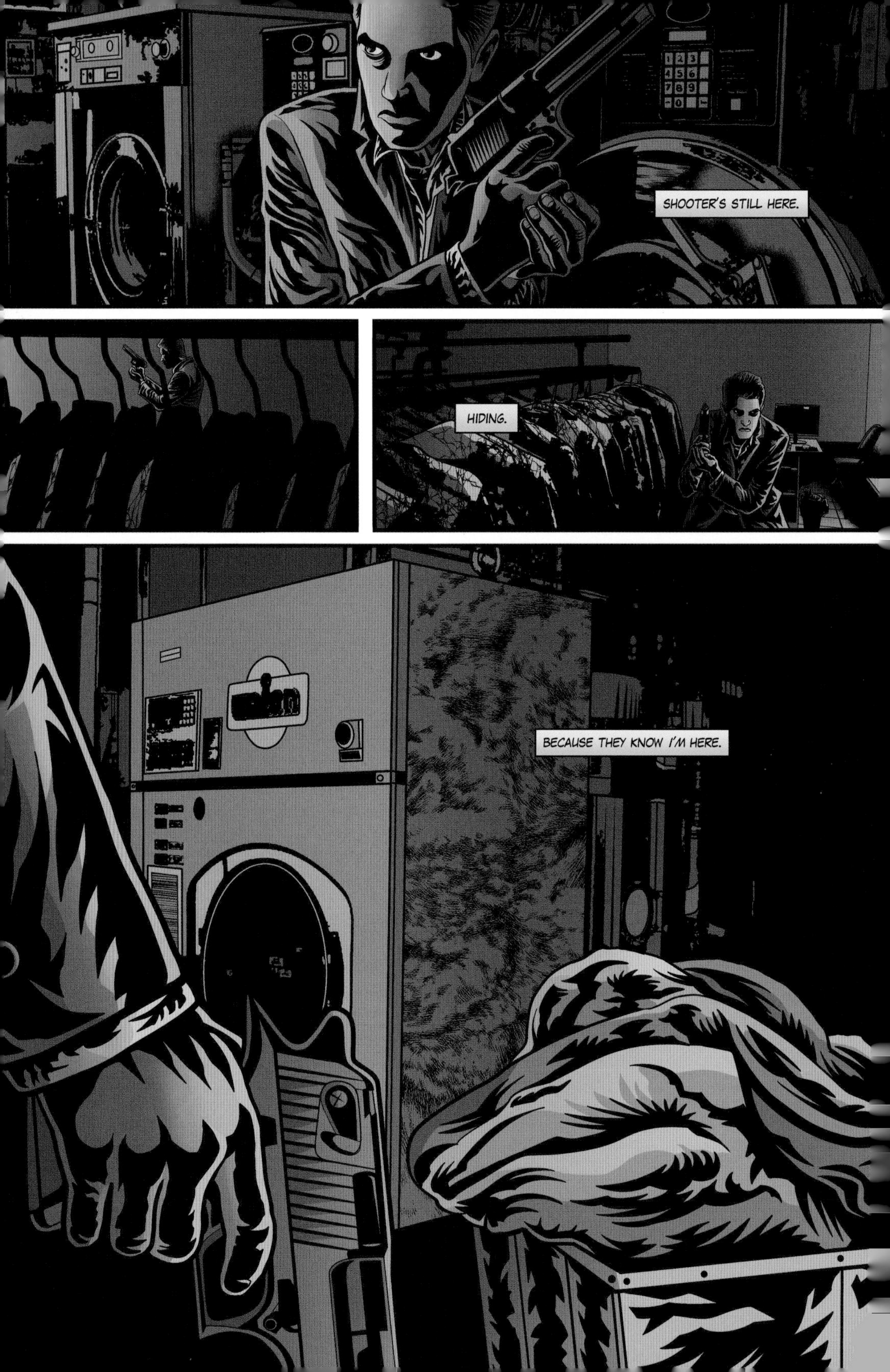
SHOOTER'S STILL HERE.
HIDING.
BECAUSE THEY KNOW I'M HERE.

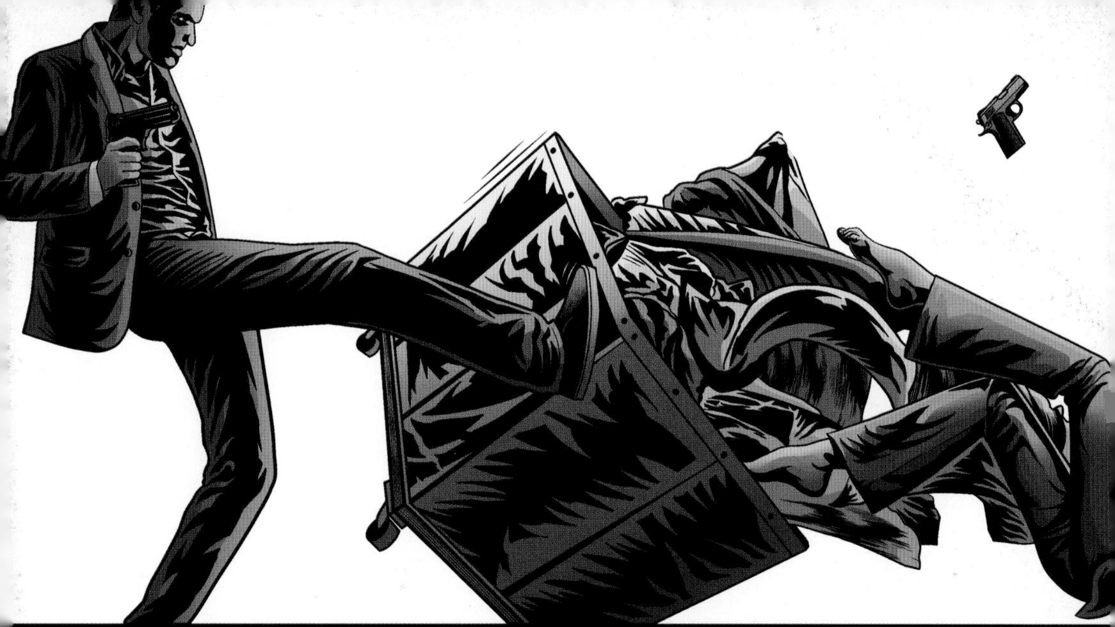

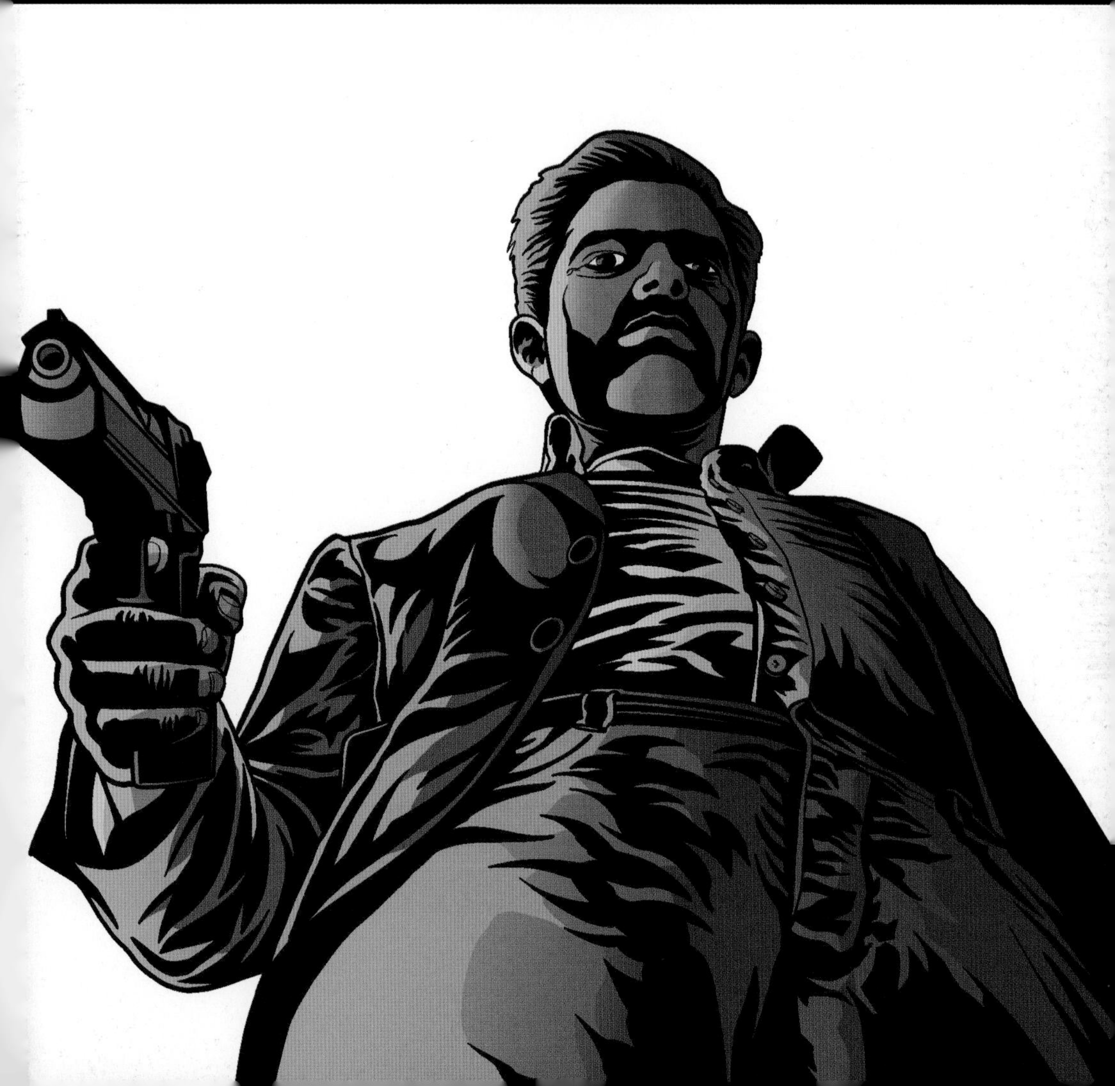

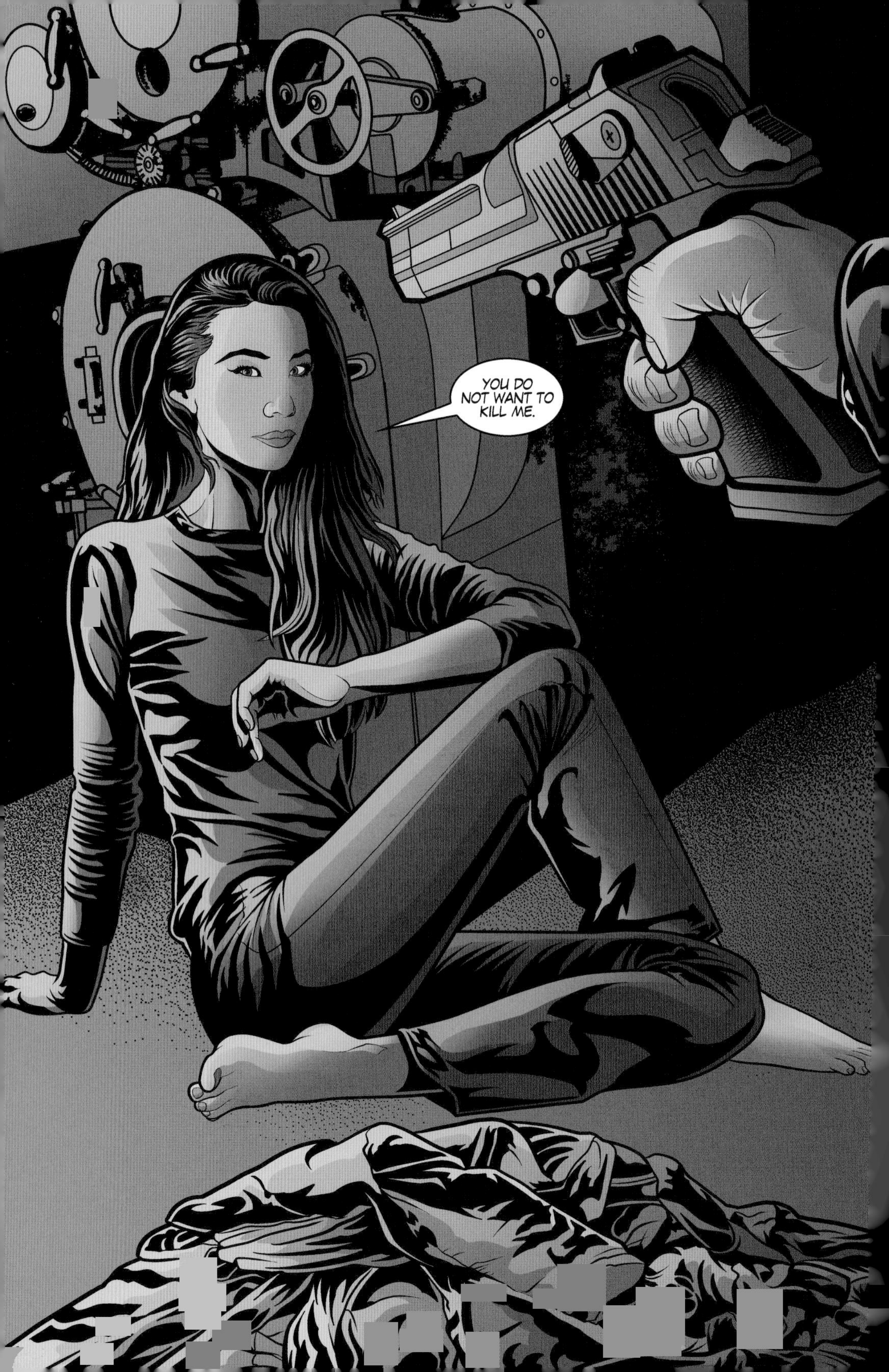
YOU DO NOT WANT TO KILL ME.

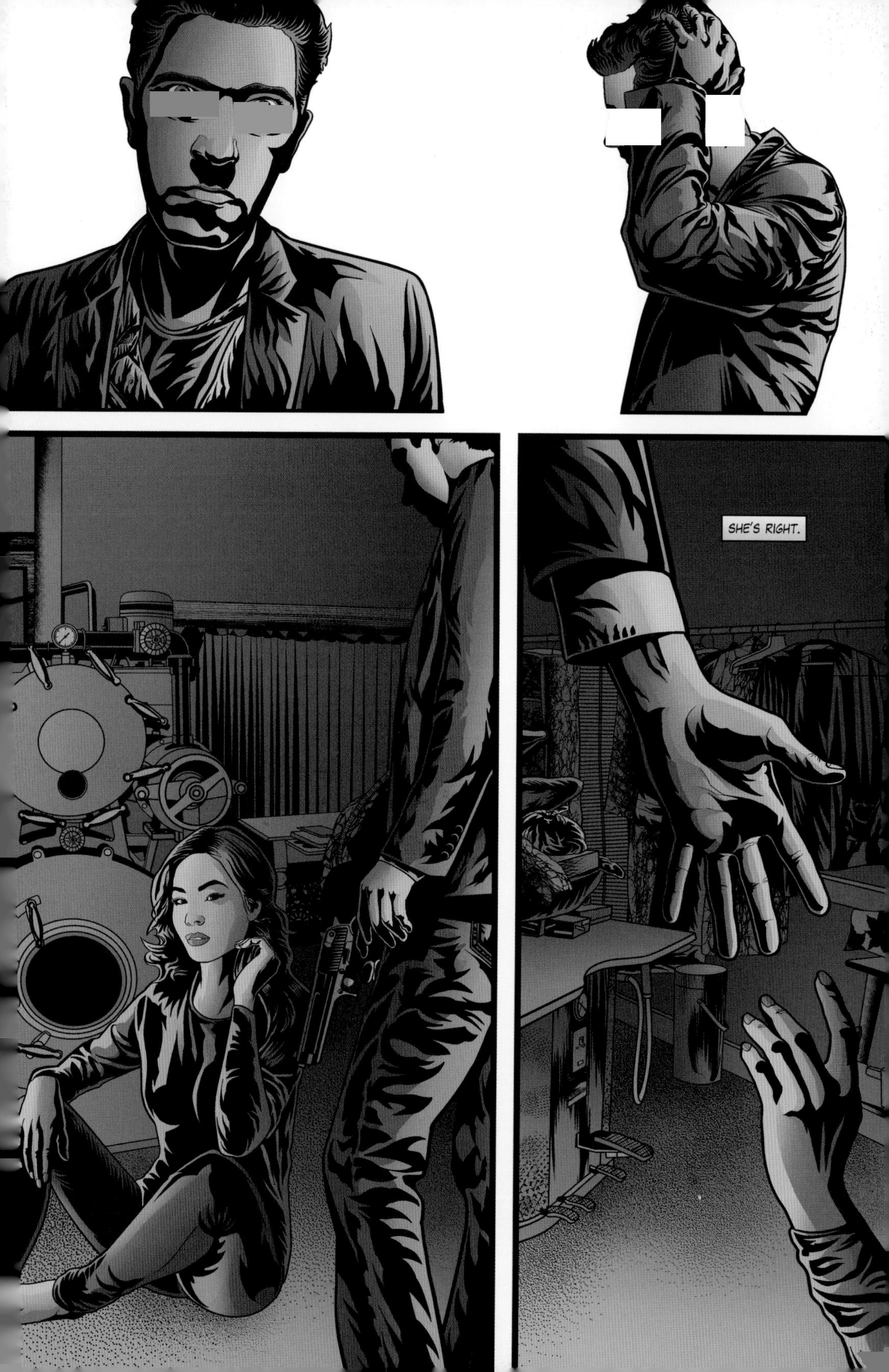
SHE'S RIGHT.

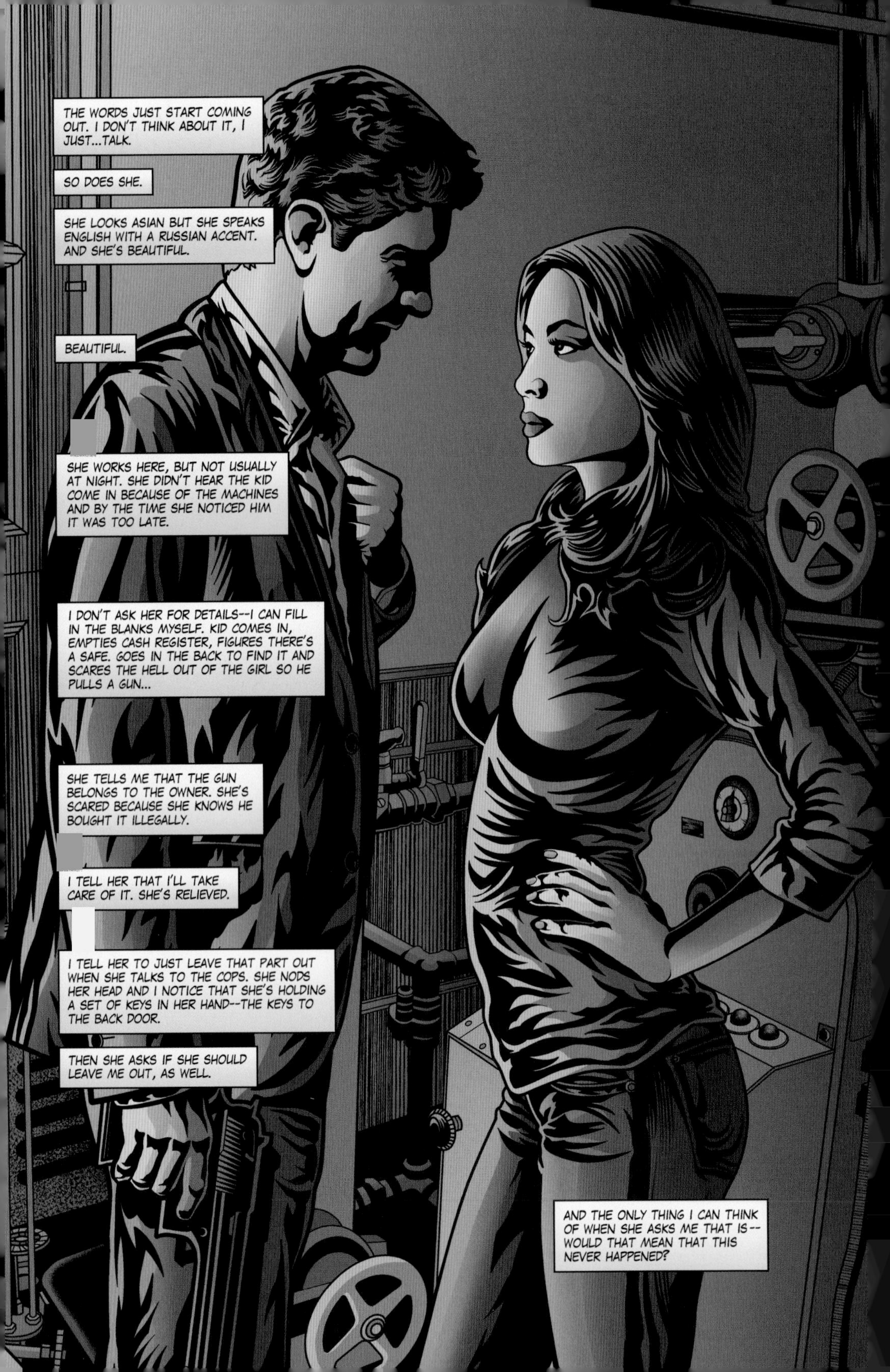
THE WORDS JUST START COMING OUT. I DON'T THINK ABOUT IT, I JUST...TALK.
SO DOES SHE.
SHE LOOKS ASIAN BUT SHE SPEAKS ENGLISH WITH A RUSSIAN ACCENT. AND SHE'S BEAUTIFUL.
BEAUTIFUL.
SHE WORKS HERE, BUT NOT USUALLY AT NIGHT. SHE DIDN'T HEAR THE KID COME IN BECAUSE OF THE MACHINES AND BY THE TIME SHE NOTICED HIM IT WAS TOO LATE.
I DON'T ASK HER FOR DETAILS--I CAN FILL IN THE BLANKS MYSELF. KID COMES IN, EMPTIES CASH REGISTER, FIGURES THERE'S A SAFE. GOES IN THE BACK TO FIND IT AND SCARES THE HELL OUT OF THE GIRL SO HE PULLS A GUN...
SHE TELLS ME THAT THE GUN BELONGS TO THE OWNER. SHE'S SCARED BECAUSE SHE KNOWS HE BOUGHT IT ILLEGALLY.
I TELL HER THAT I'LL TAKE CARE OF IT. SHE'S RELIEVED.
I TELL HER TO JUST LEAVE THAT PART OUT WHEN SHE TALKS TO THE COPS. SHE NODS HER HEAD AND I NOTICE THAT SHE'S HOLDING A SET OF KEYS IN HER HAND--THE KEYS TO THE BACK DOOR.
THEN SHE ASKS IF SHE SHOULD LEAVE ME OUT, AS WELL.
AND THE ONLY THING I CAN THINK OF WHEN SHE ASKS ME THAT IS--WOULD THAT MEAN THAT THIS NEVER HAPPENED?

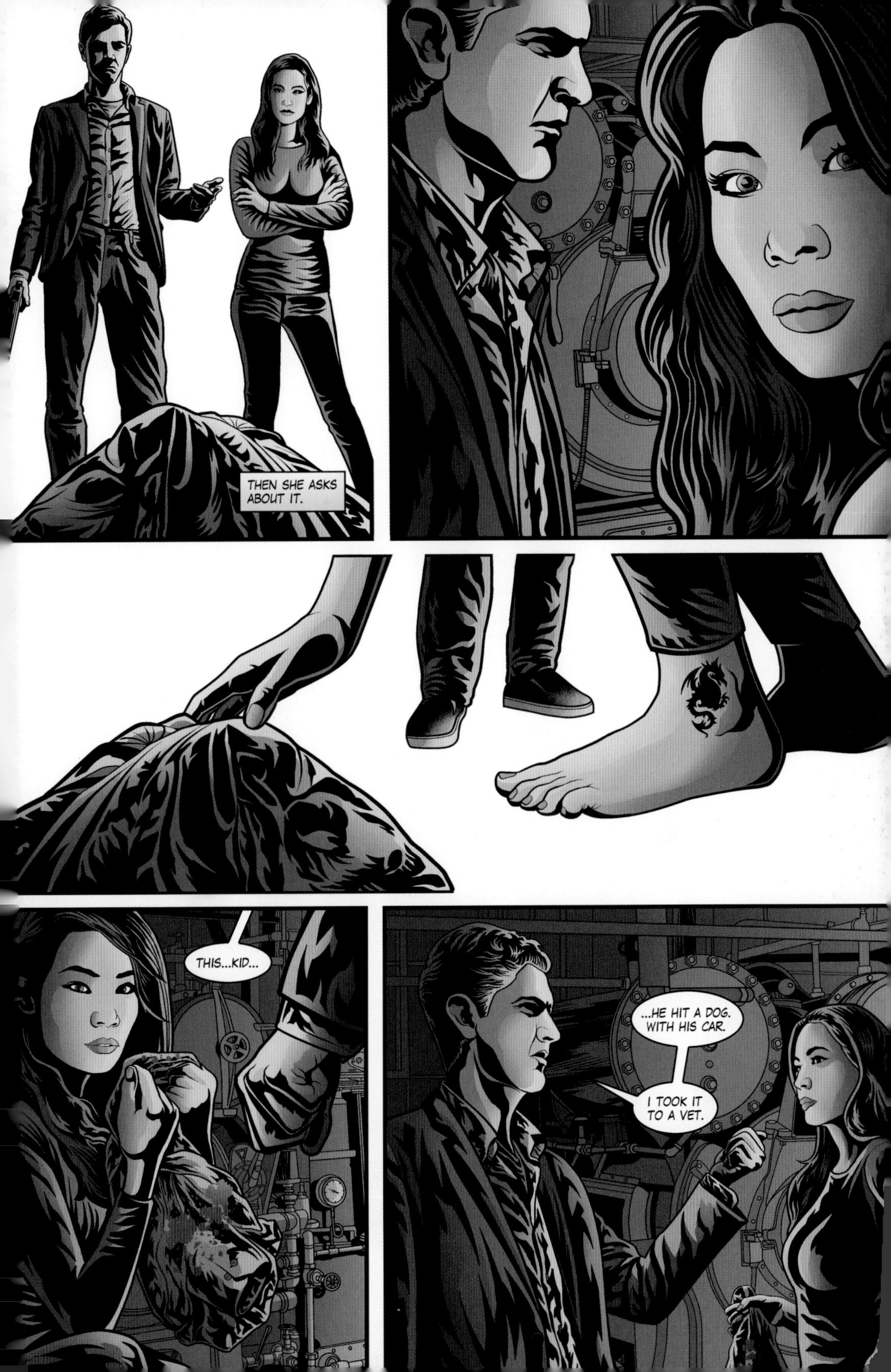
THEN SHE ASKS ABOUT IT.
THIS...KID...
...HE HIT A DOG. WITH HIS CAR.
I TOOK IT TO A VET.

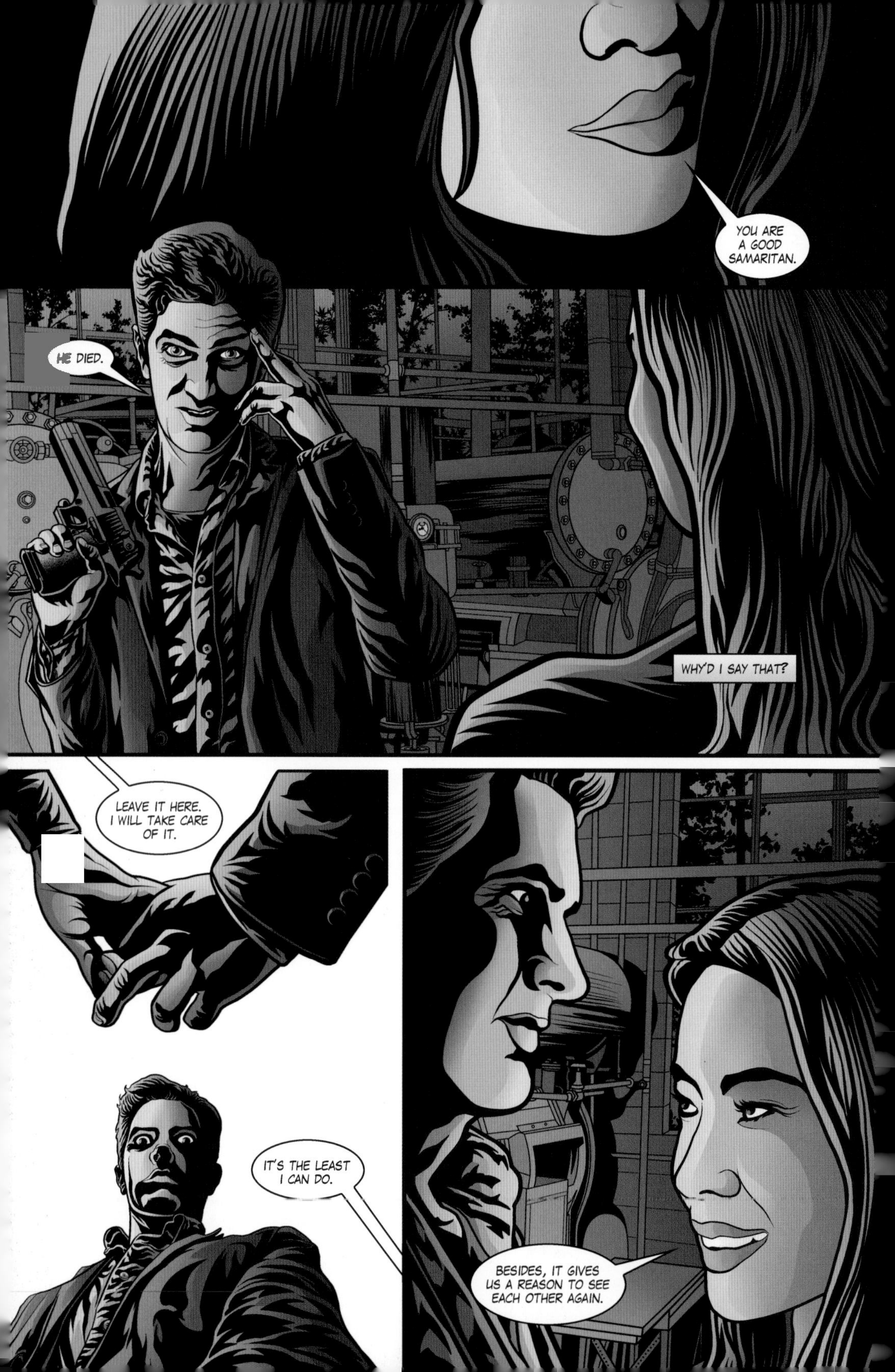
YOU ARE A GOOD SAMARITAN.
HE DIED.
WHY'D I SAY THAT?
LEAVE IT HERE. I WILL TAKE CARE OF IT.
IT'S THE LEAST I CAN DO.
BESIDES, IT GIVES US A REASON TO SEE EACH OTHER AGAIN.

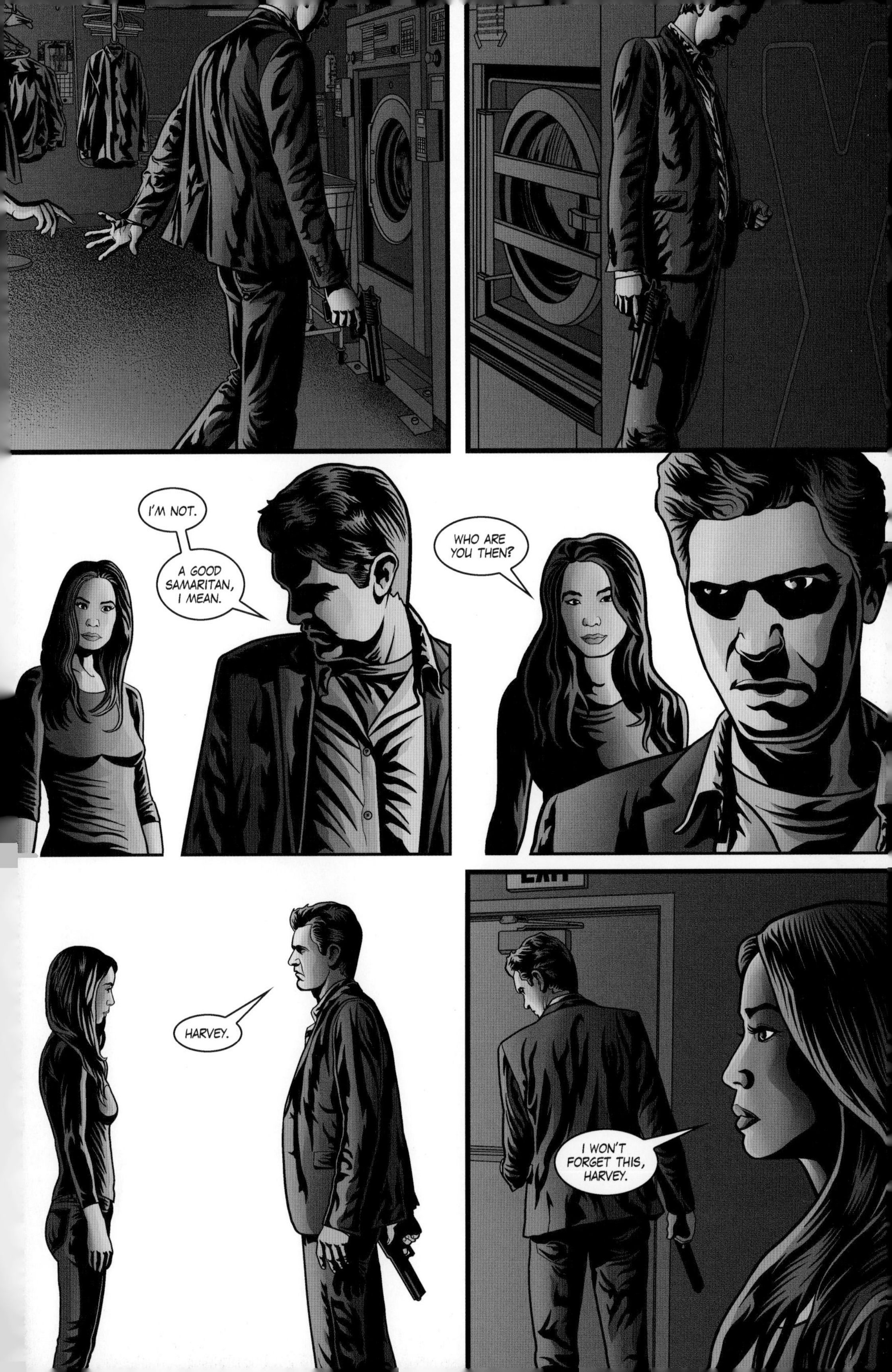
I'M NOT.
A GOOD SAMARITAN, I MEAN.
WHO ARE YOU THEN?
HARVEY.
I WON'T FORGET THIS, HARVEY.

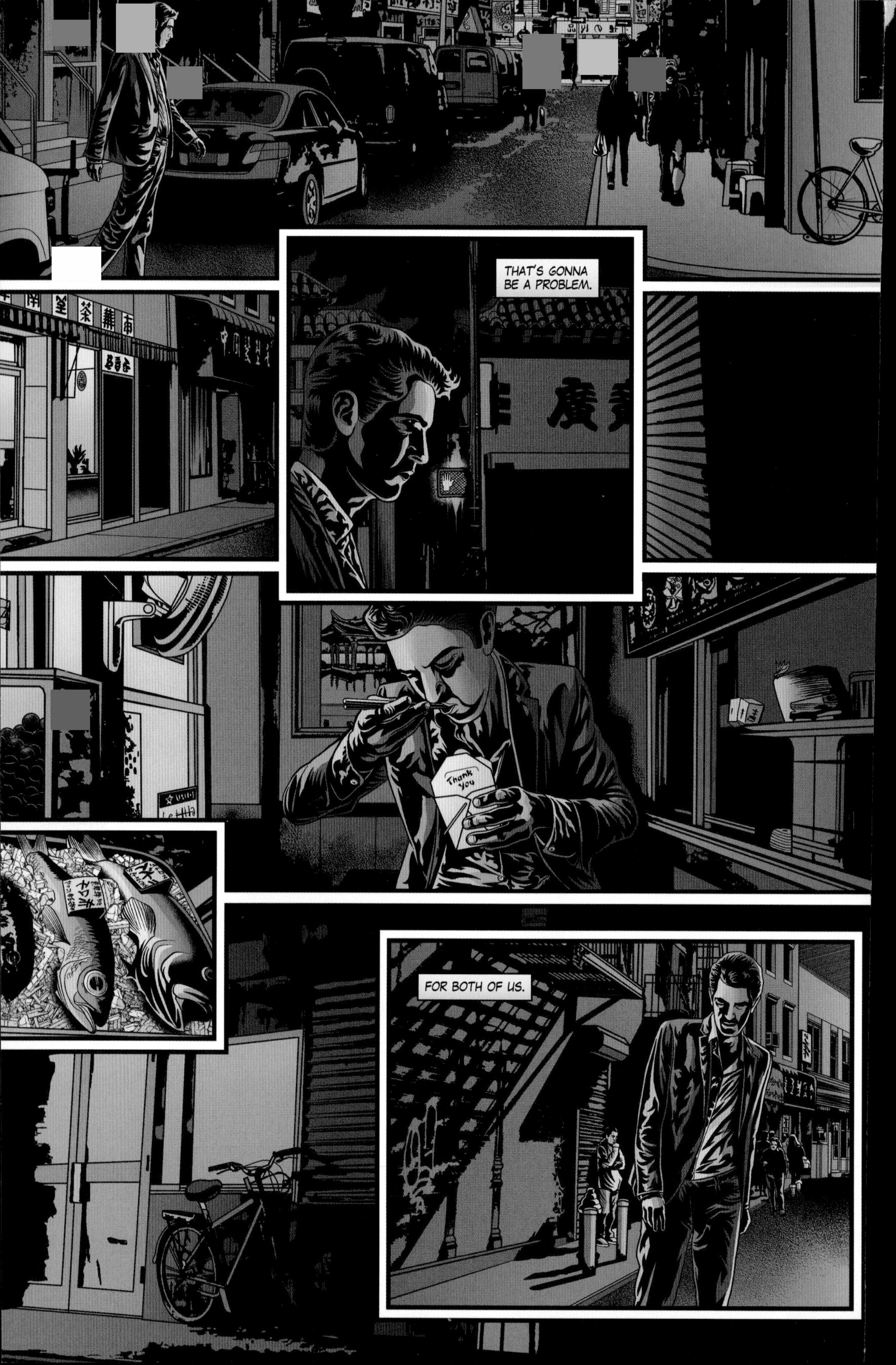
THAT'S GONNA
BE A PROBLEM.
Thank you
FOR BOTH OF US.

SATURDAY

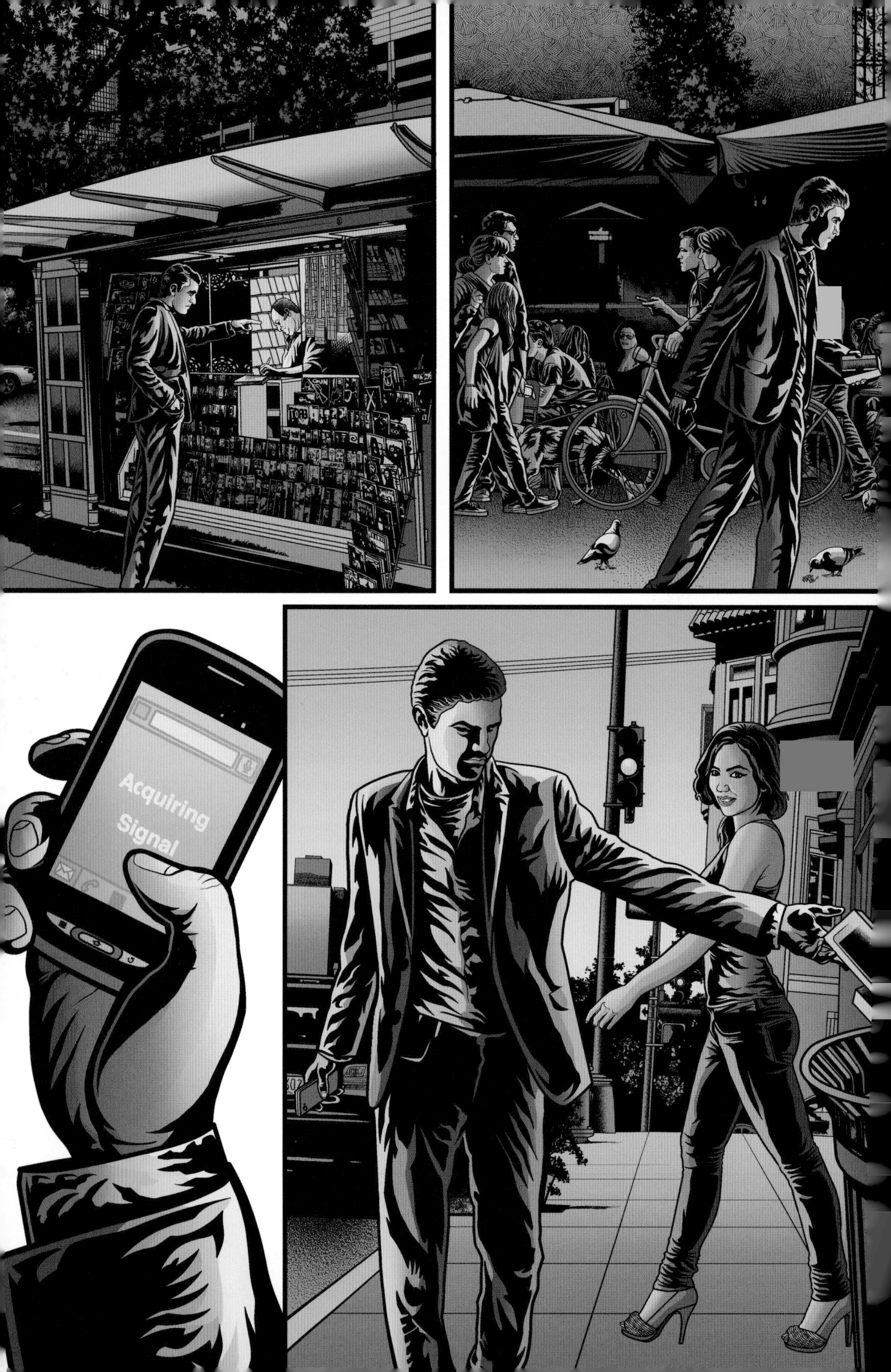
Acquiring
Signal

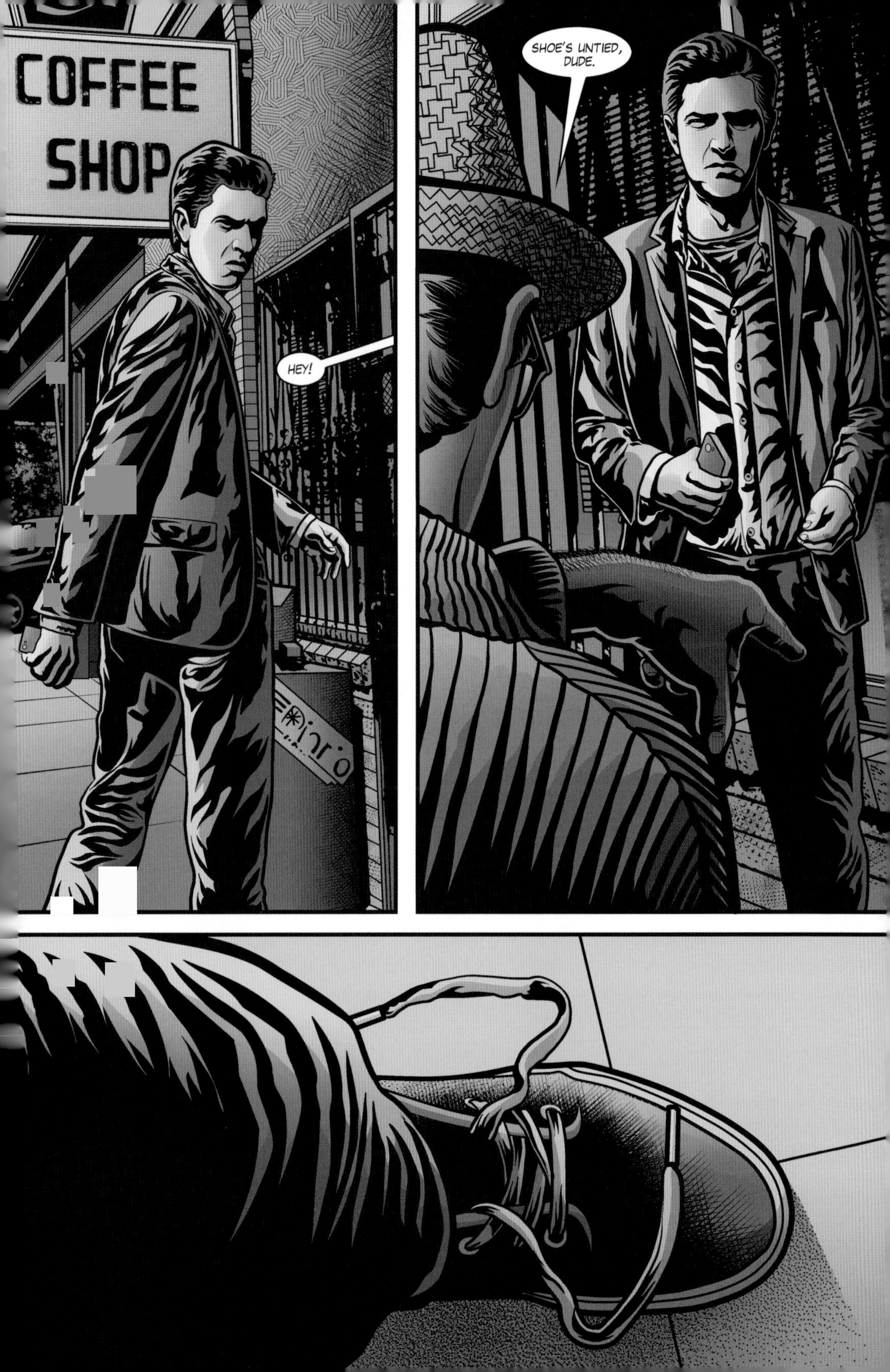
COFFEE SHOP
HEY!
SHOE'S UNTIED, DUDE.

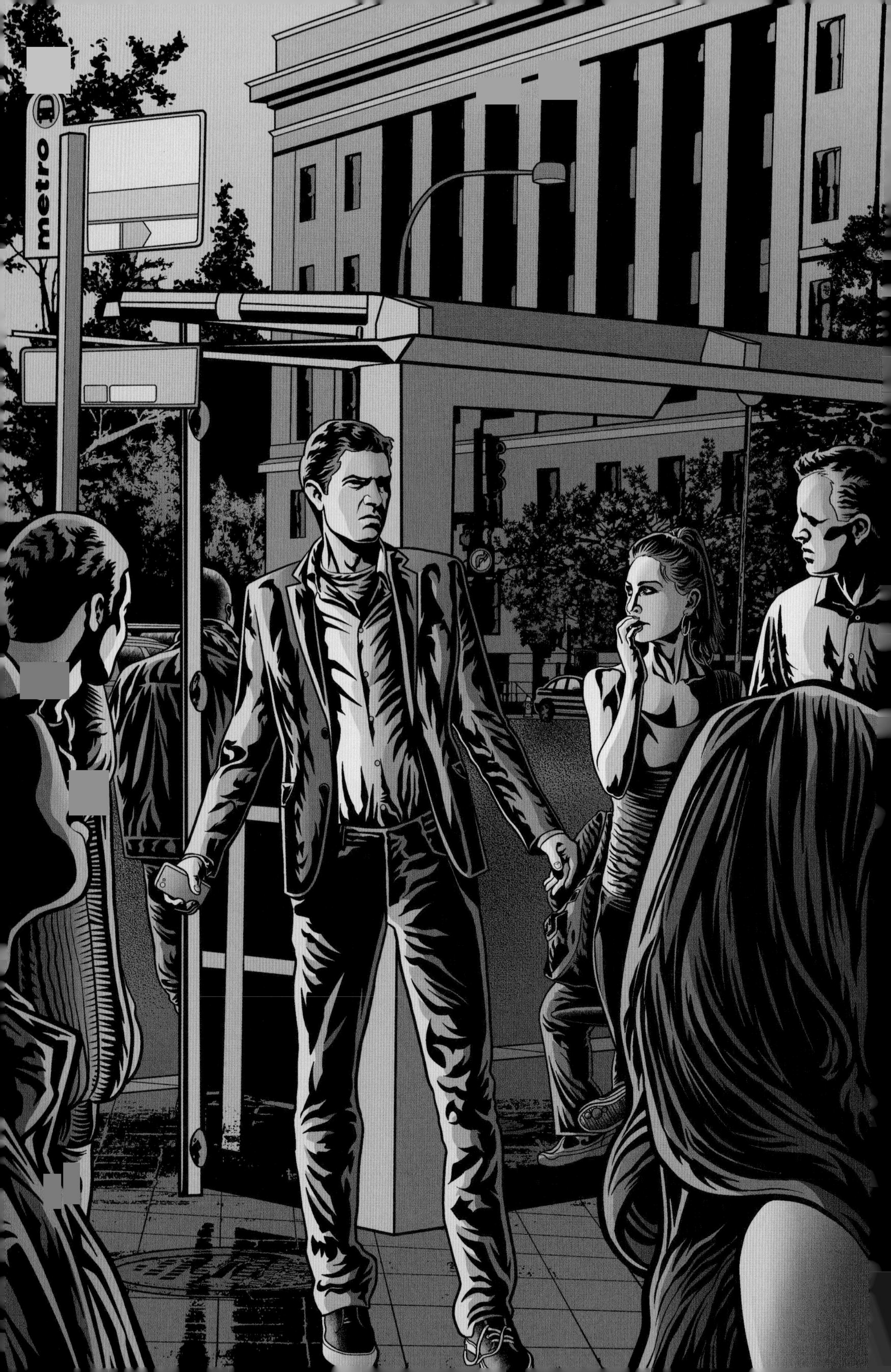
metro

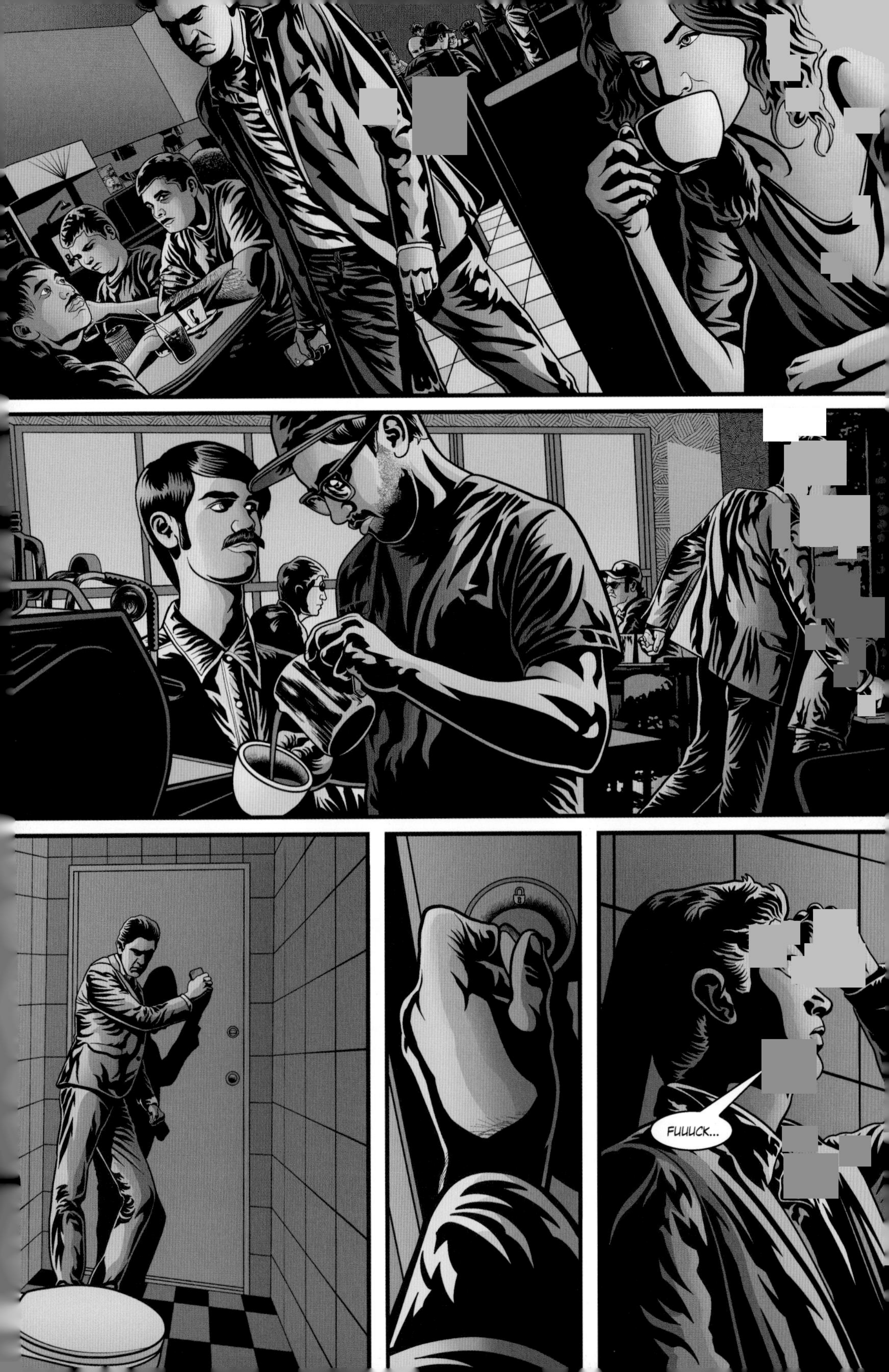
FUUUCK...

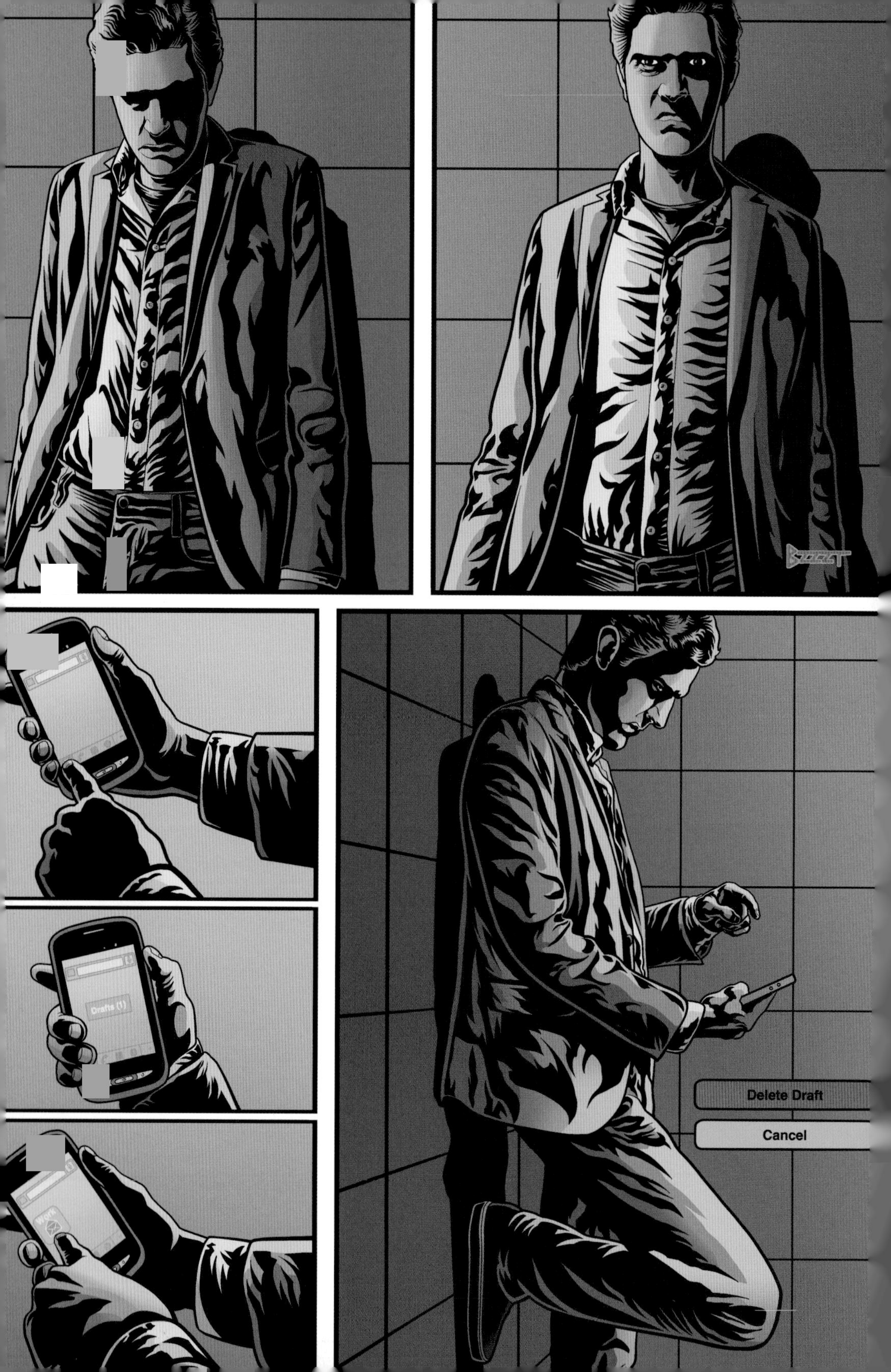
Drafts (1)
Work
Delete Draft
Cancel

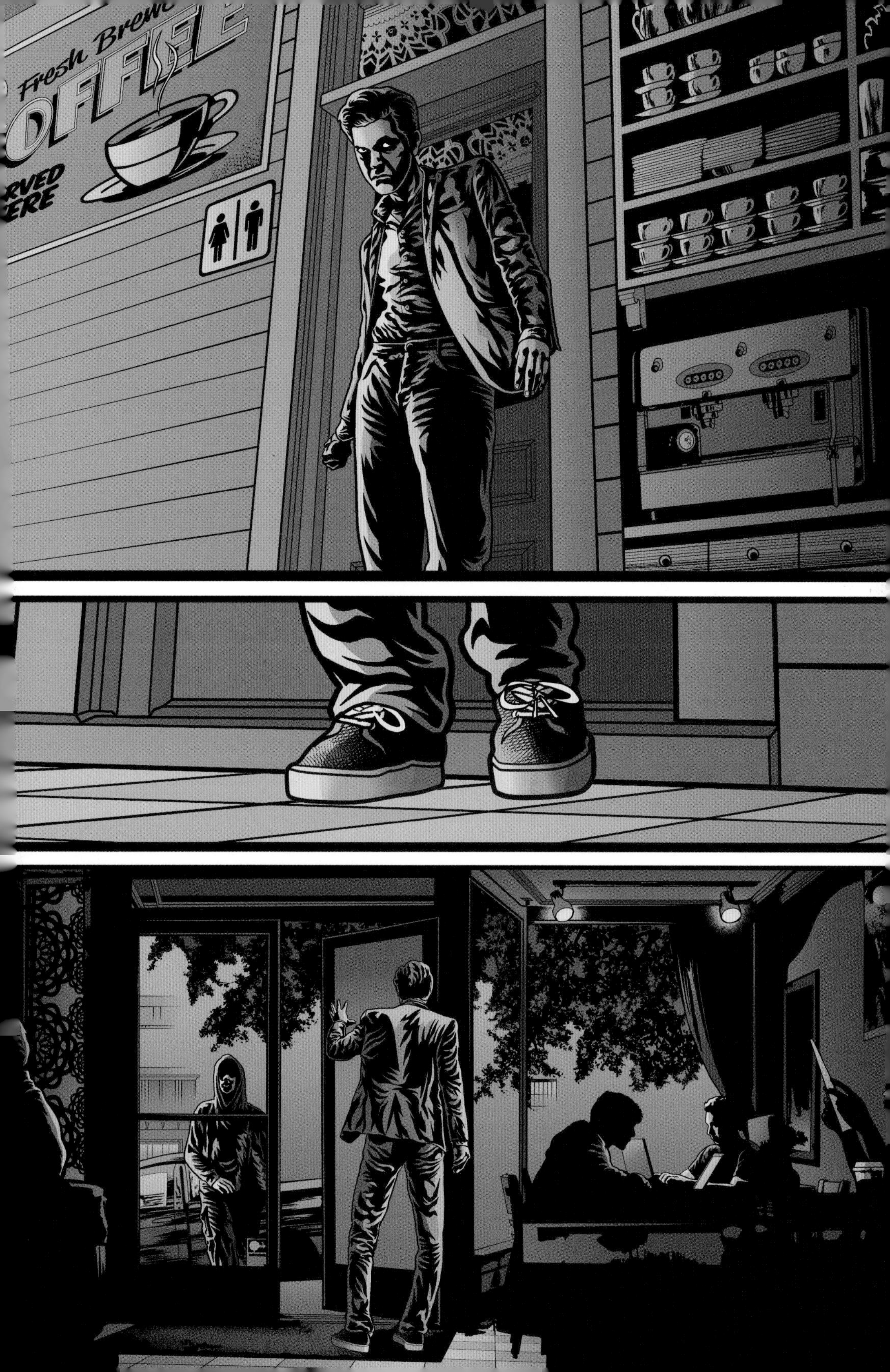

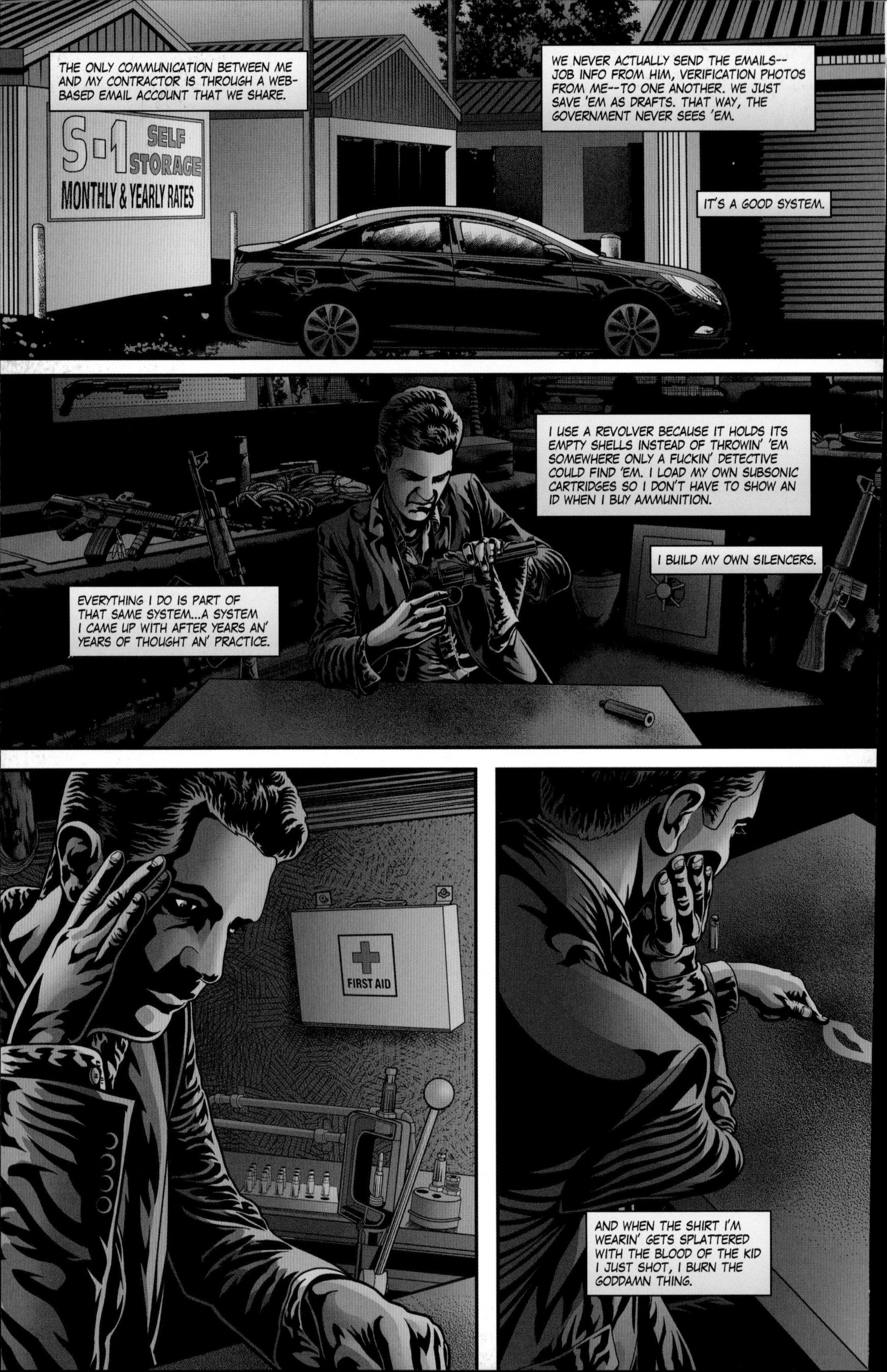

THE ONLY COMMUNICATION BETWEEN ME AND MY CONTRACTOR IS THROUGH A WEB-BASED EMAIL ACCOUNT THAT WE SHARE.
S-1 SELF STORAGE
MONTHLY & YEARLY RATES
WE NEVER ACTUALLY SEND THE EMAILS-- JOB INFO FROM HIM, VERIFICATION PHOTOS FROM ME--TO ONE ANOTHER. WE JUST SAVE 'EM AS DRAFTS. THAT WAY, THE GOVERNMENT NEVER SEES 'EM.
IT'S A GOOD SYSTEM.
I USE A REVOLVER BECAUSE IT HOLDS ITS EMPTY SHELLS INSTEAD OF THROWIN' 'EM SOMEWHERE ONLY A FUCKIN' DETECTIVE COULD FIND 'EM. I LOAD MY OWN SUBSONIC CARTRIDGES SO I DON'T HAVE TO SHOW AN ID WHEN I BUY AMMUNITION.
I BUILD MY OWN SILENCERS.
EVERYTHING I DO IS PART OF THAT SAME SYSTEM...A SYSTEM I CAME UP WITH AFTER YEARS AN' YEARS OF THOUGHT AN' PRACTICE.
FIRST AID
AND WHEN THE SHIRT I'M WEARIN' GETS SPLATTERED WITH THE BLOOD OF THE KID I JUST SHOT, I BURN THE GODDAMN THING.

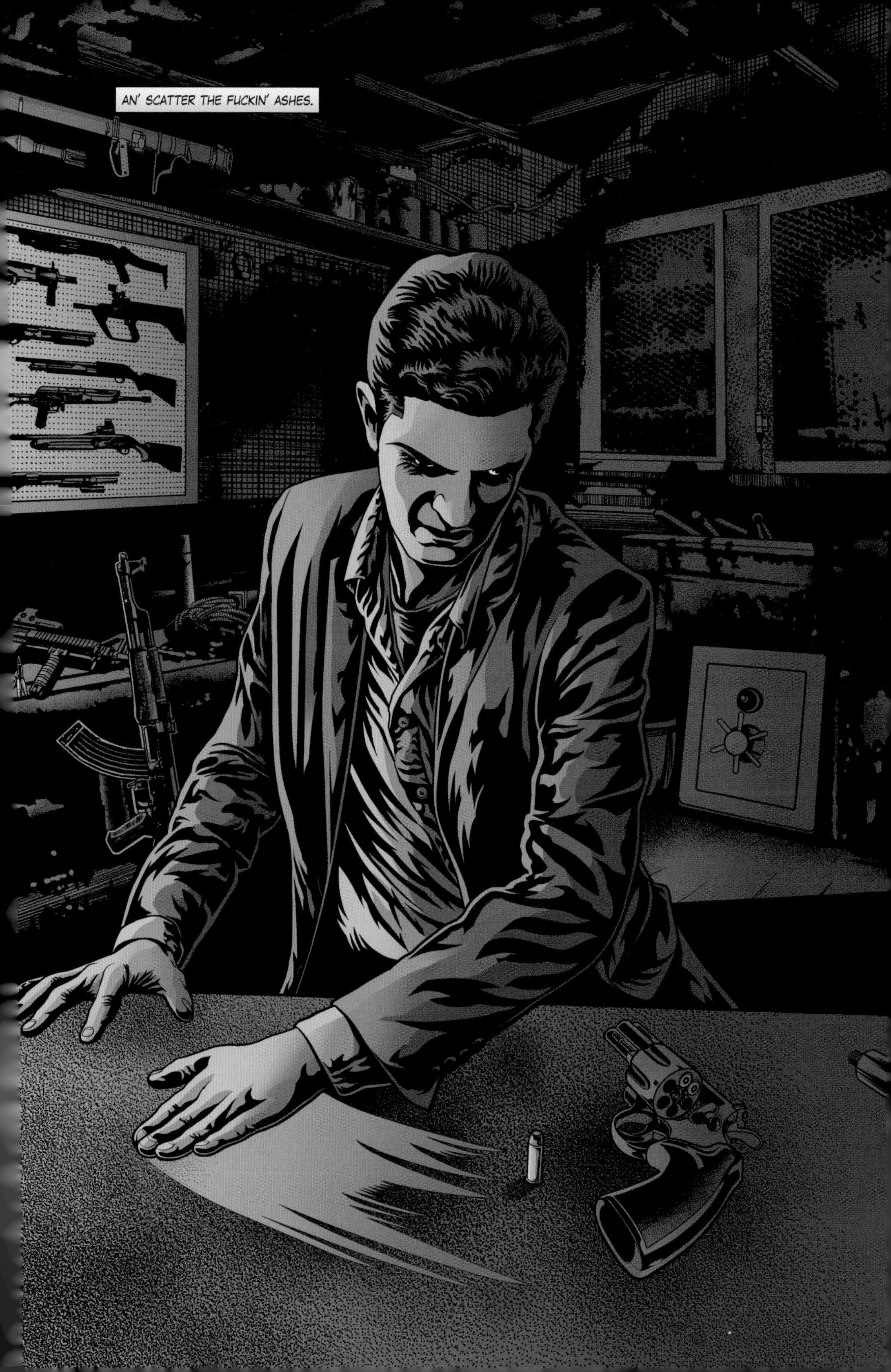
AN' SCATTER THE FUCKIN' ASHES.

SUNDAY

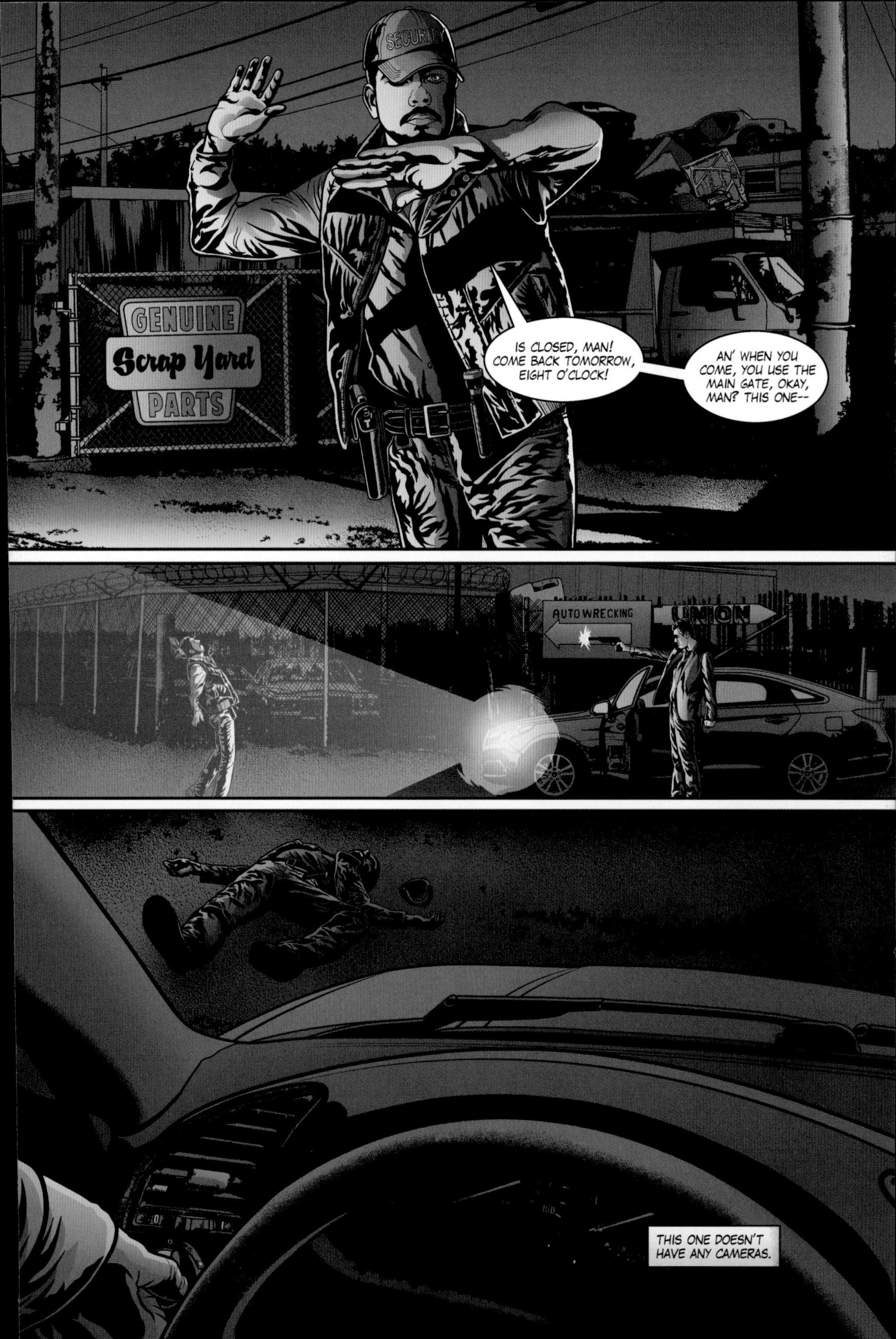
SECURITY
GENUINE
Scrap Yard
PARTS
IS CLOSED, MAN! COME BACK TOMORROW, EIGHT O'CLOCK!
AN' WHEN YOU COME, YOU USE THE MAIN GATE, OKAY, MAN? THIS ONE--
AUTO WRECKING
UNION
THIS ONE DOESN'T HAVE ANY CAMERAS.

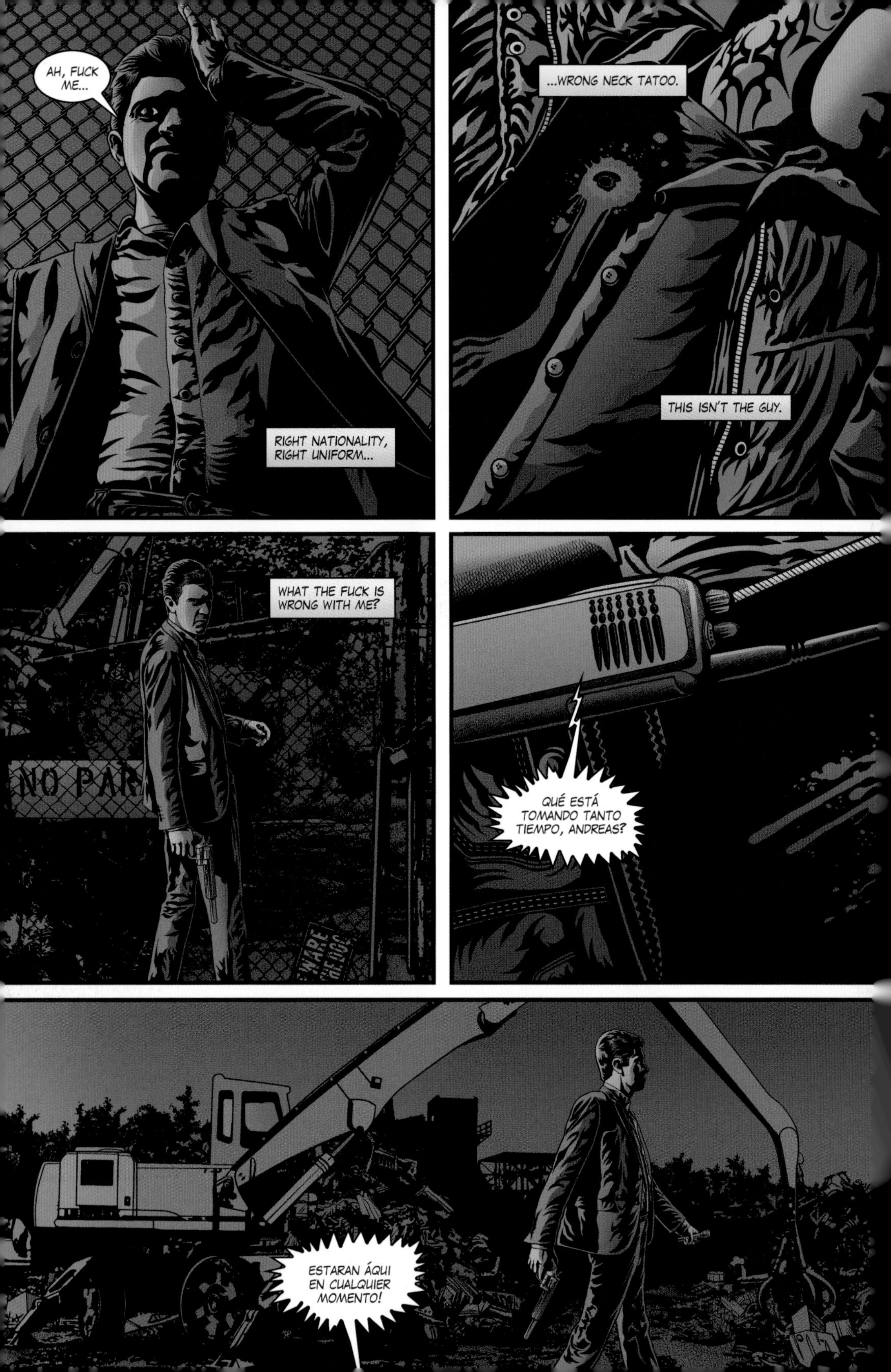
AH, FUCK ME...
RIGHT NATIONALITY, RIGHT UNIFORM...
...WRONG NECK TATOO.
THIS ISN'T THE GUY.
WHAT THE FUCK IS WRONG WITH ME?
NO PAR
QUÉ ESTÁ TOMANDO TANTO TIEMPO, ANDREAS?
ESTARAN ÁQUI EN CUALQUIER MOMENTO!

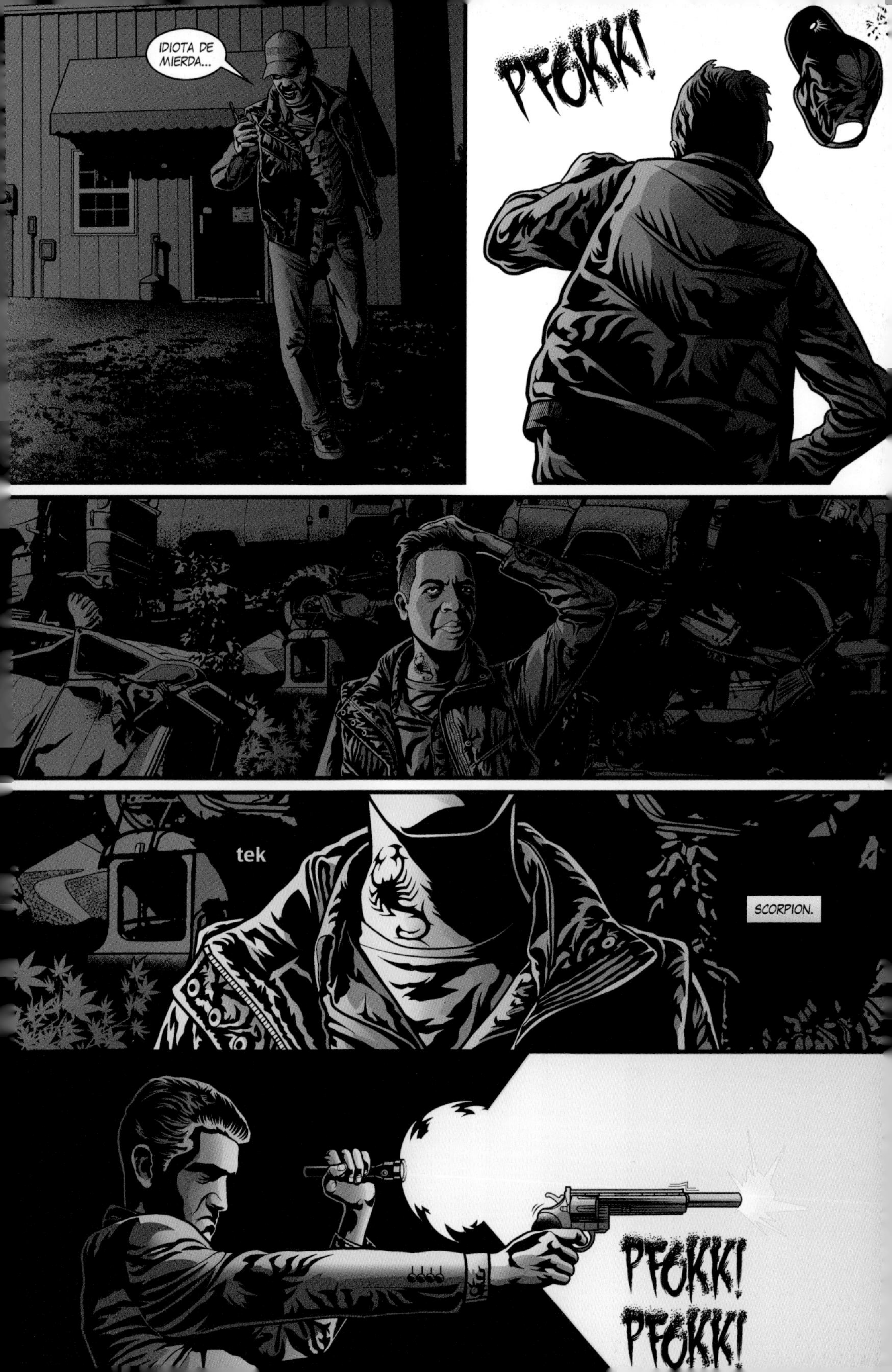
IDIOTA DE MIERDA...
PFOKK!
tek
SCORPION.
PFOKK!
PFOKK!

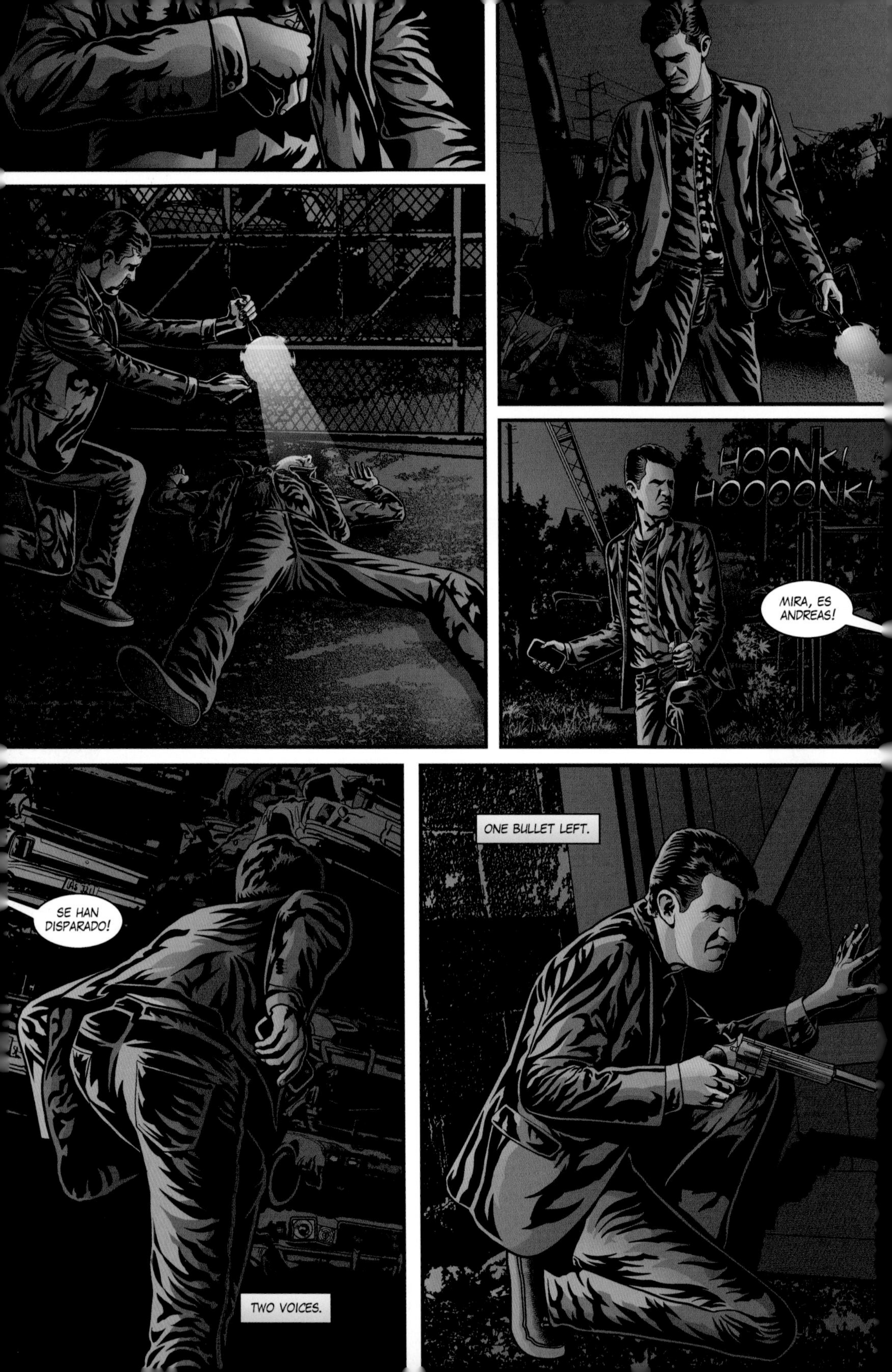
HOONK! HOOOOONK!
MIRA, ES ANDREAS!
SE HAN DISPARADO!
TWO VOICES.
ONE BULLET LEFT.

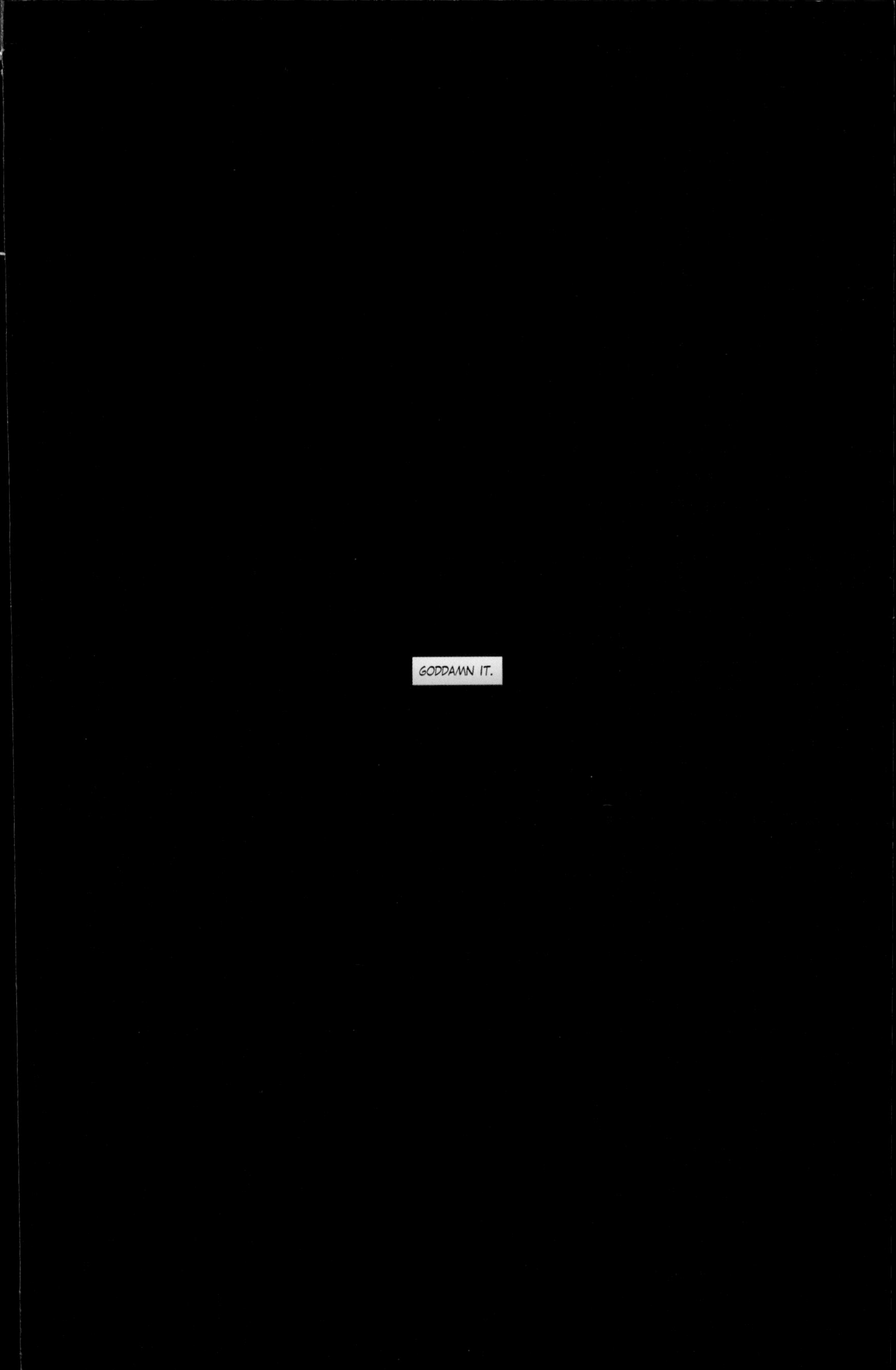
GODDAMN IT.

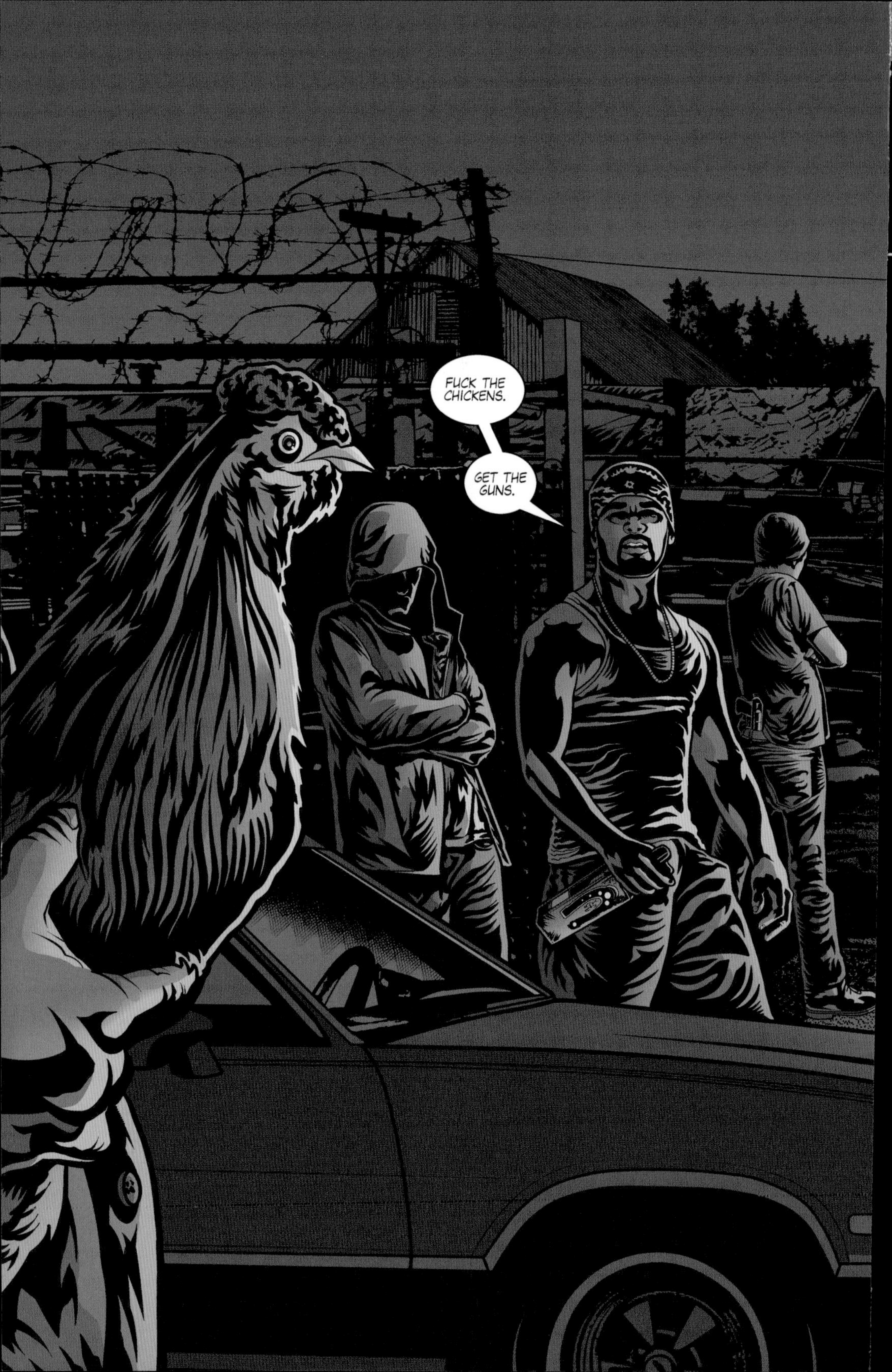
FUCK THE CHICKENS.
GET THE GUNS.

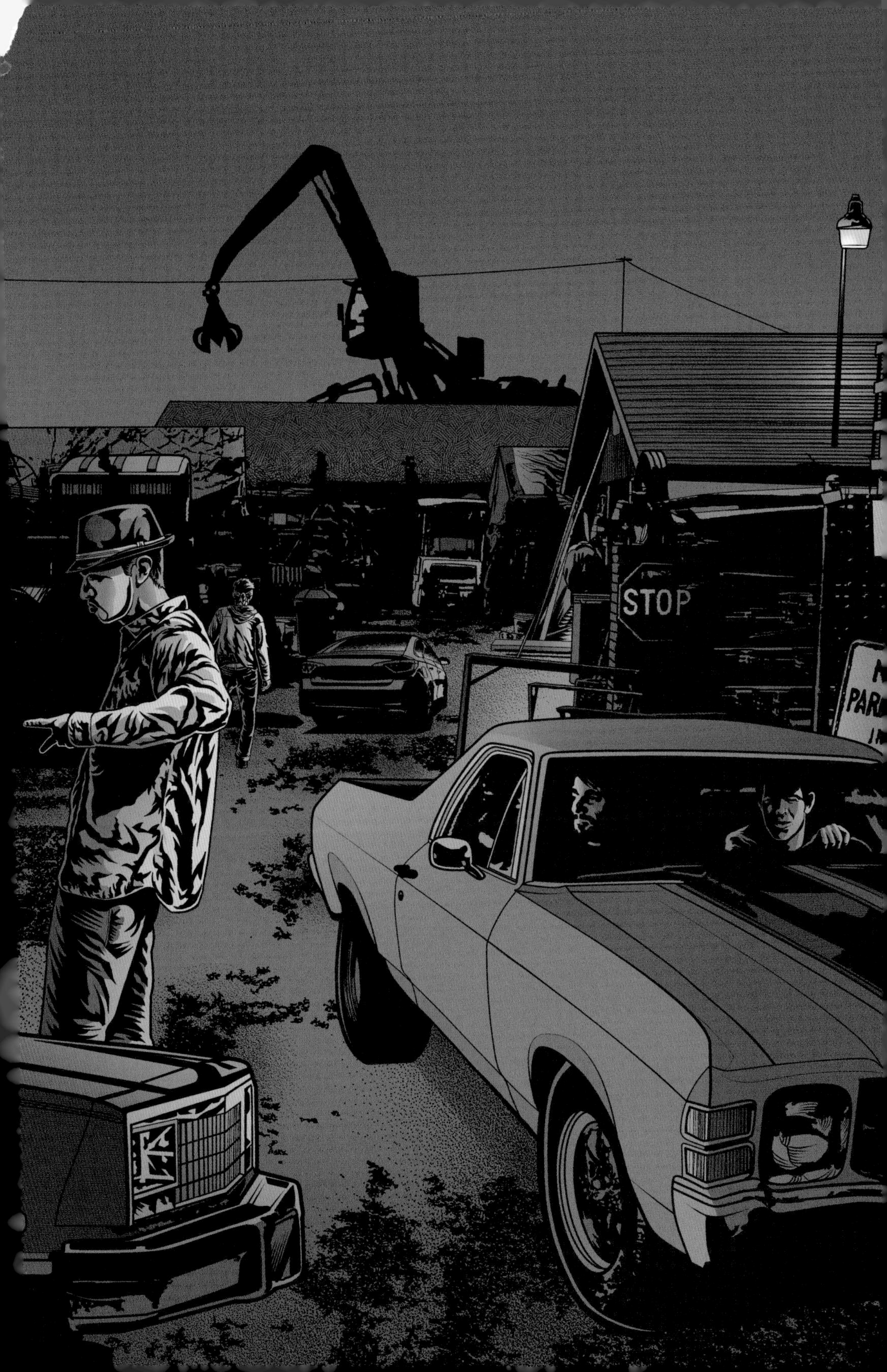
STOP

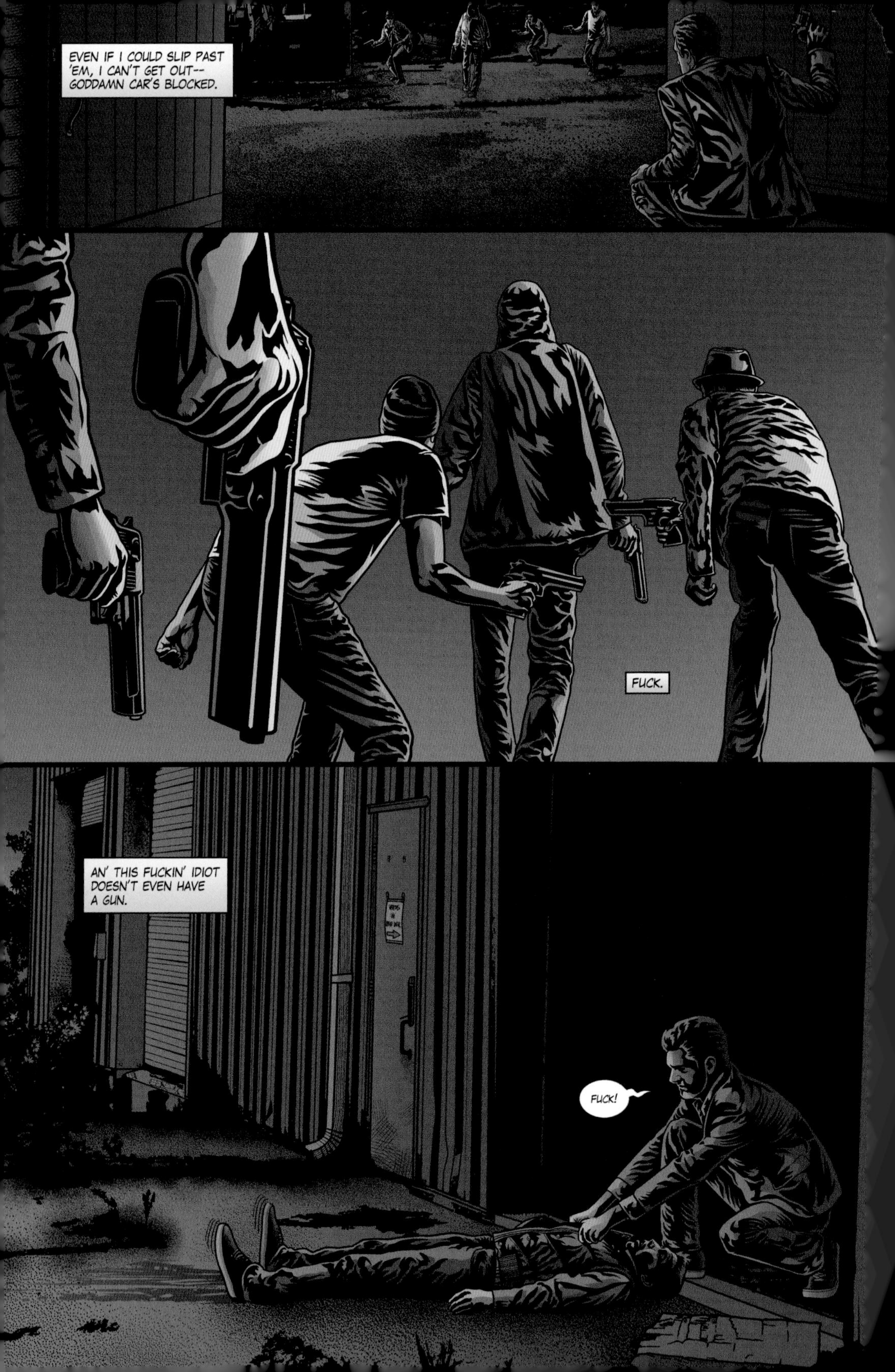
EVEN IF I COULD SLIP PAST 'EM, I CAN'T GET OUT-- GODDAMN CAR'S BLOCKED.
FUCK.
AN' THIS FUCKIN' IDIOT DOESN'T EVEN HAVE A GUN.
FUCK!

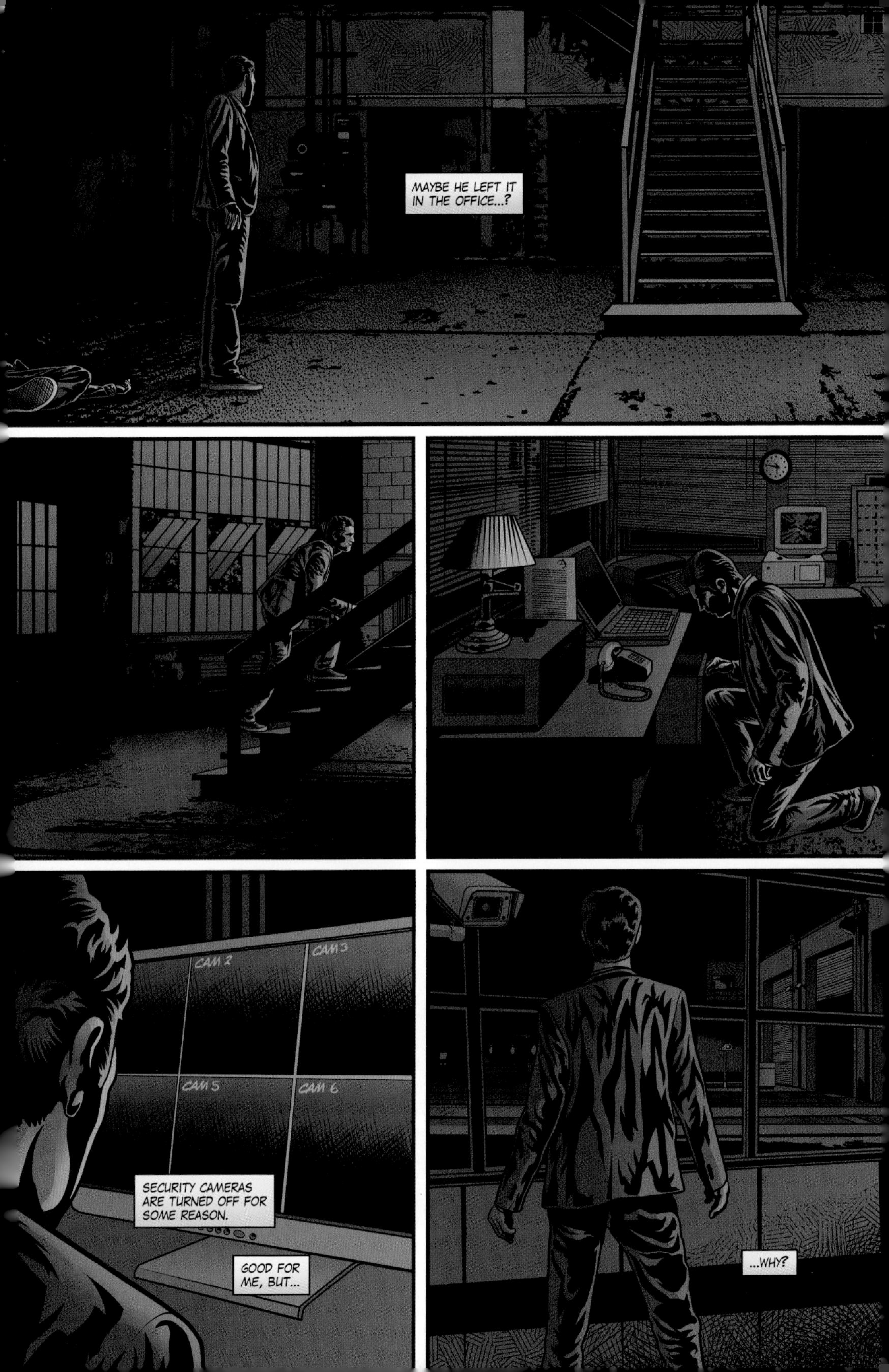
MAYBE HE LEFT IT IN THE OFFICE...?
CAM 2
CAM 3
CAM 5
CAM 6
SECURITY CAMERAS ARE TURNED OFF FOR SOME REASON.
GOOD FOR ME, BUT...
...WHY?

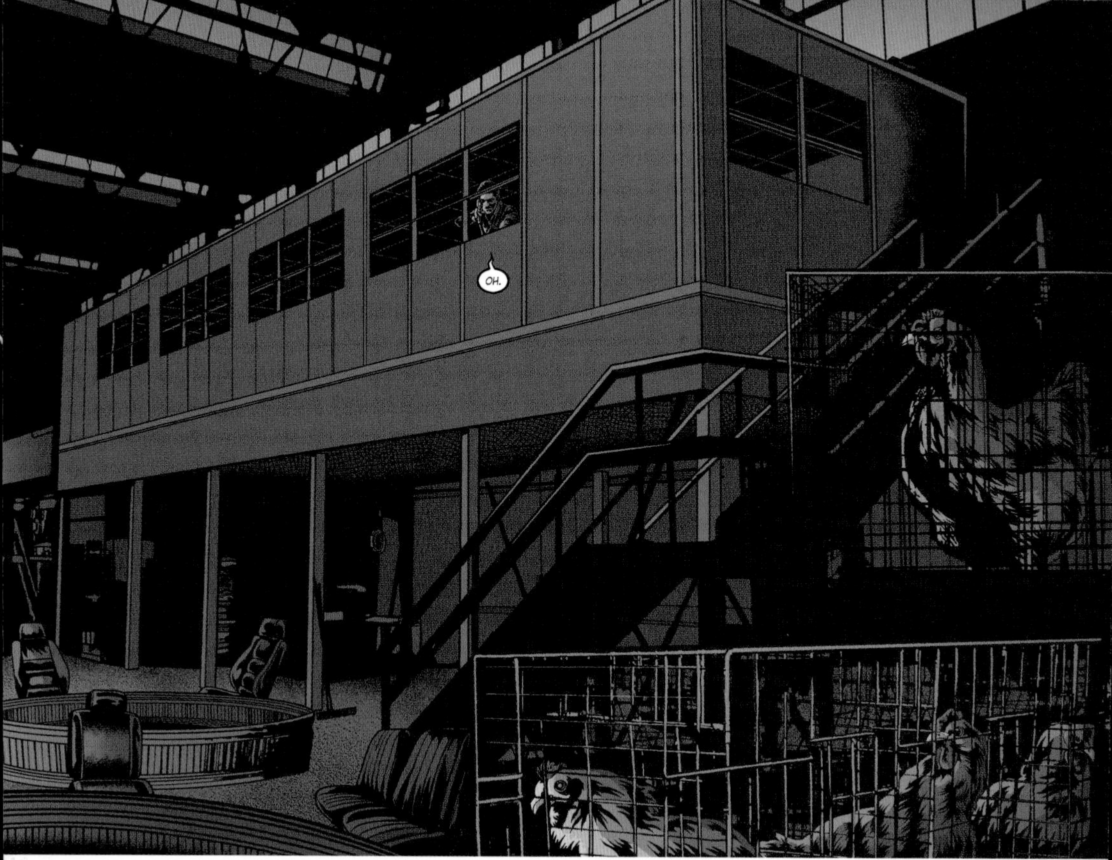
OH.

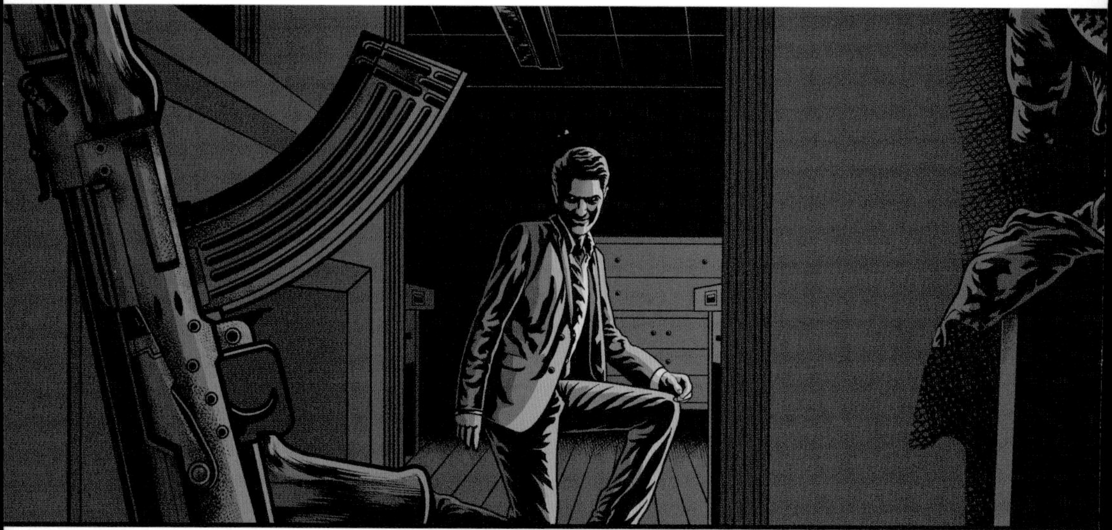

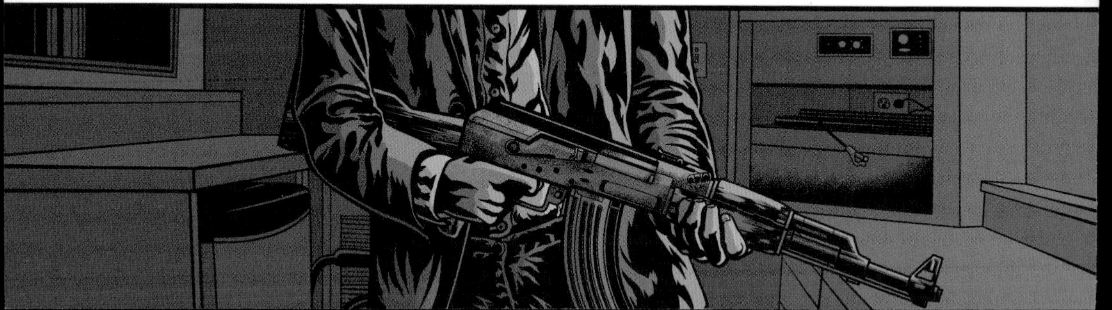

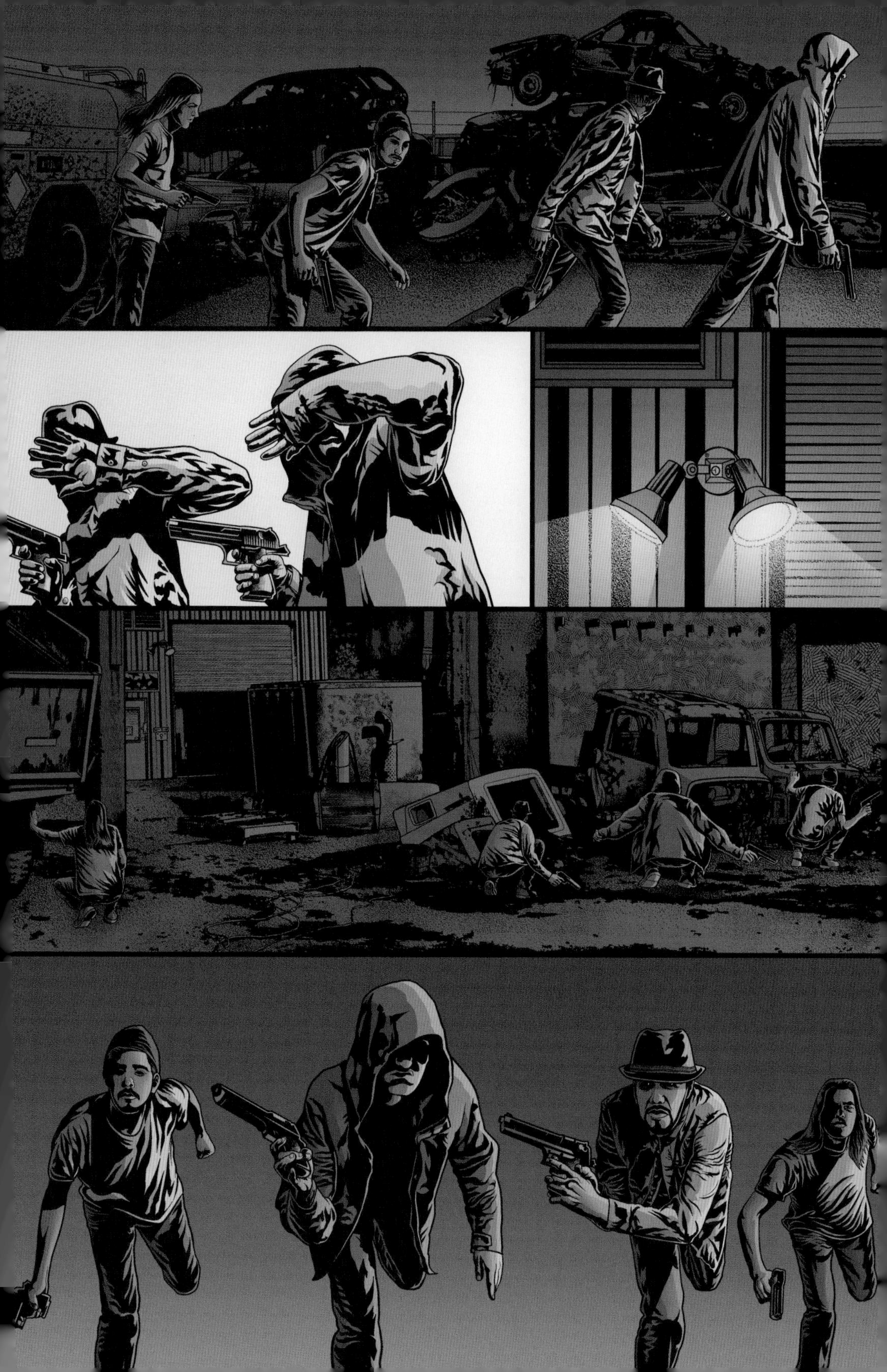

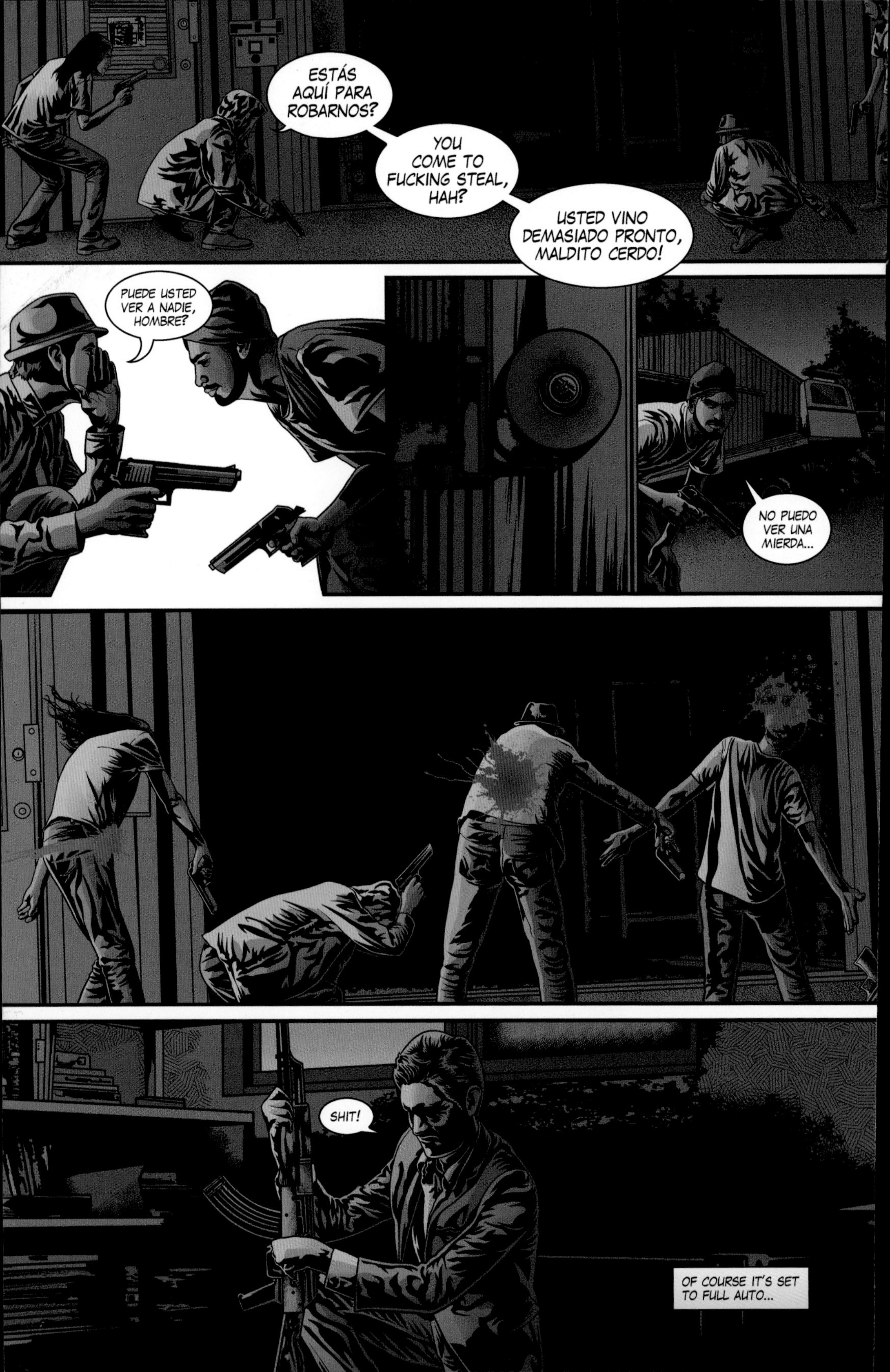
ESTÁS AQUÍ PARA ROBARNOS?
YOU COME TO FUCKING STEAL, HAH?
USTED VINO DEMASIADO PRONTO, MALDITO CERDO!
PUEDE USTED VER A NADIE, HOMBRE?
NO PUEDO VER UNA MIERDA...
SHIT!
OF COURSE IT'S SET TO FULL AUTO...

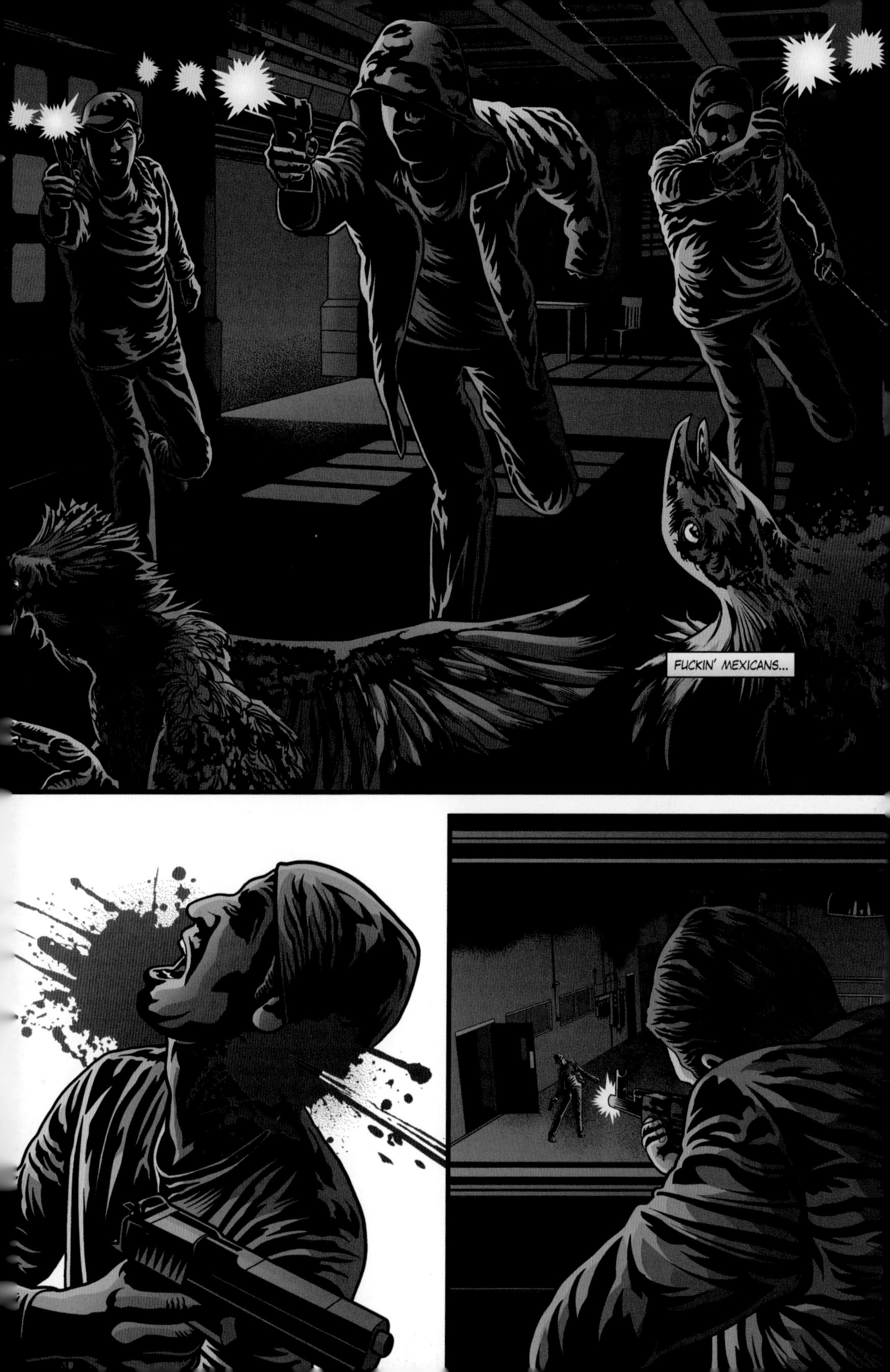
FUCKIN' MEXICANS...

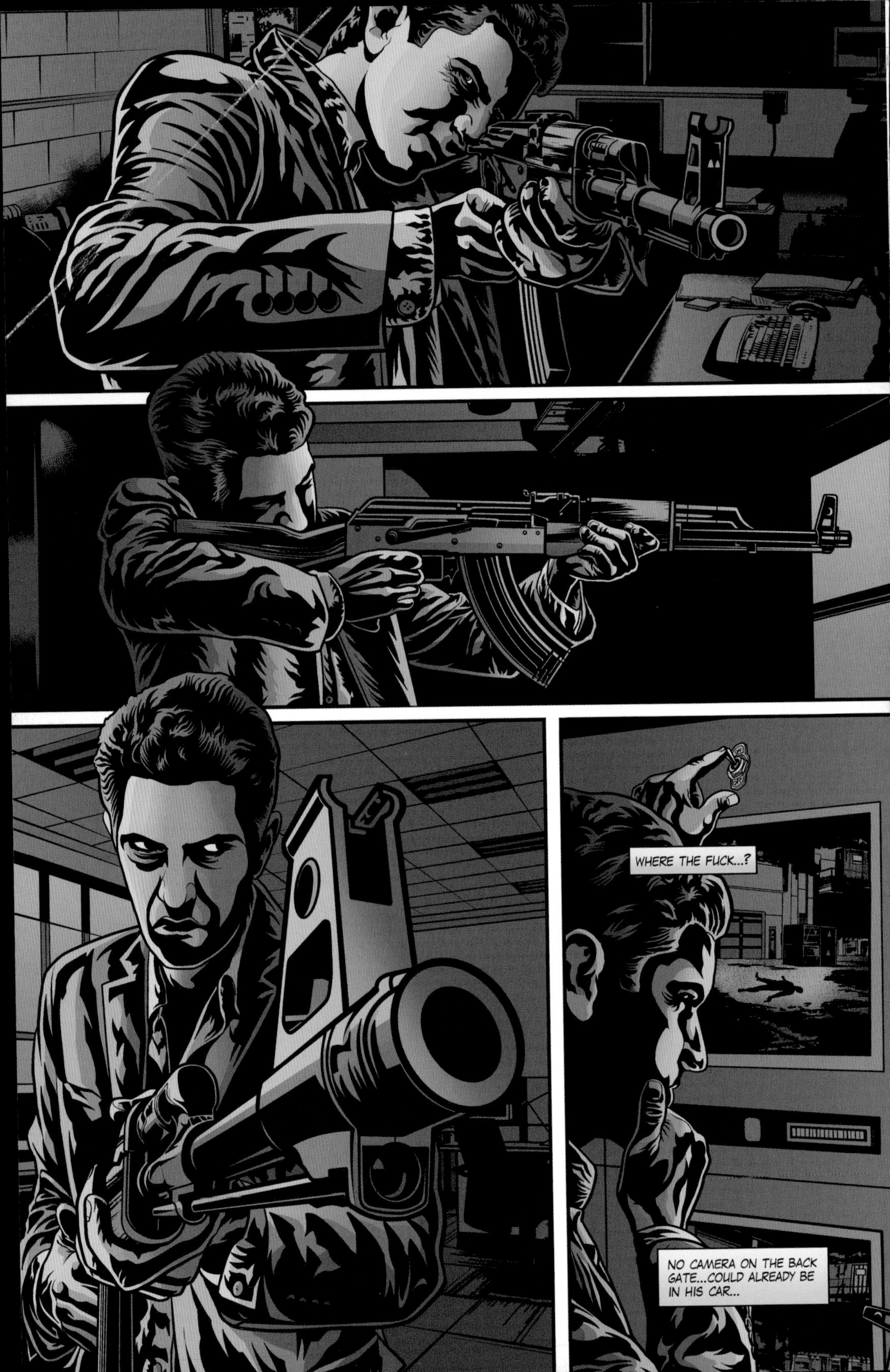
WHERE THE FUCK...?
NO CAMERA ON THE BACK GATE...COULD ALREADY BE IN HIS CAR...

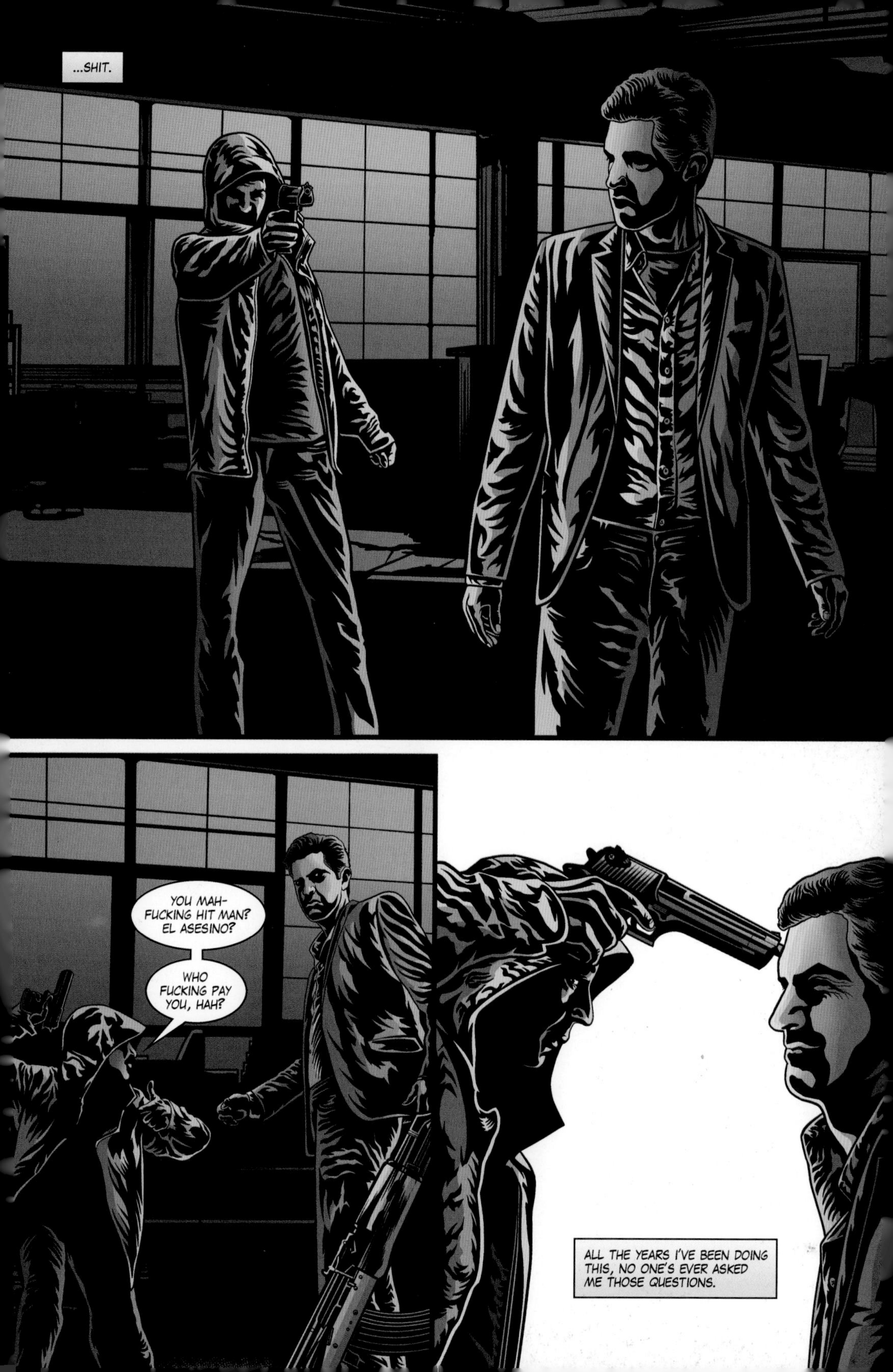
...SHIT.
YOU MAH-FUCKING HIT MAN? EL ASESINO?
WHO FUCKING PAY YOU, HAH?
ALL THE YEARS I'VE BEEN DOING THIS, NO ONE'S EVER ASKED ME THOSE QUESTIONS.

BECAUSE EITHER THEY WERE DEAD WITHIN SECONDS OF SEEING ME OR BECAUSE THEY NEVER FUCKING SAW ME AT ALL.

BUT THIS ASSHOLE... HE SEES ME, CLEAR AS DAY. HE CAN SEE EXACTLY WHAT I AM BECAUSE I LET HIM SEE EXACTLY WHAT I AM.

WHEN MY MIND'S ON THE JOB I'M INVISIBLE. A GHOST. BUT I WASN'T THINKING ABOUT THE JOB. I WAS THINKING ABOUT HER.

I'VE BEEN THINKING ABOUT HER SINCE THE SECOND I LAID EYES ON HER.

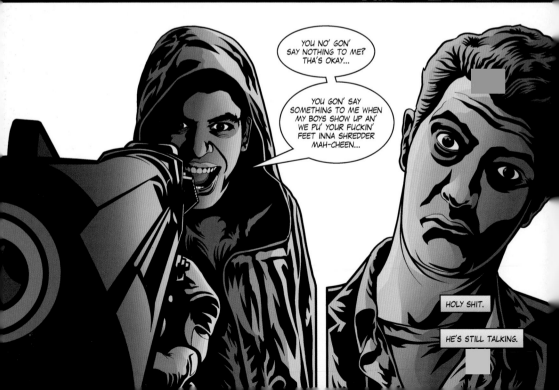

YOU NO' GON' SAY NOTHING TO ME? THA'S OKAY...

YOU GON' SAY SOMETHING TO ME WHEN MY BOYS SHOW UP AN' WE PU' YOUR FUCKIN' FEET INNA SHREDDER MAH-CHEEN...

HOLY SHIT.

HE'S STILL TALKING.

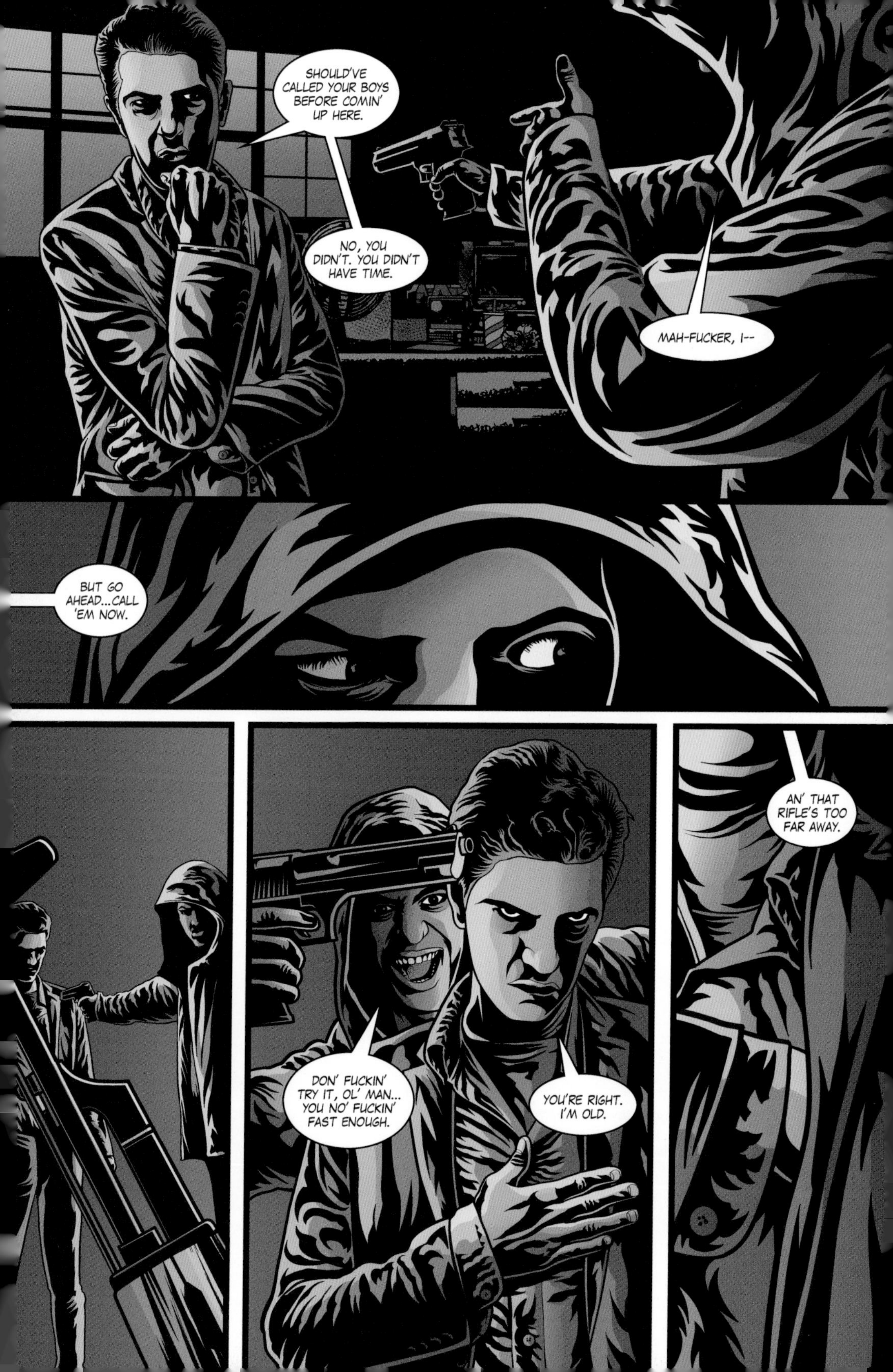
SHOULD'VE CALLED YOUR BOYS BEFORE COMIN' UP HERE.
NO, YOU DIDN'T. YOU DIDN'T HAVE TIME.
MAH-FUCKER, I--
BUT GO AHEAD...CALL 'EM NOW.
DON' FUCKIN' TRY IT, OL' MAN... YOU NO' FUCKIN' FAST ENOUGH.
YOU'RE RIGHT. I'M OLD.
AN' THAT RIFLE'S TOO FAR AWAY.

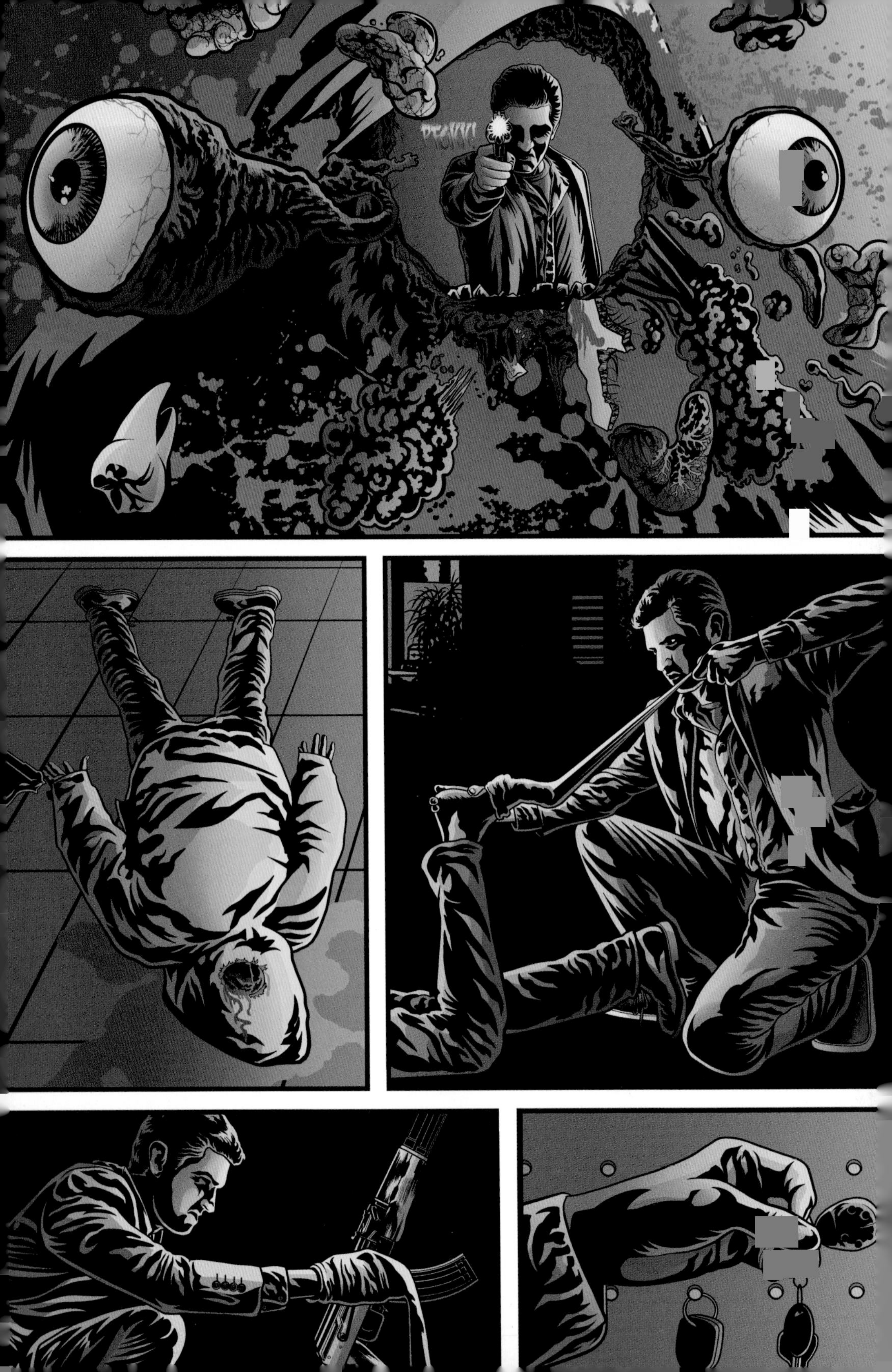

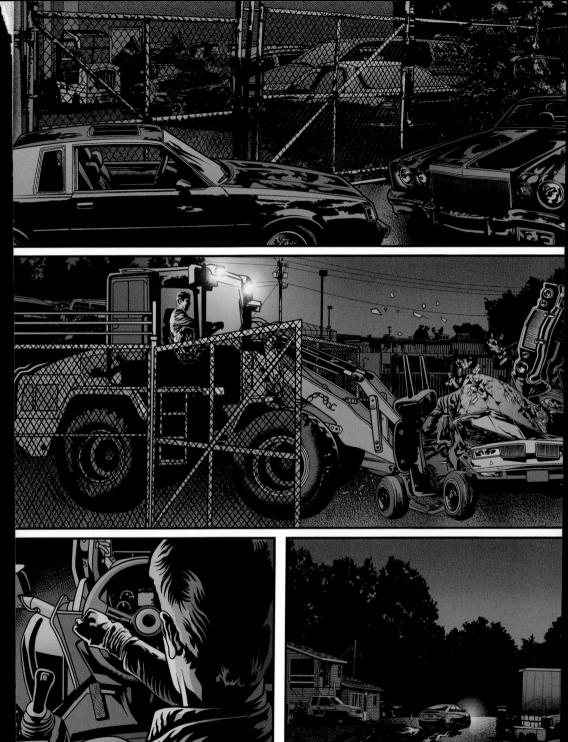

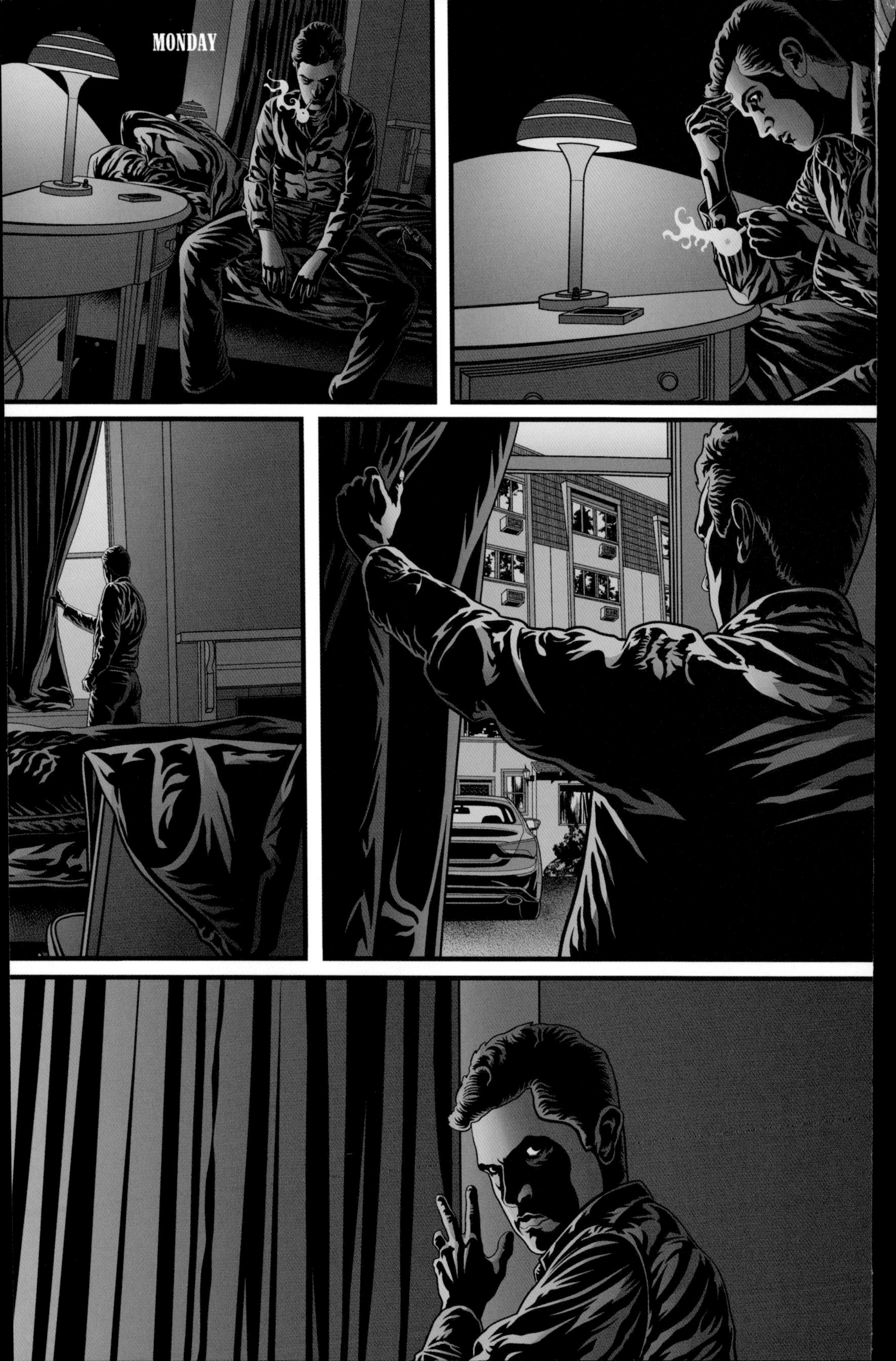
MONDAY

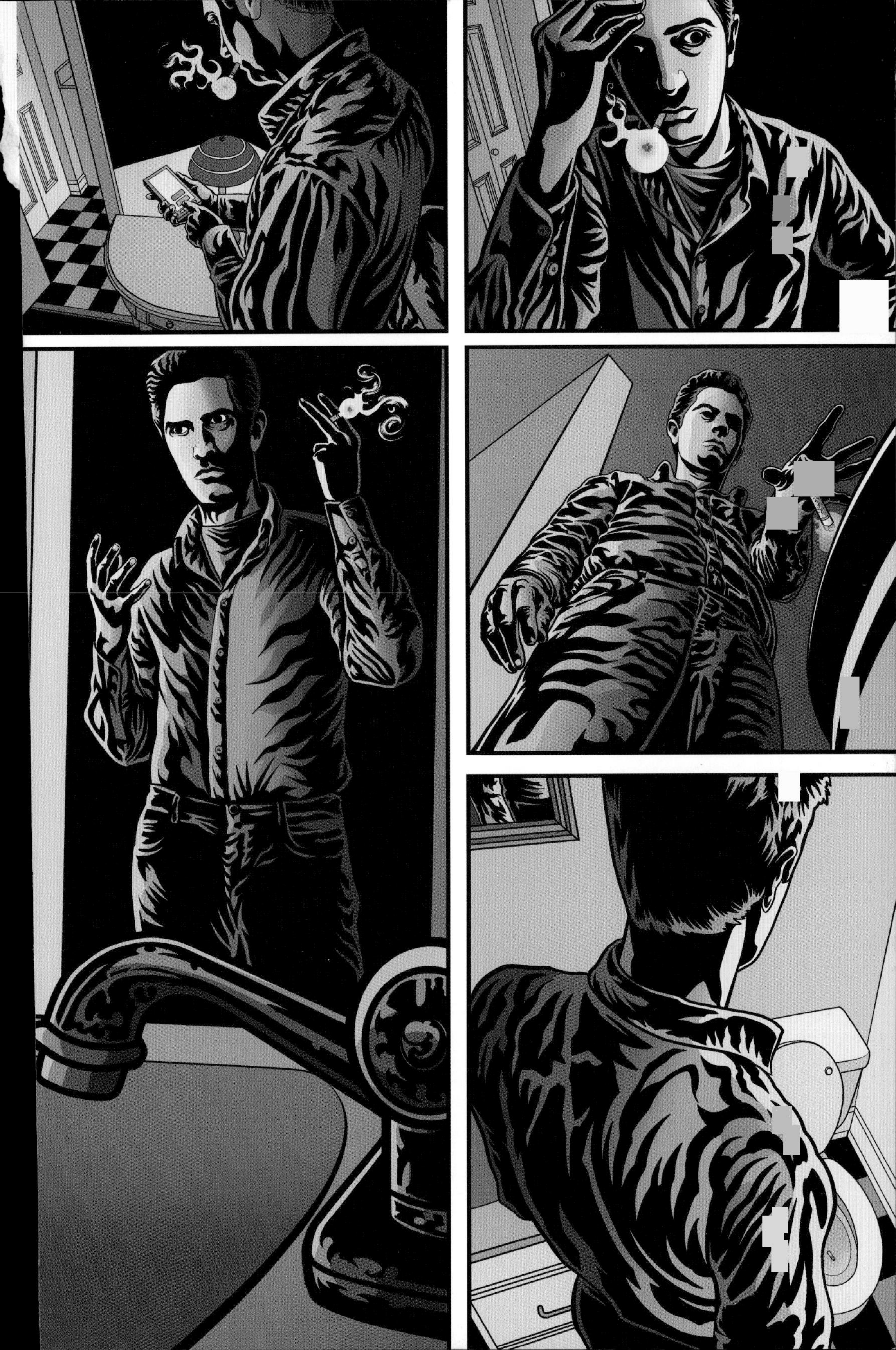

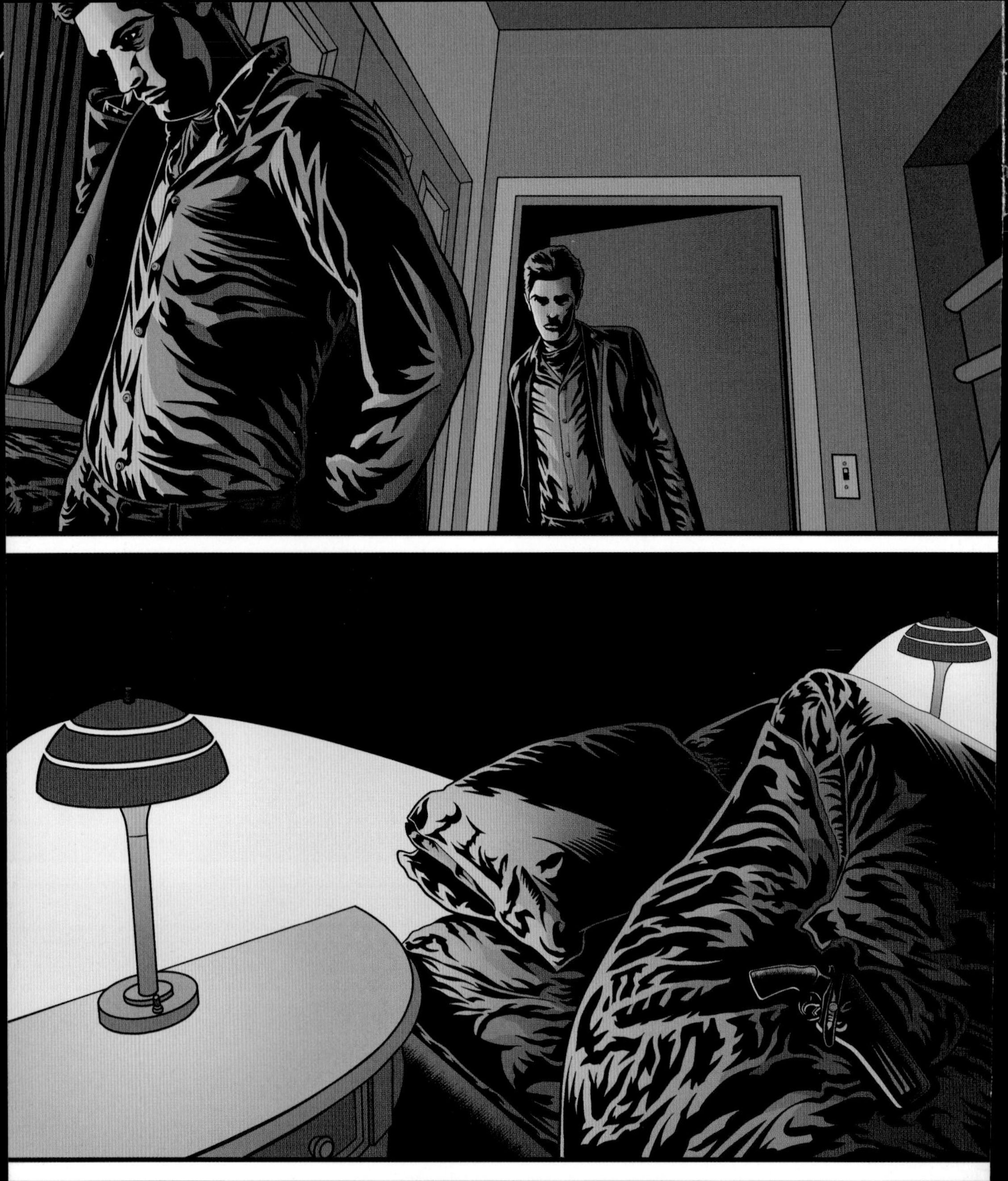

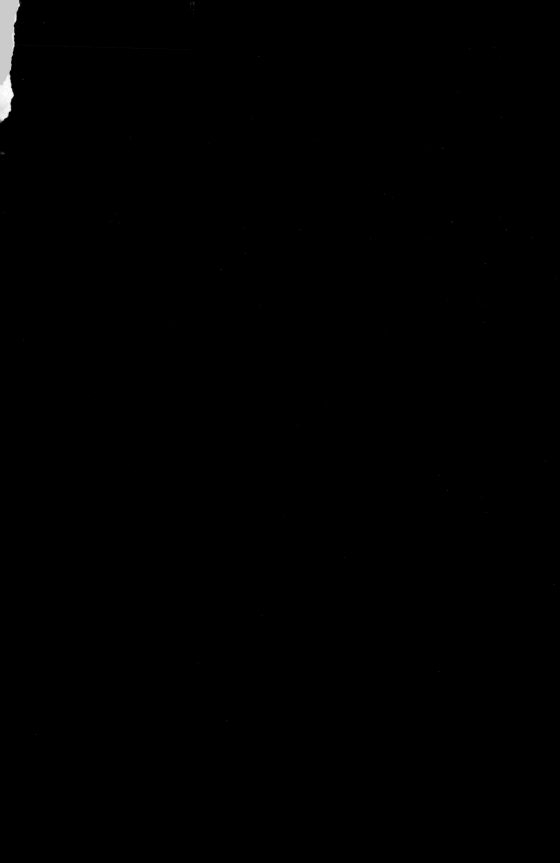

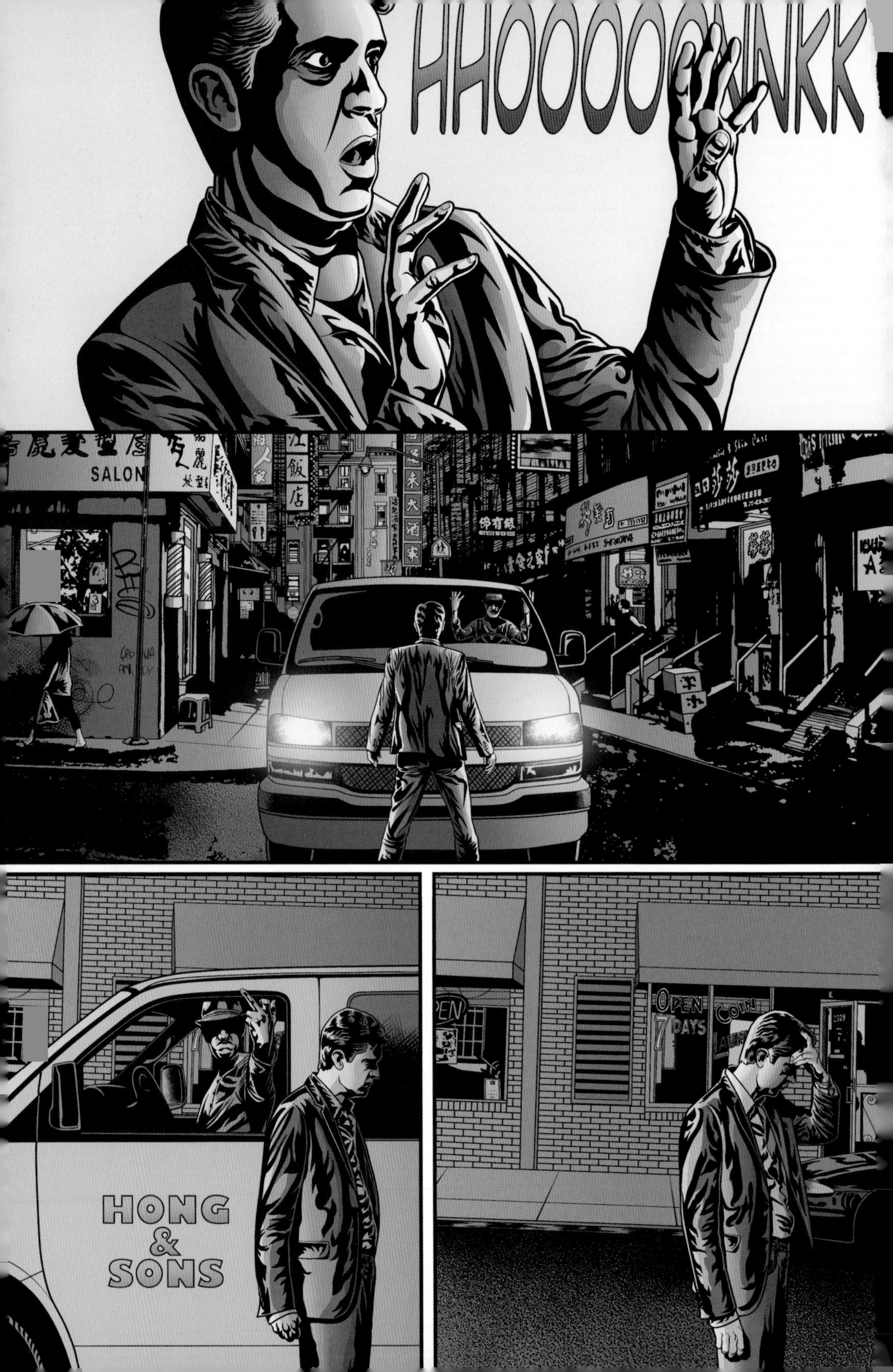

HHOOOOONKK
SALON
HONG & SONS
OPEN 7 DAYS
COIN

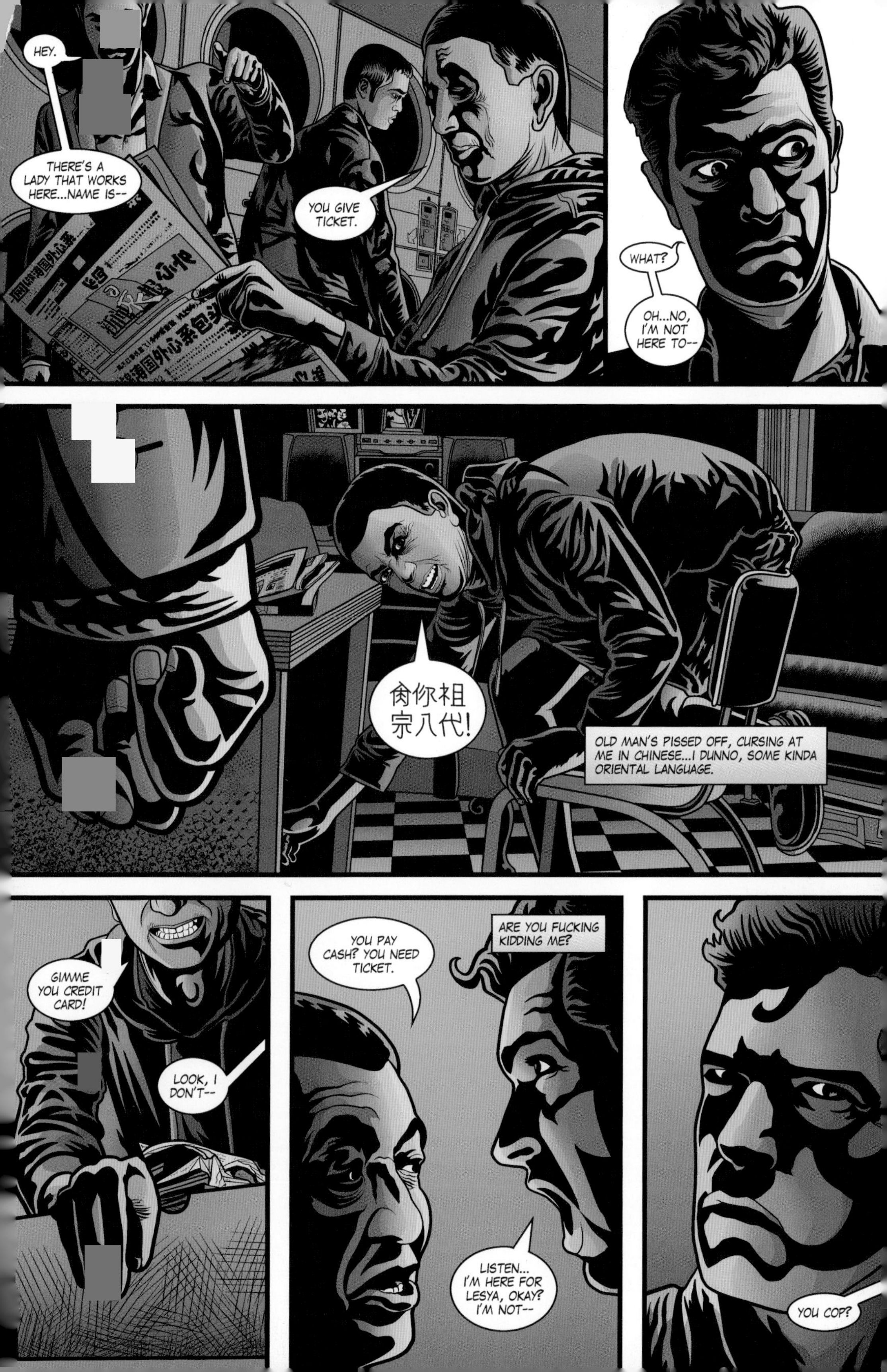
HEY.
THERE'S A LADY THAT WORKS HERE...NAME IS--
YOU GIVE TICKET.
WHAT?
OH...NO, I'M NOT HERE TO--
肏你祖宗八代!
OLD MAN'S PISSED OFF, CURSING AT ME IN CHINESE...I DUNNO, SOME KINDA ORIENTAL LANGUAGE.
GIMME YOU CREDIT CARD!
LOOK, I DON'T--
YOU PAY CASH? YOU NEED TICKET.
ARE YOU FUCKING KIDDING ME?
LISTEN... I'M HERE FOR LESYA, OKAY? I'M NOT--
YOU COP?

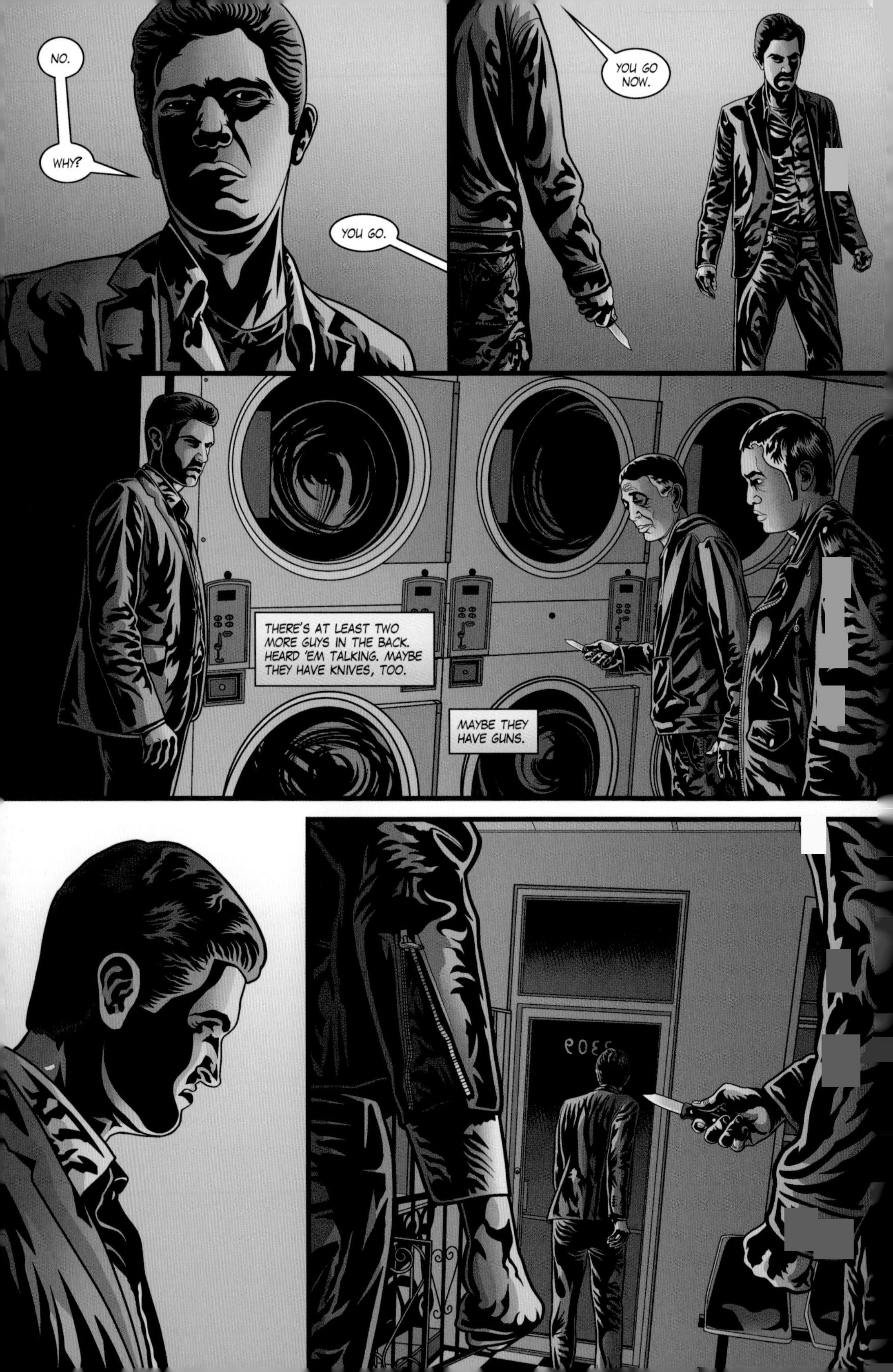
NO.
WHY?
YOU GO.
YOU GO NOW.
THERE'S AT LEAST TWO MORE GUYS IN THE BACK. HEARD 'EM TALKING. MAYBE THEY HAVE KNIVES, TOO.
MAYBE THEY HAVE GUNS.

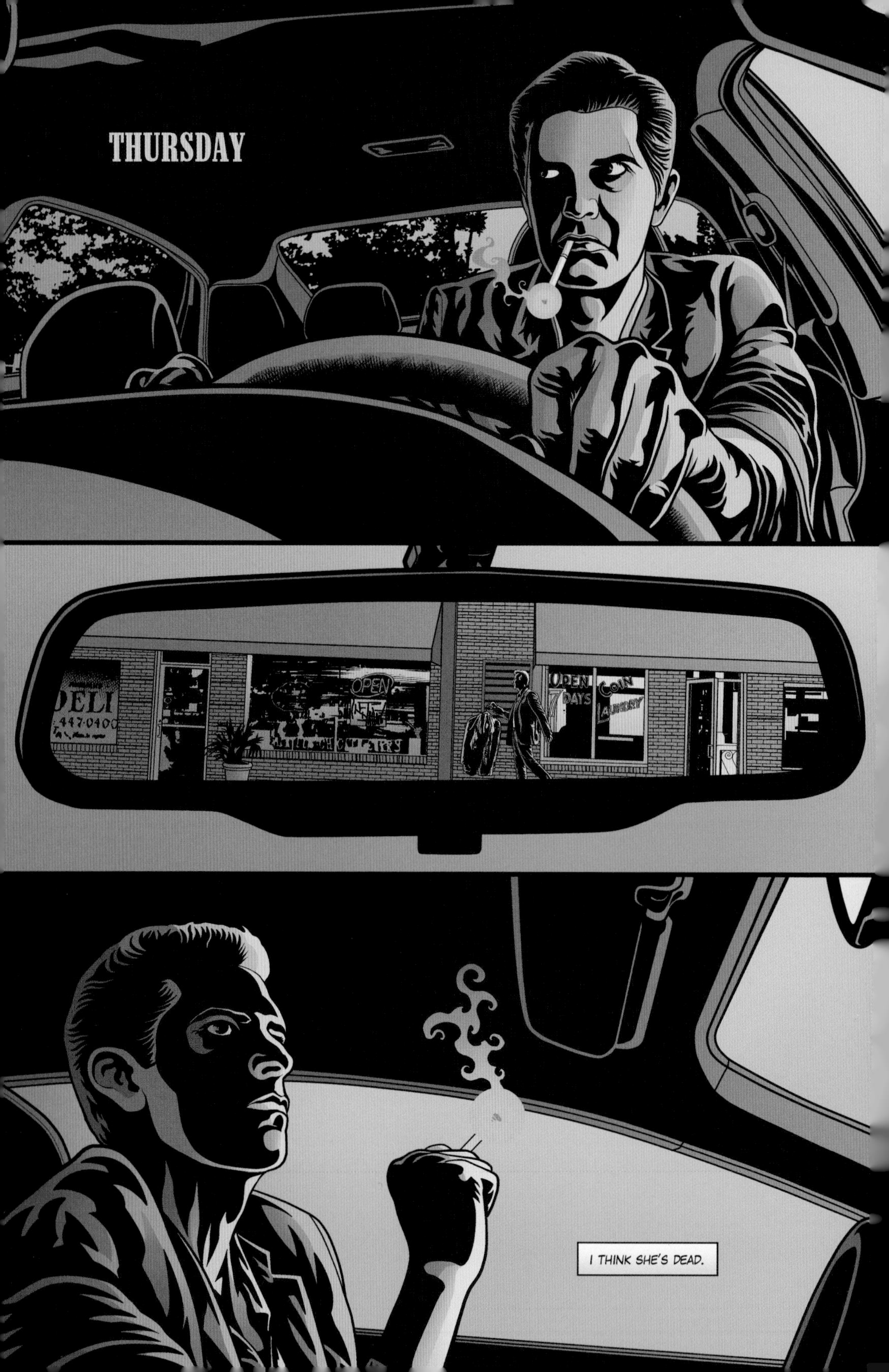
THURSDAY
DELI
447-0400
OPEN
OPEN 7 DAYS
COIN LAUNDRY
I THINK SHE'S DEAD.

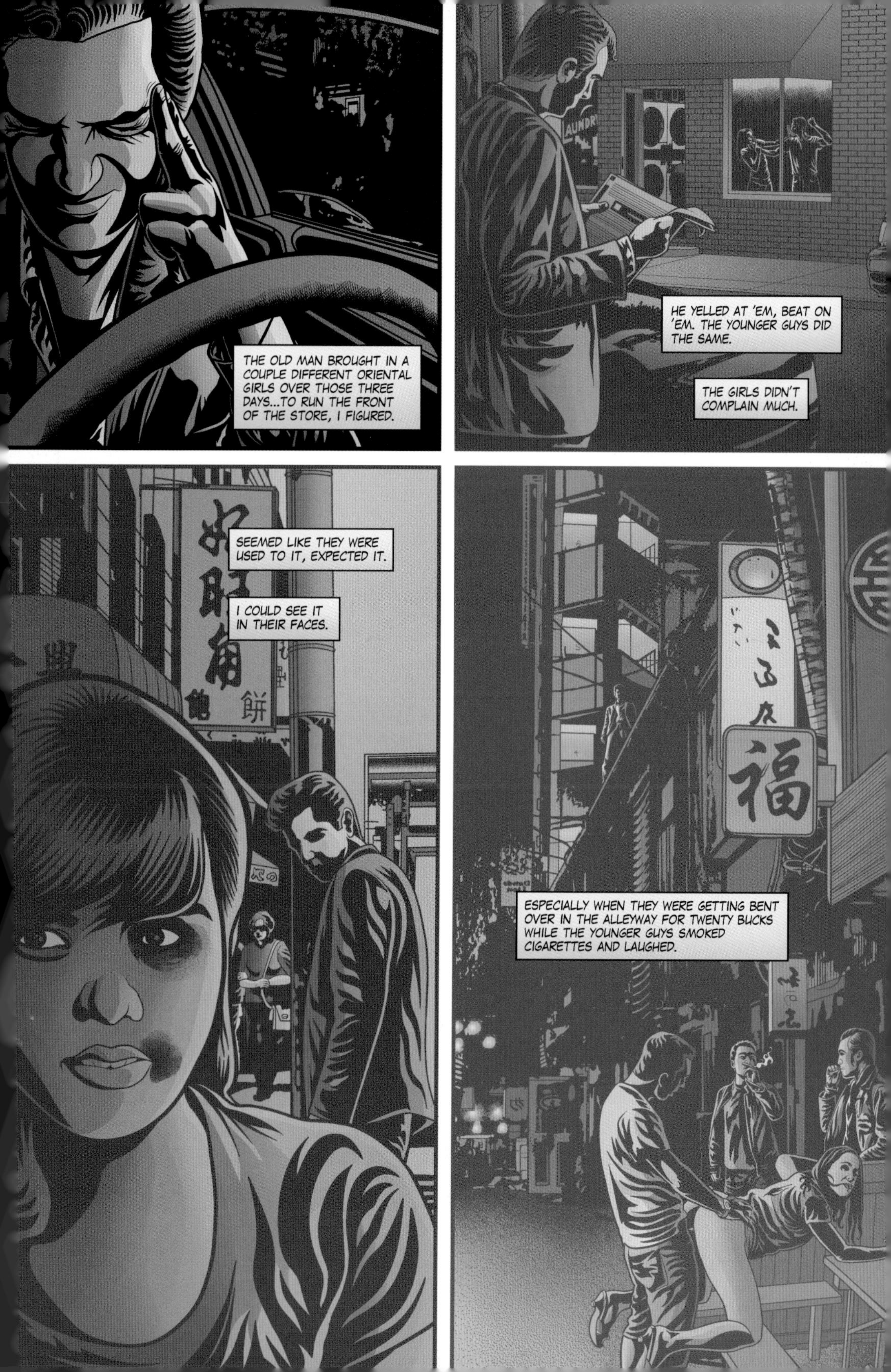
THE OLD MAN BROUGHT IN A COUPLE DIFFERENT ORIENTAL GIRLS OVER THOSE THREE DAYS...TO RUN THE FRONT OF THE STORE, I FIGURED.
HE YELLED AT 'EM, BEAT ON 'EM. THE YOUNGER GUYS DID THE SAME.
THE GIRLS DIDN'T COMPLAIN MUCH.
SEEMED LIKE THEY WERE USED TO IT, EXPECTED IT.
I COULD SEE IT IN THEIR FACES.
ESPECIALLY WHEN THEY WERE GETTING BENT OVER IN THE ALLEYWAY FOR TWENTY BUCKS WHILE THE YOUNGER GUYS SMOKED CIGARETTES AND LAUGHED.
福

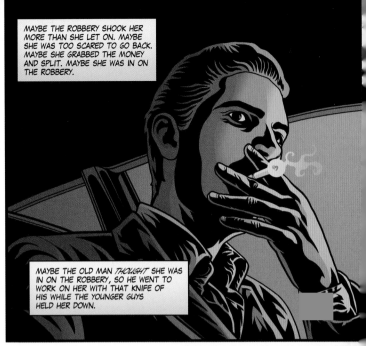

MAYBE THE ROBBERY SHOOK HER MORE THAN SHE LET ON. MAYBE SHE WAS TOO SCARED TO GO BACK. MAYBE SHE GRABBED THE MONEY AND SPLIT. MAYBE SHE WAS IN ON THE ROBBERY.

MAYBE THE OLD MAN *THOUGHT* SHE WAS IN ON THE ROBBERY, SO HE WENT TO WORK ON HER WITH THAT KNIFE OF HIS WHILE THE YOUNGER GUYS HELD HER DOWN.

MAYBE I SHOULD JUST GET THE HELL OUTTA HERE BECAUSE THE GIRL IS GONE AN' MY PROBLEM IS FUCKIN' SOLVED.

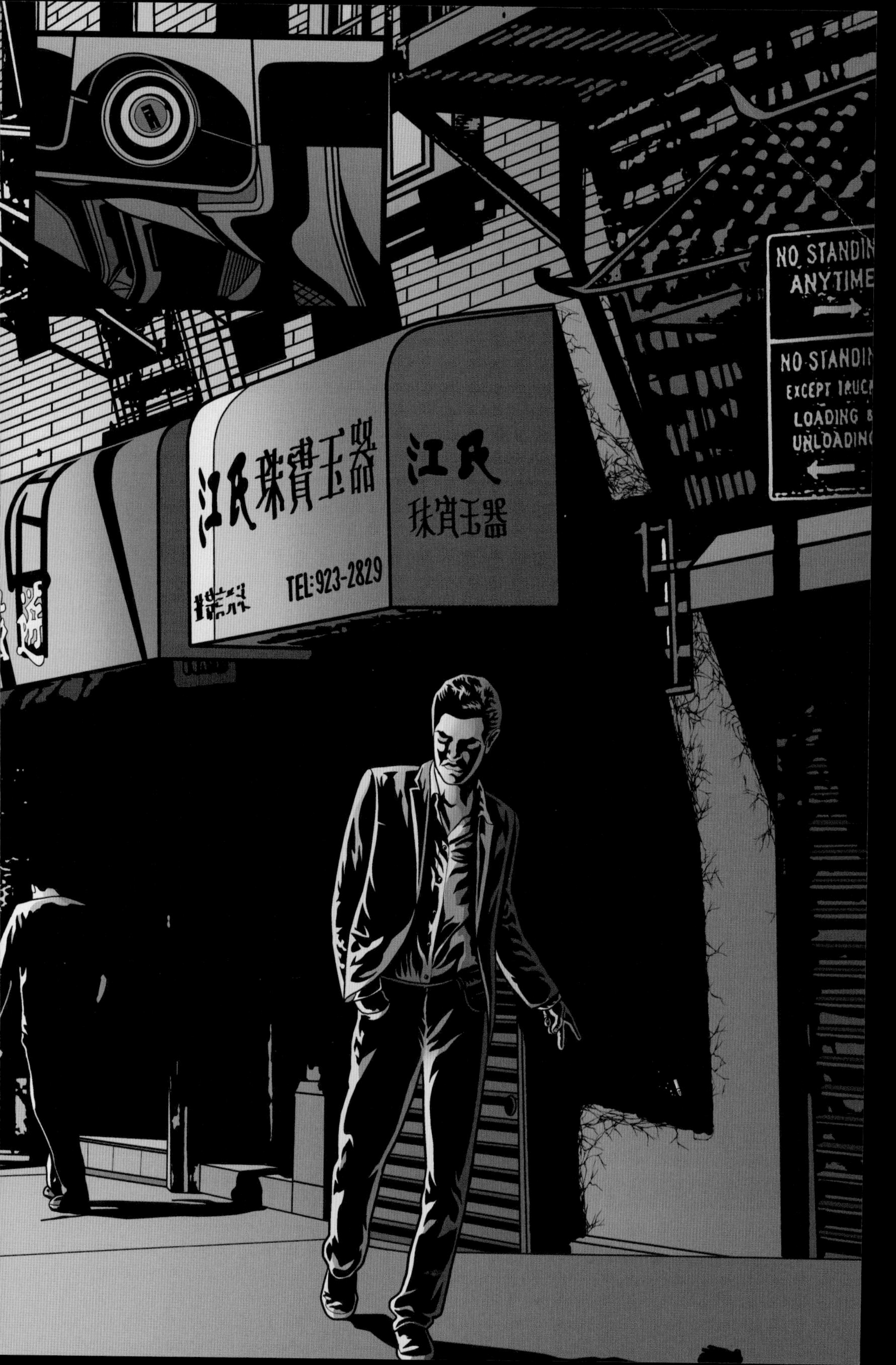
江氏珠寶玉器
江氏
珠寶玉器
TEL:923-2829
NO STANDIN
ANYTIME
NO STANDIN
LOADING
UNLOADIN

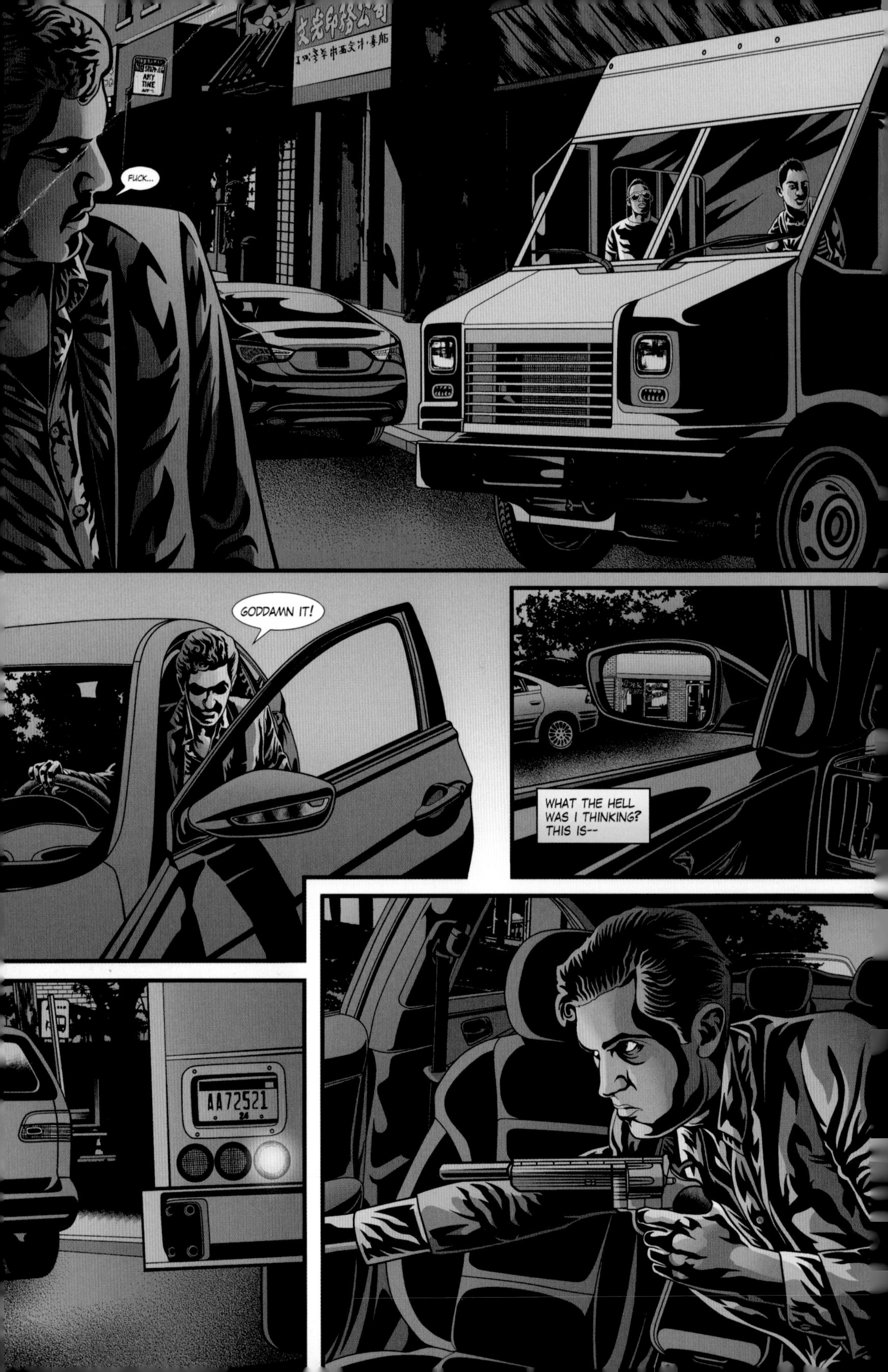
FUCK...
GODDAMN IT!
WHAT THE HELL WAS I THINKING? THIS IS--
AA72521

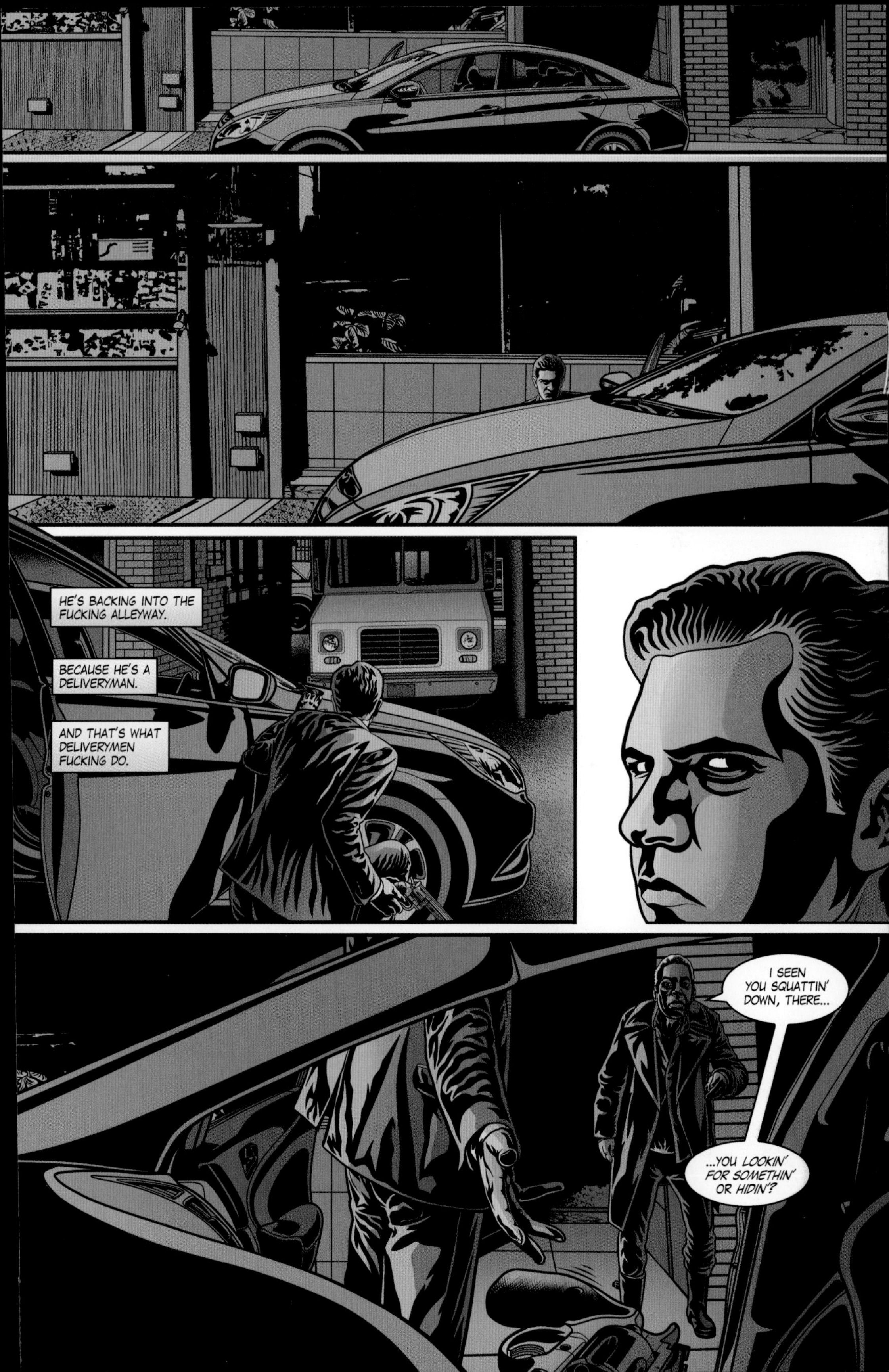

HE'S BACKING INTO THE FUCKING ALLEYWAY.
BECAUSE HE'S A DELIVERYMAN.
AND THAT'S WHAT DELIVERYMEN FUCKING DO.
I SEEN YOU SQUATTIN' DOWN, THERE...
...YOU LOOKIN' FOR SOMETHIN' OR HIDIN'?

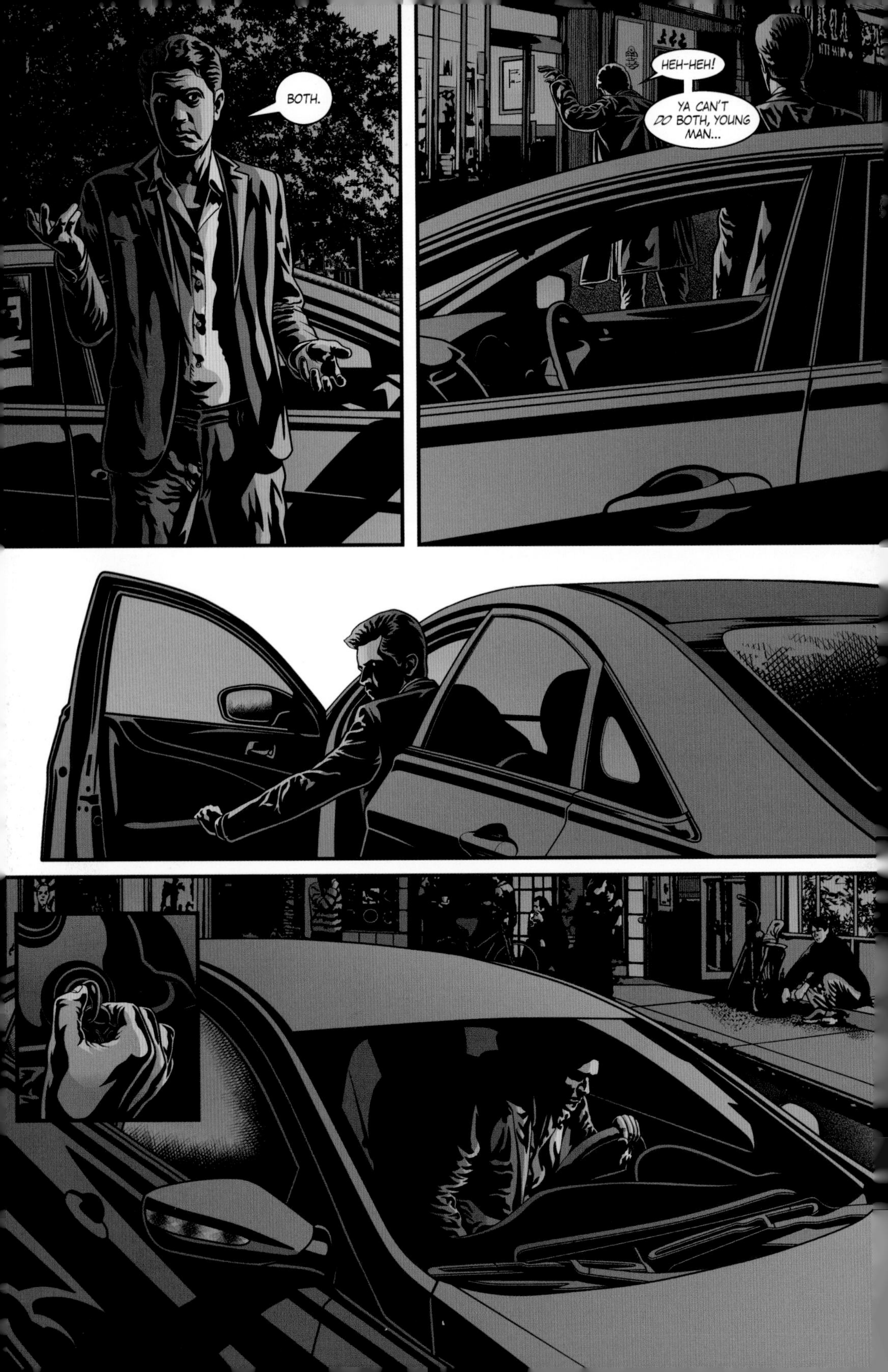
BOTH.
HEH-HEH!
YA CAN'T *DO* BOTH, YOUNG MAN...

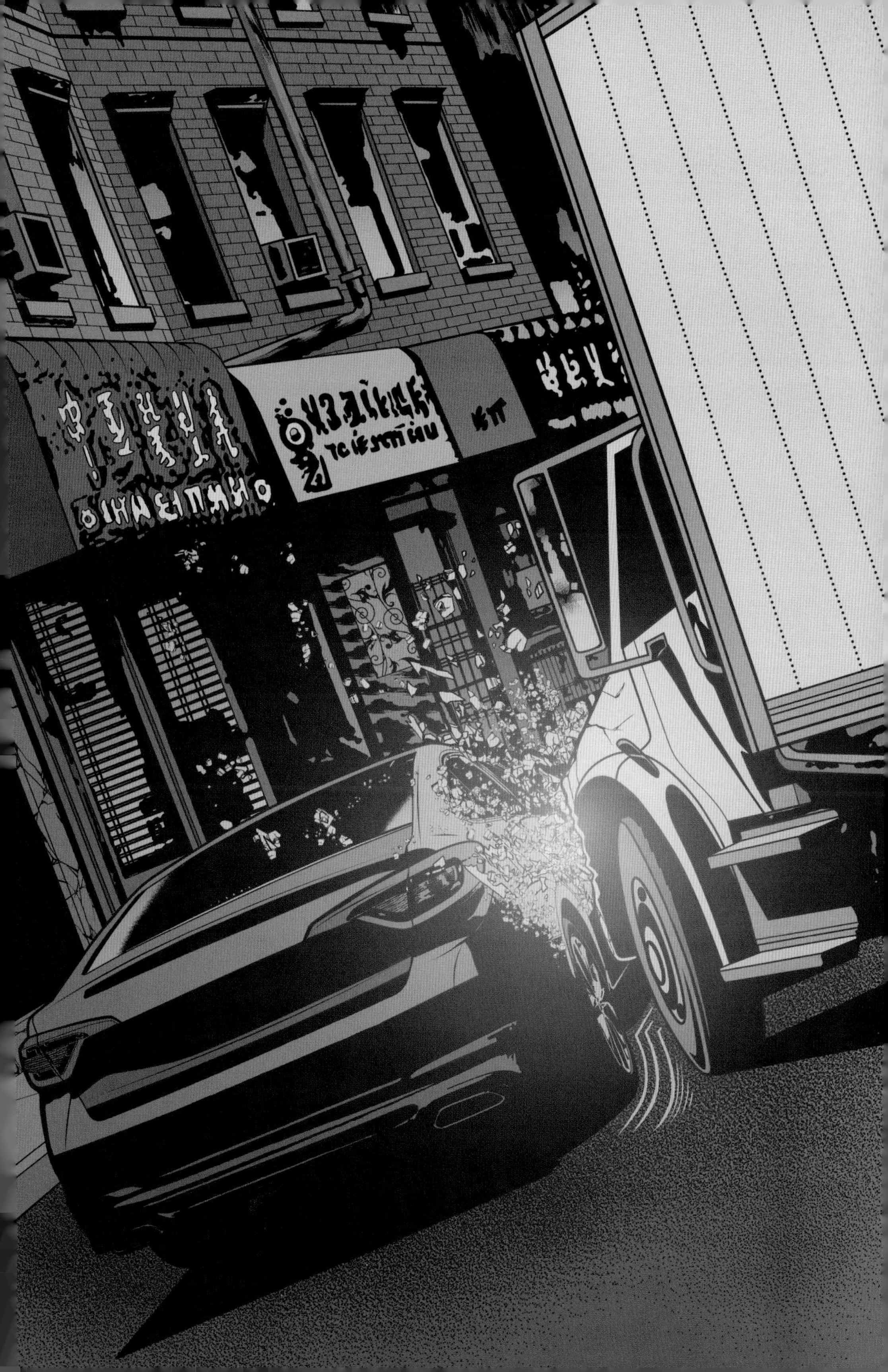

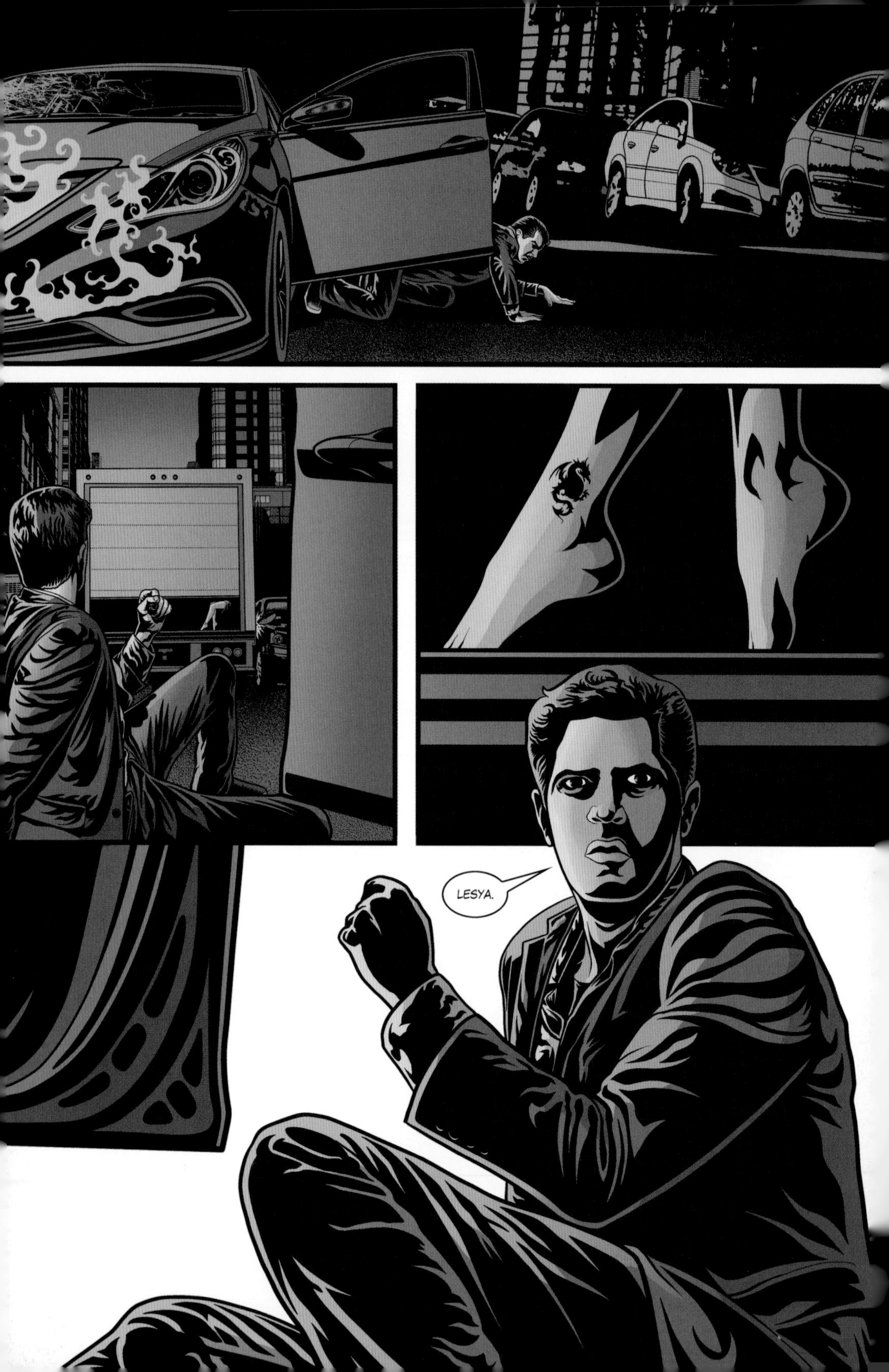
LESYA.

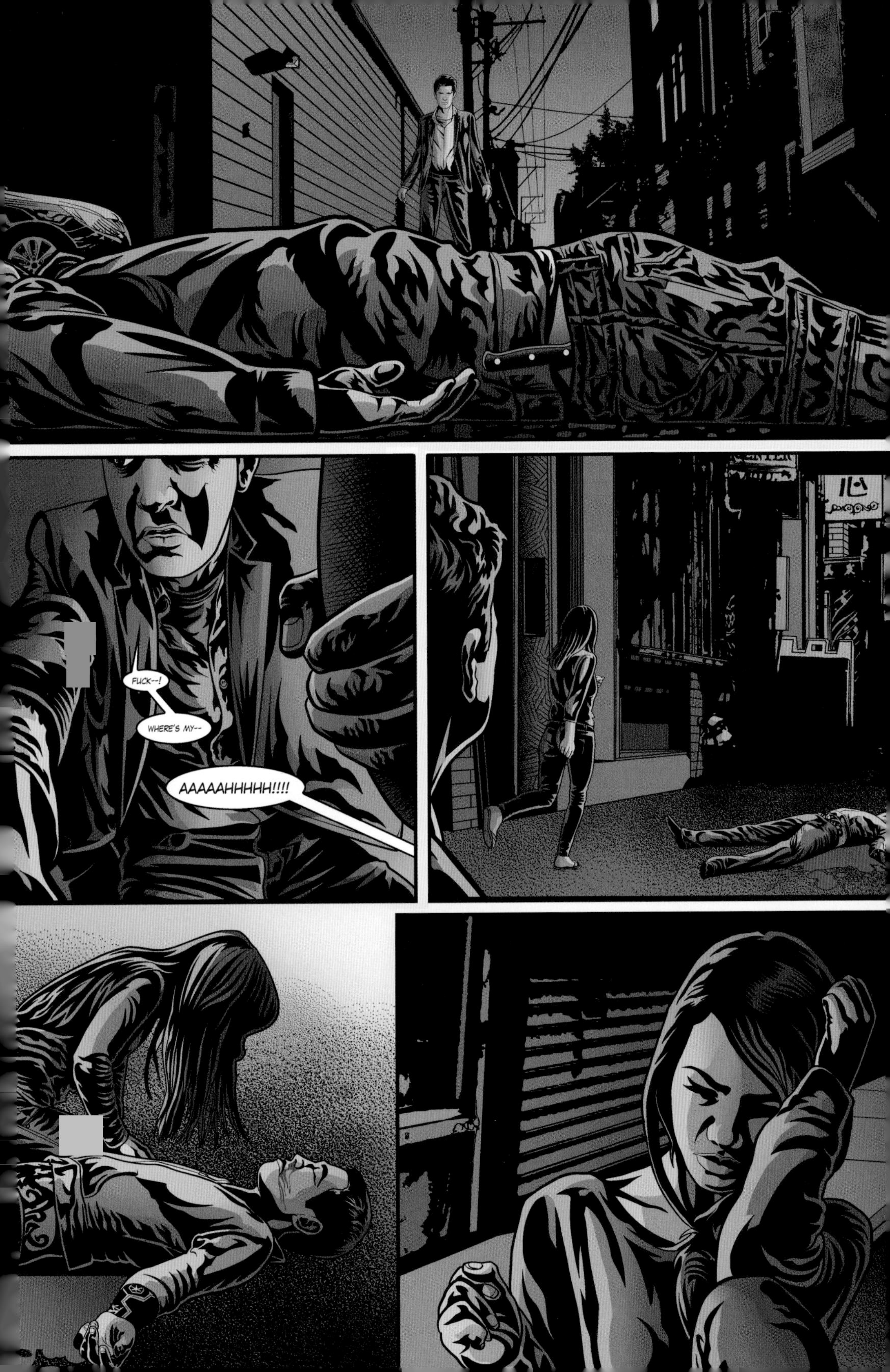
FUCK--!
WHERE'S MY--
AAAAAHHHHH!!!!
心

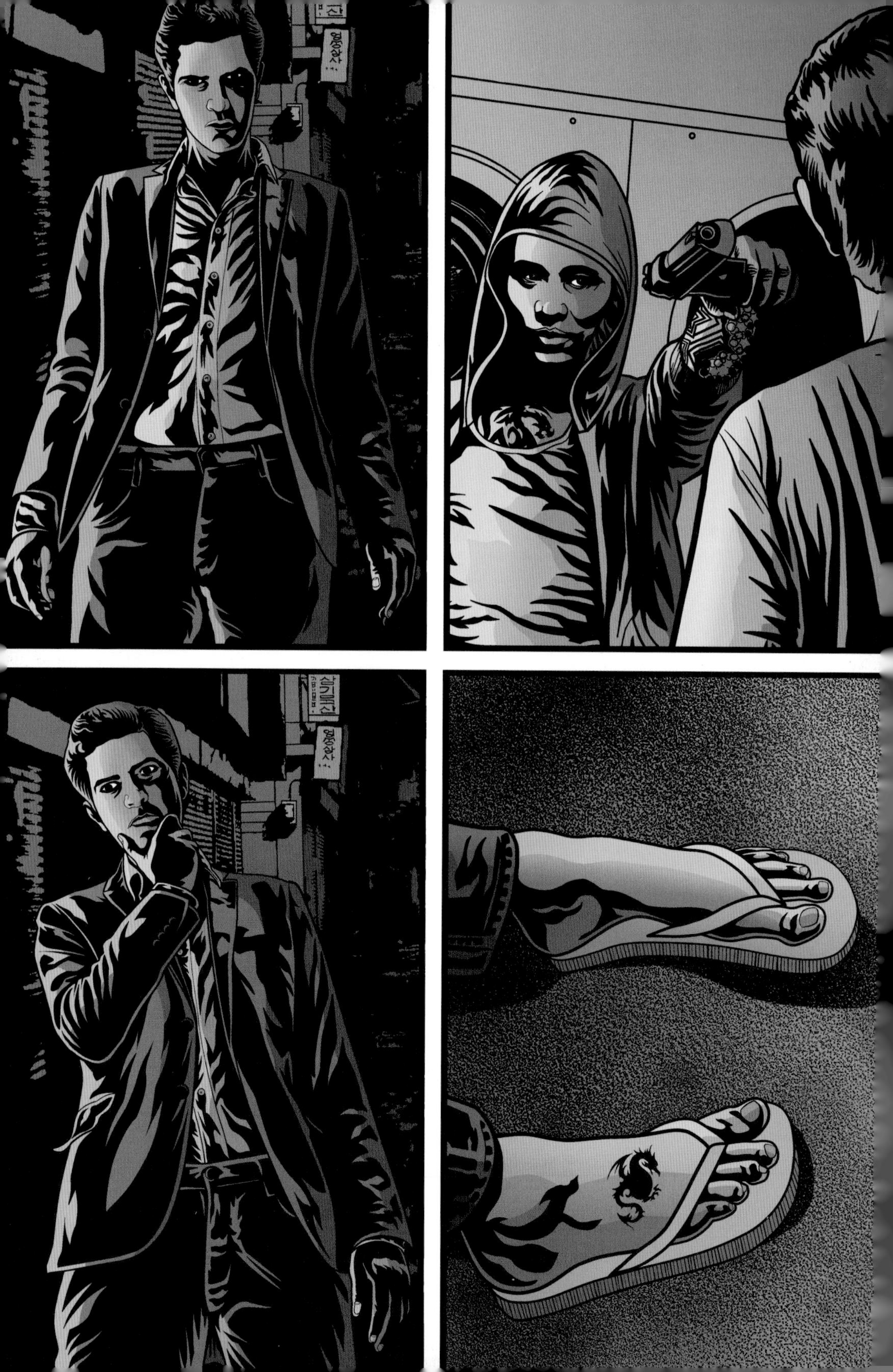

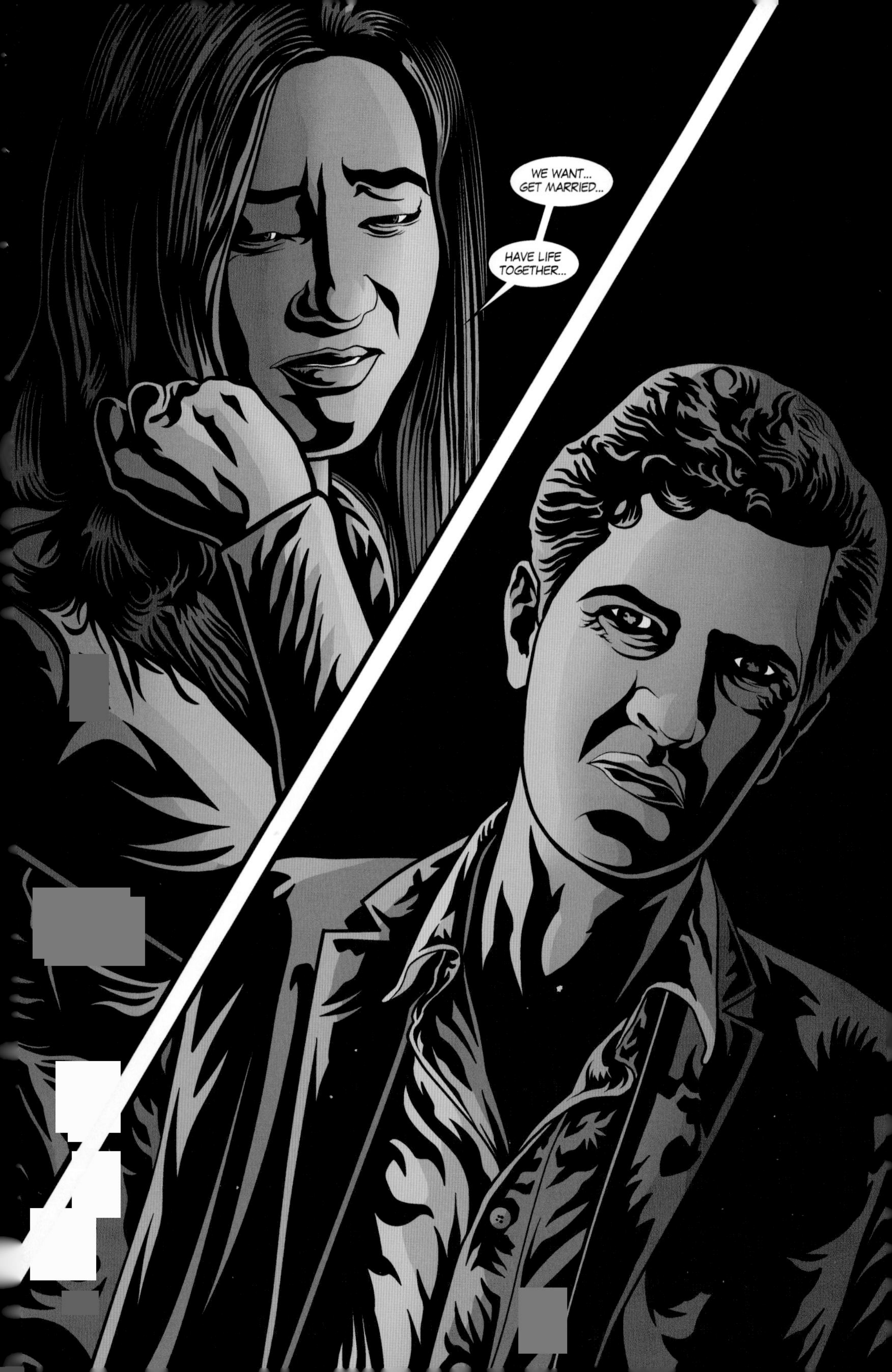
WE WANT... GET MARRIED...
HAVE LIFE TOGETHER...

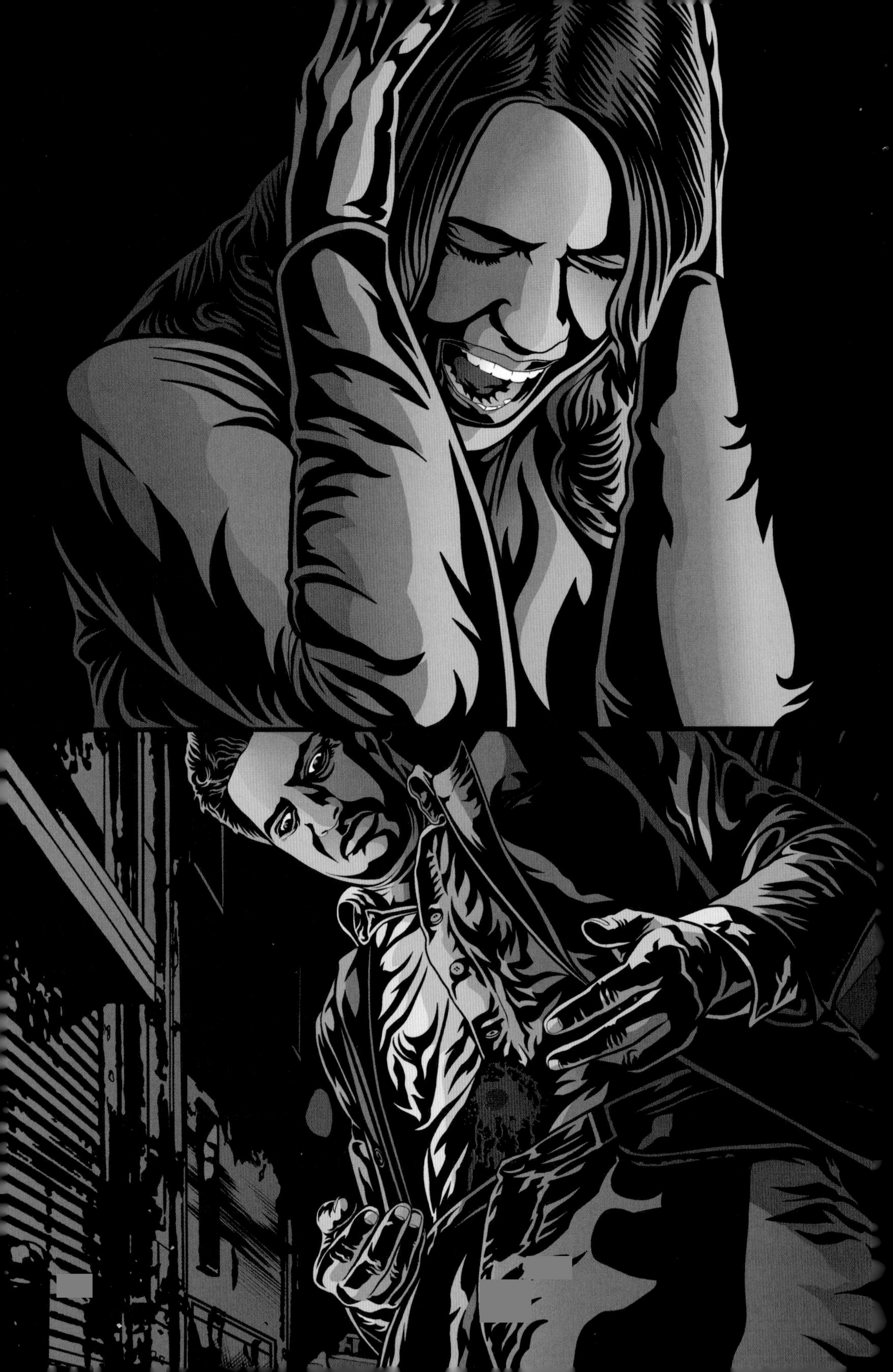

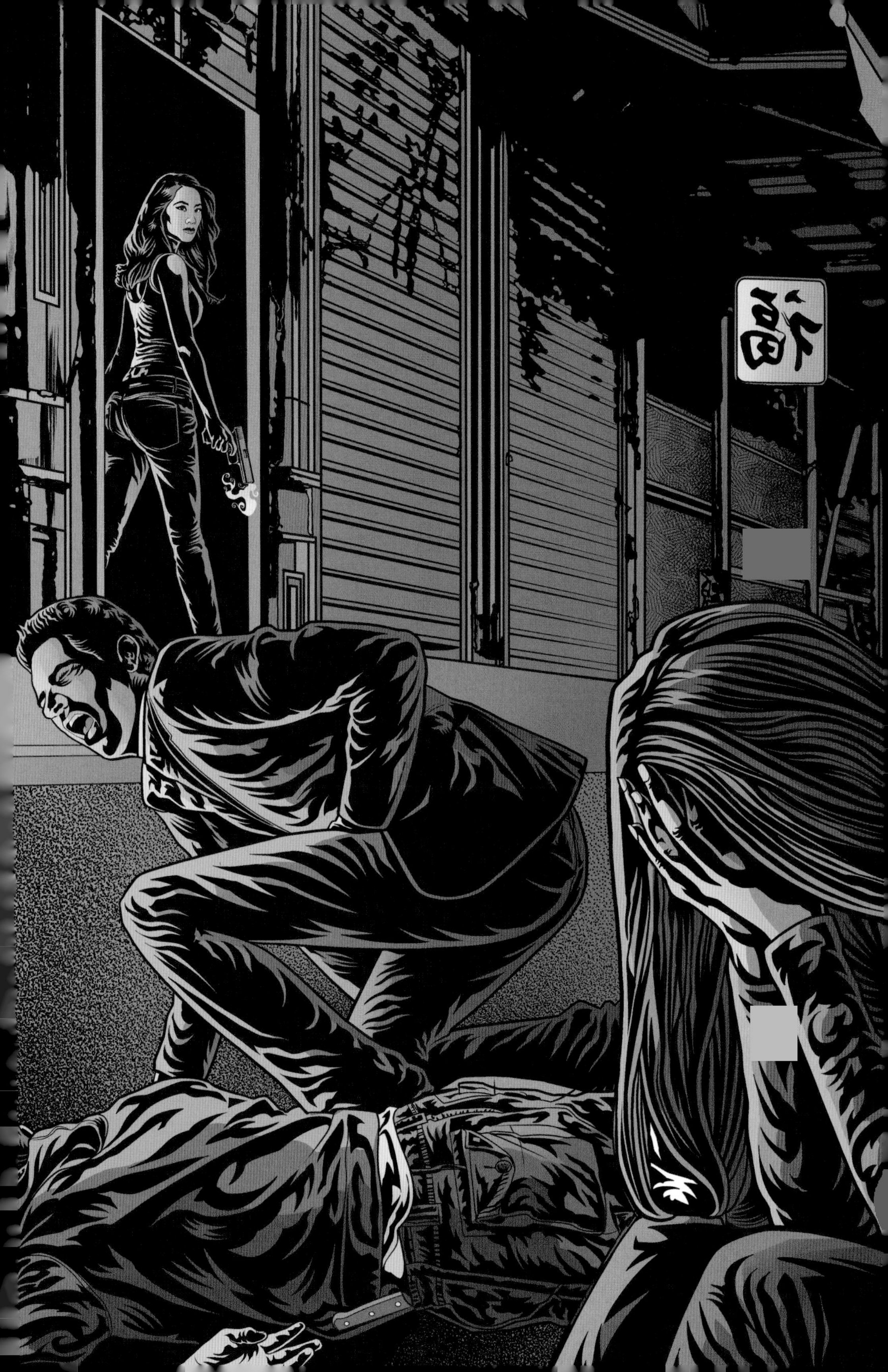

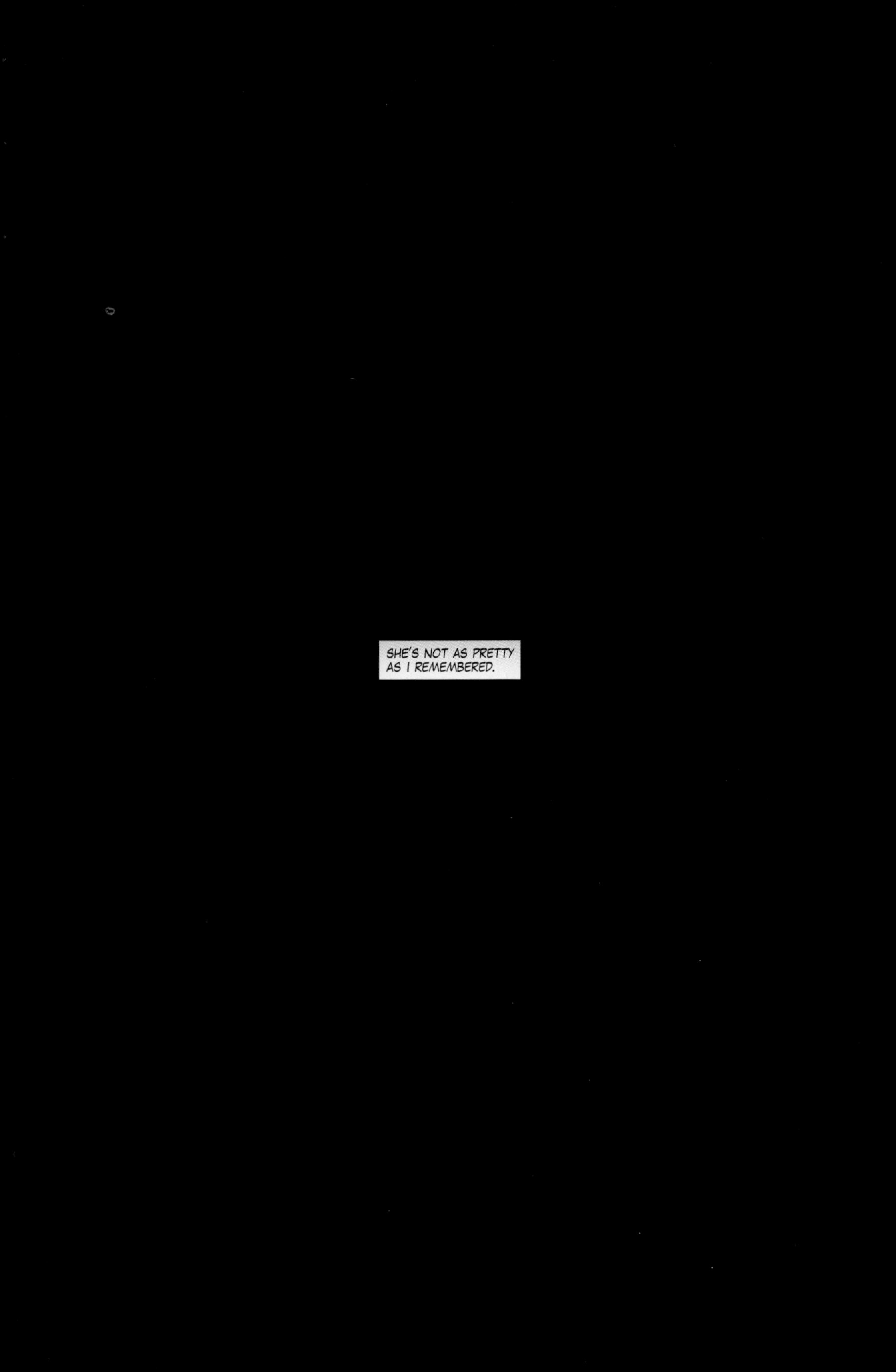
SHE'S NOT AS PRETTY AS I REMEMBERED.

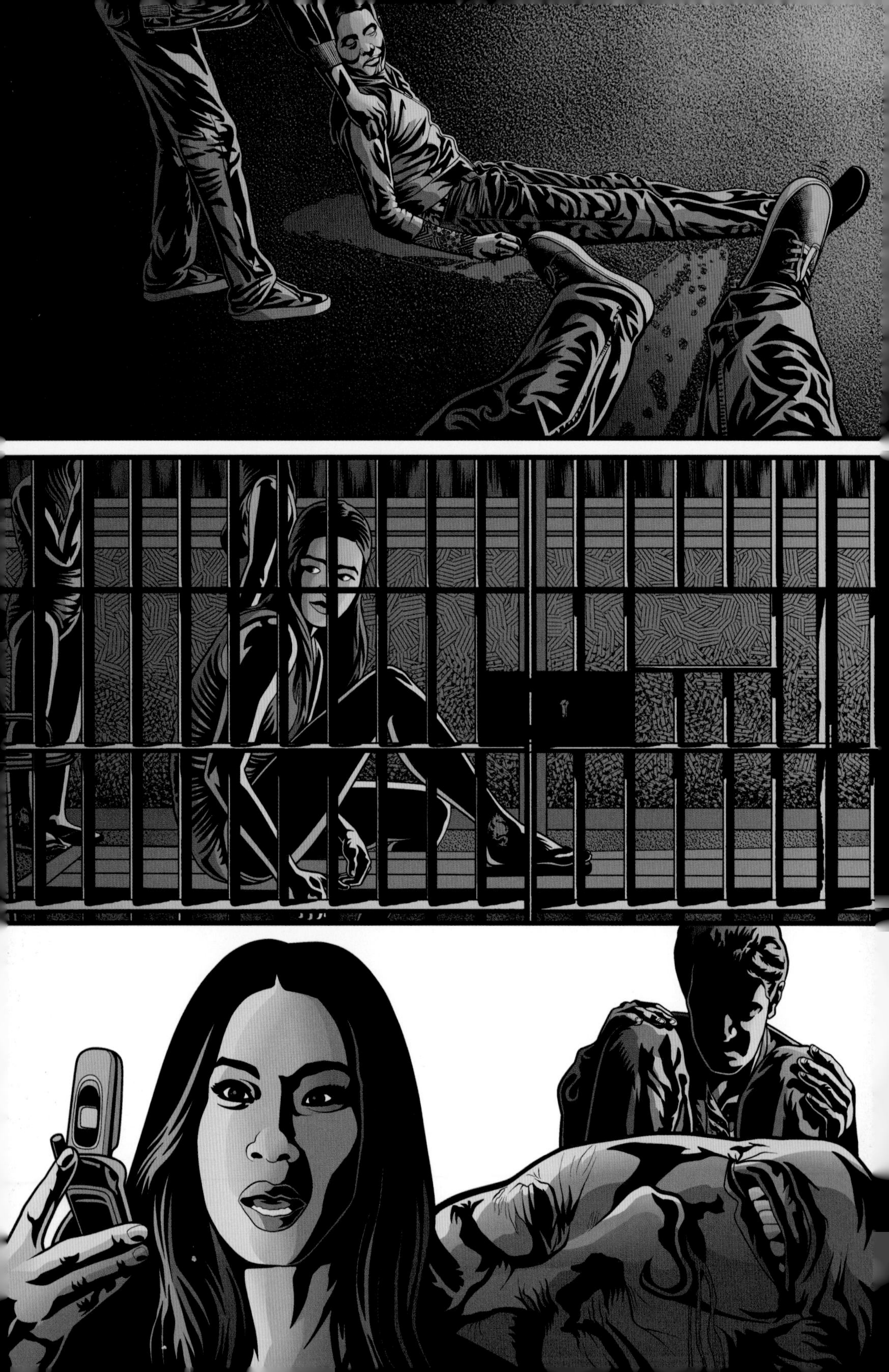

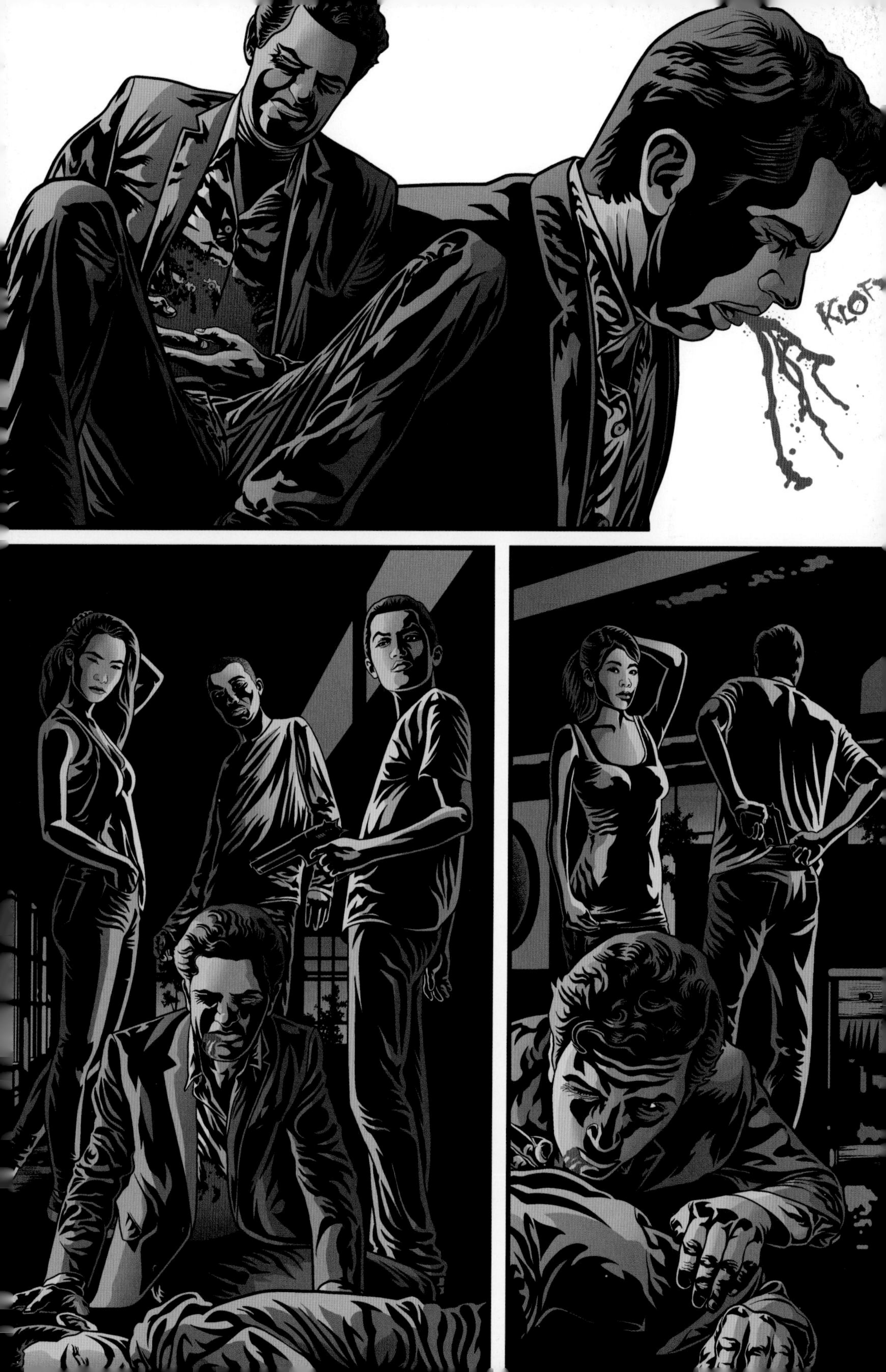
KLOF

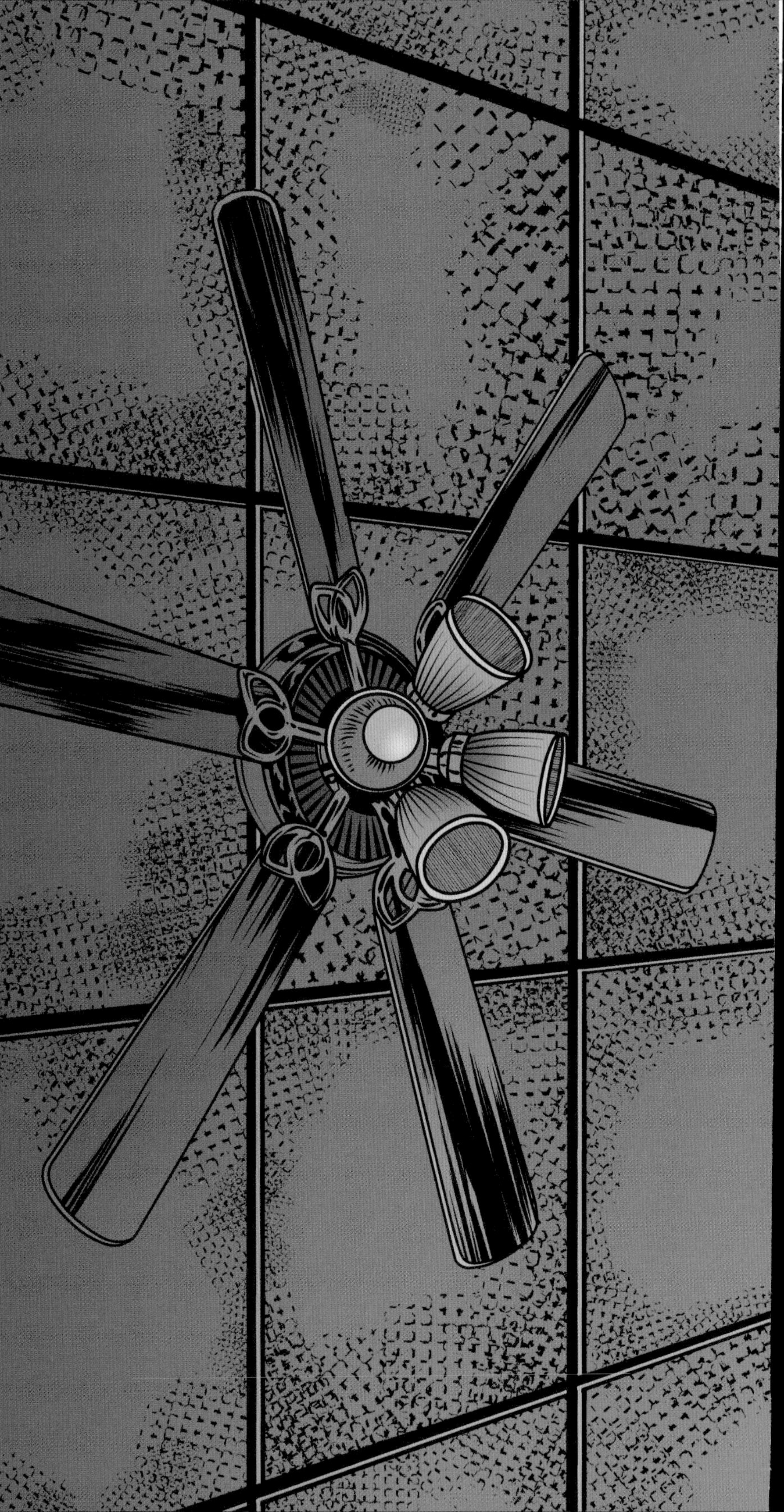

I HEAR THE TRUCK COME BACK, THE GIRLS GETTING HERDED INTO IT. I HEAR THEM CRY, PLEAD IN A LANGUAGE I DON'T UNDERSTAND. I HEAR THEM GET PUNCHED, SLAPPED. THE CRYING AND PLEADING STOPS.

I HEAR LESYA YELLING, SEVERAL MEN YELLING BACK. LESYA YELLS BACK, LOUDER. NONE OF IT'S IN ENGLISH. FOUR OF THE MEN STAY. THE OTHERS LEAVE WITH THE GIRLS.

I HEAR WATER SLOSHING AROUND IN A METAL BUCKET AS IT'S BEING CARRIED PAST ME. I SMELL BLEACH AND CIGARETTE SMOKE.

MOST OF MY BODY GOES COLD, NUMB...ALL EXCEPT MY GUT. EVERY TIME I TAKE A BREATH, I FEEL MY INSIDES STRETCHING, TEARING, BUT IT'S ALL I HAVE. I HUDDLE AROUND IT, A TINY FIRE IN A MASSIVE BLIZZARD.

I USED TO WONDER WHY THEY ALL LOOKED SO SURPRISED AT THE END. NOW I KNOW.

IT'S SO FUCKING STRANGE.

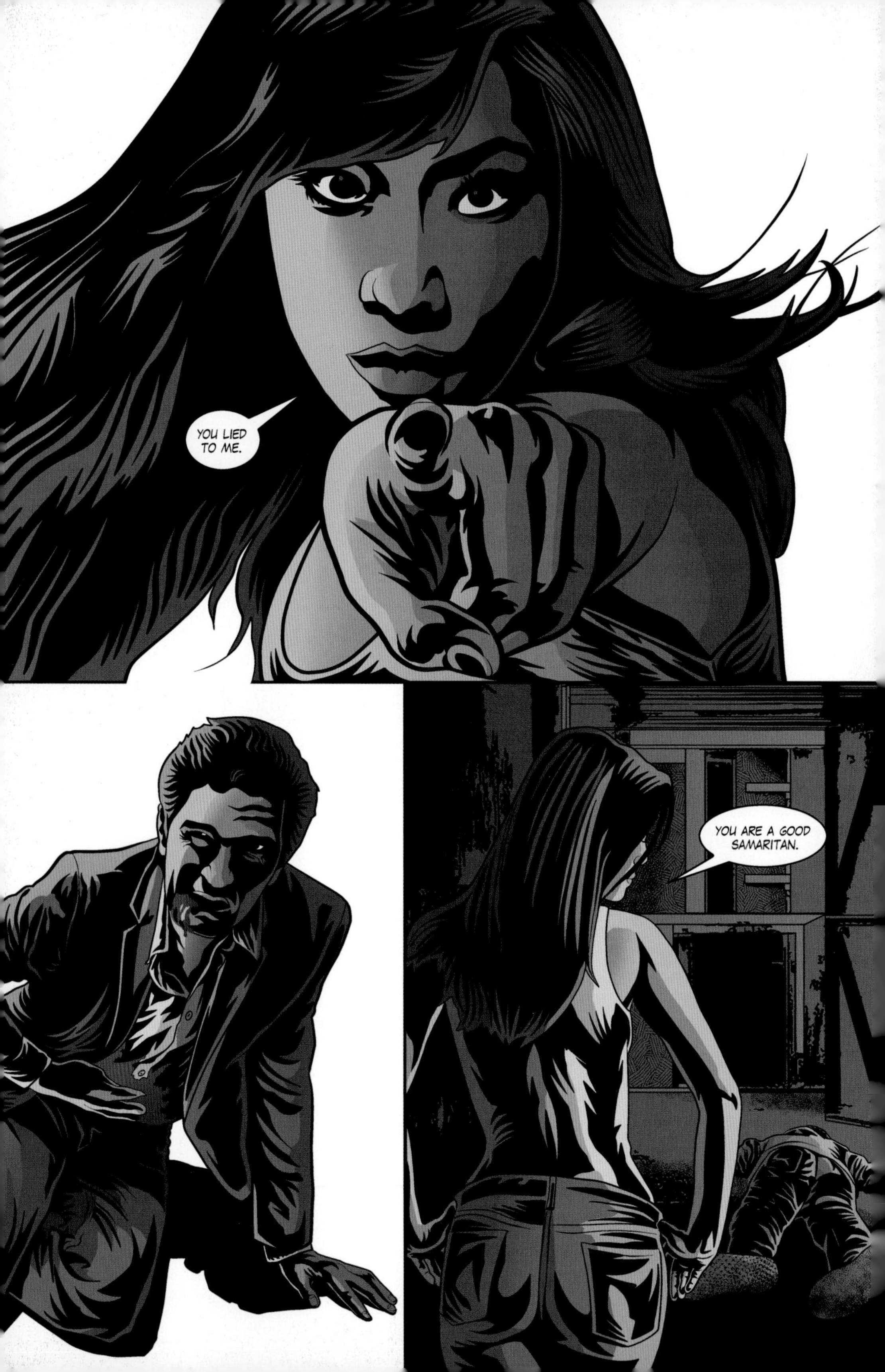
YOU LIED TO ME.
YOU ARE A GOOD SAMARITAN.

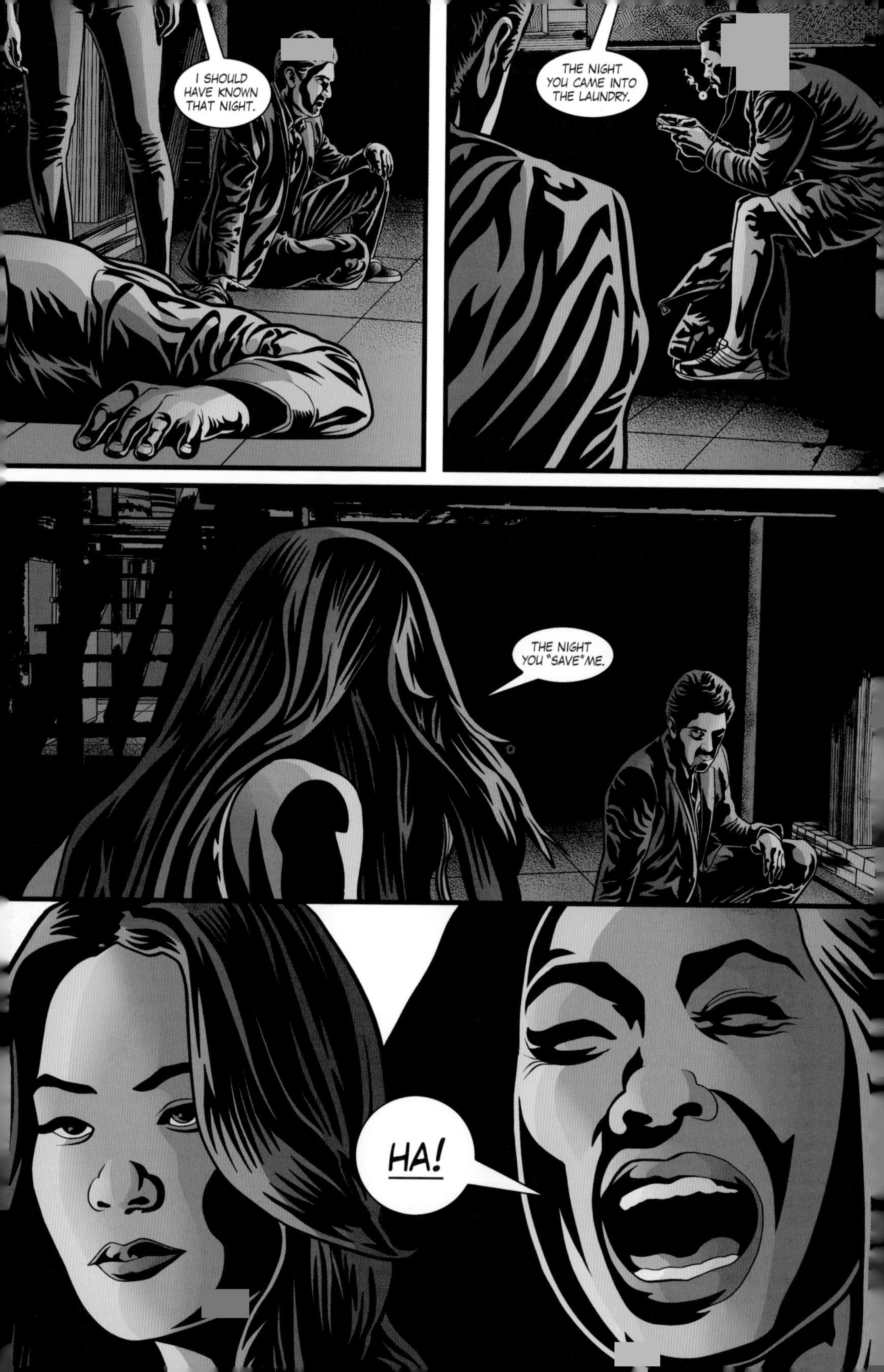
I SHOULD HAVE KNOWN THAT NIGHT.
THE NIGHT YOU CAME INTO THE LAUNDRY.
THE NIGHT YOU "SAVE" ME.
HA!

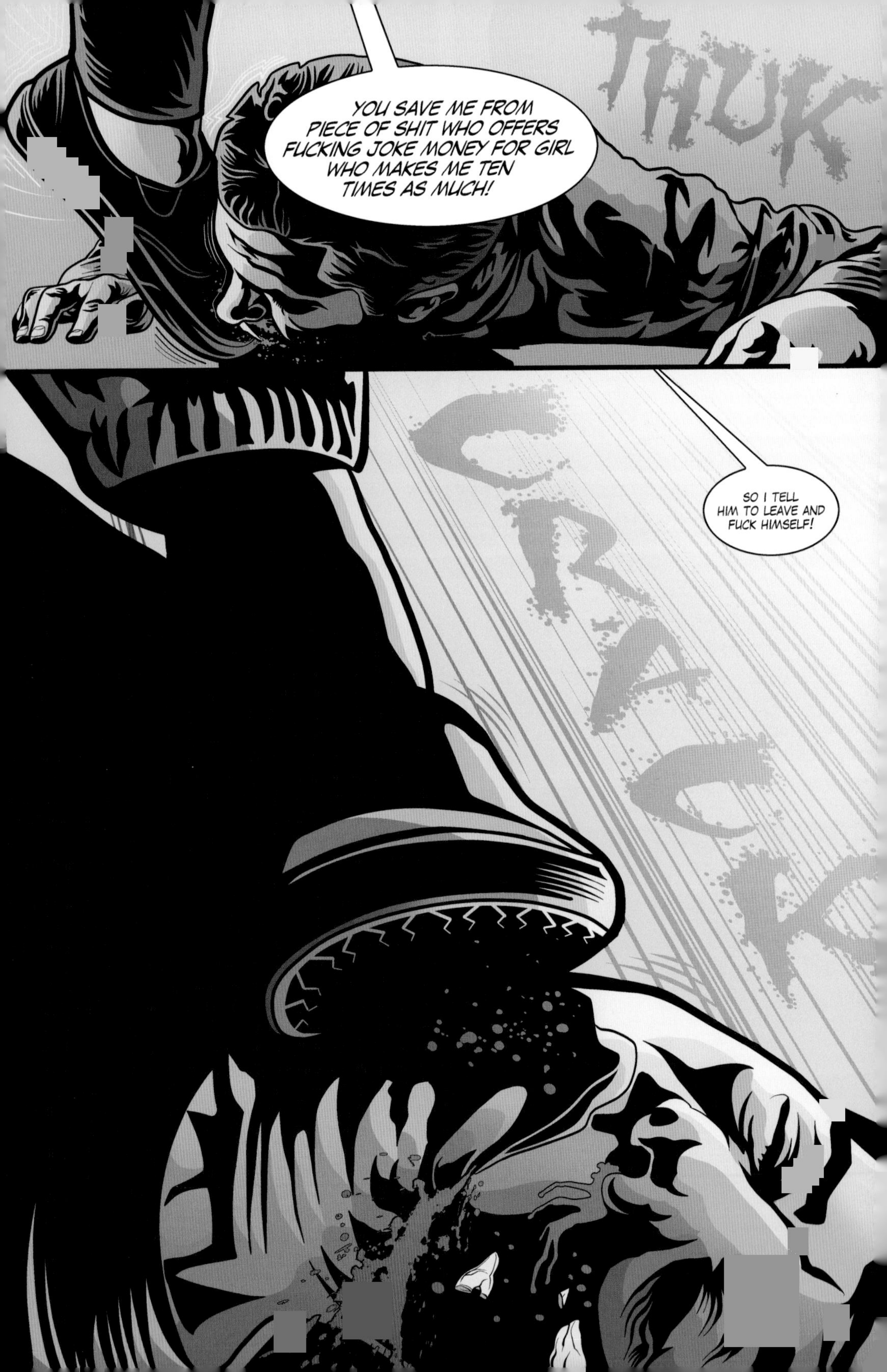
THUK
YOU SAVE ME FROM PIECE OF SHIT WHO OFFERS FUCKING JOKE MONEY FOR GIRL WHO MAKES ME TEN TIMES AS MUCH!
CRACK
SO I TELL HIM TO LEAVE AND FUCK HIMSELF!

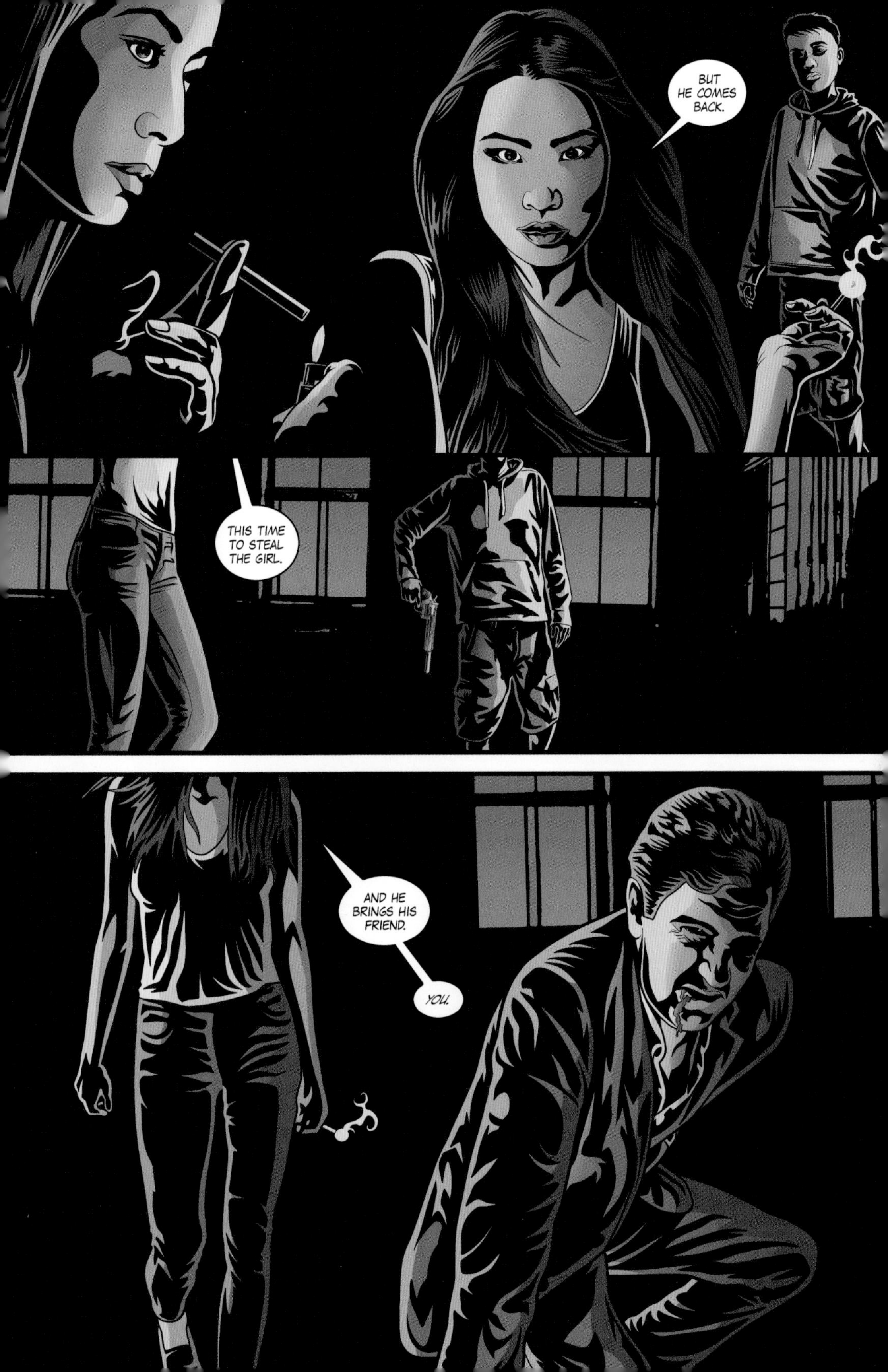
BUT HE COMES BACK.
THIS TIME TO STEAL THE GIRL.
AND HE BRINGS HIS FRIEND.
YOU.

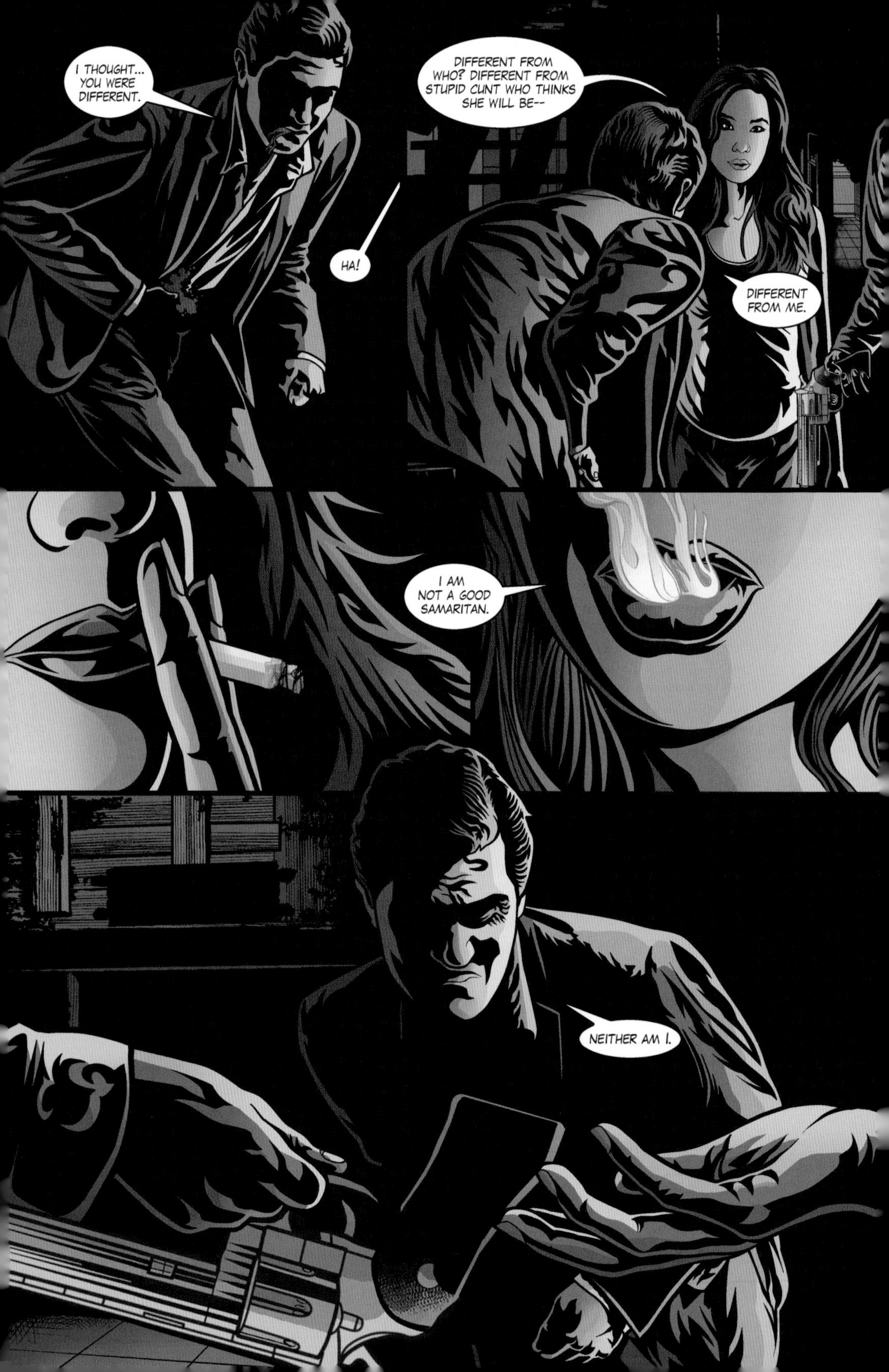
I THOUGHT... YOU WERE DIFFERENT.
DIFFERENT FROM WHO? DIFFERENT FROM STUPID CUNT WHO THINKS SHE WILL BE--
HA!
DIFFERENT FROM ME.
I AM NOT A GOOD SAMARITAN.
NEITHER AM I.

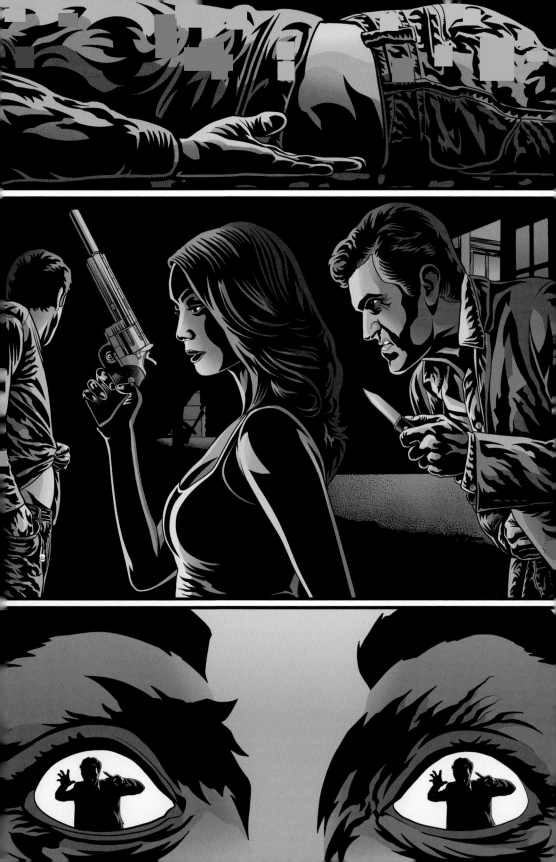

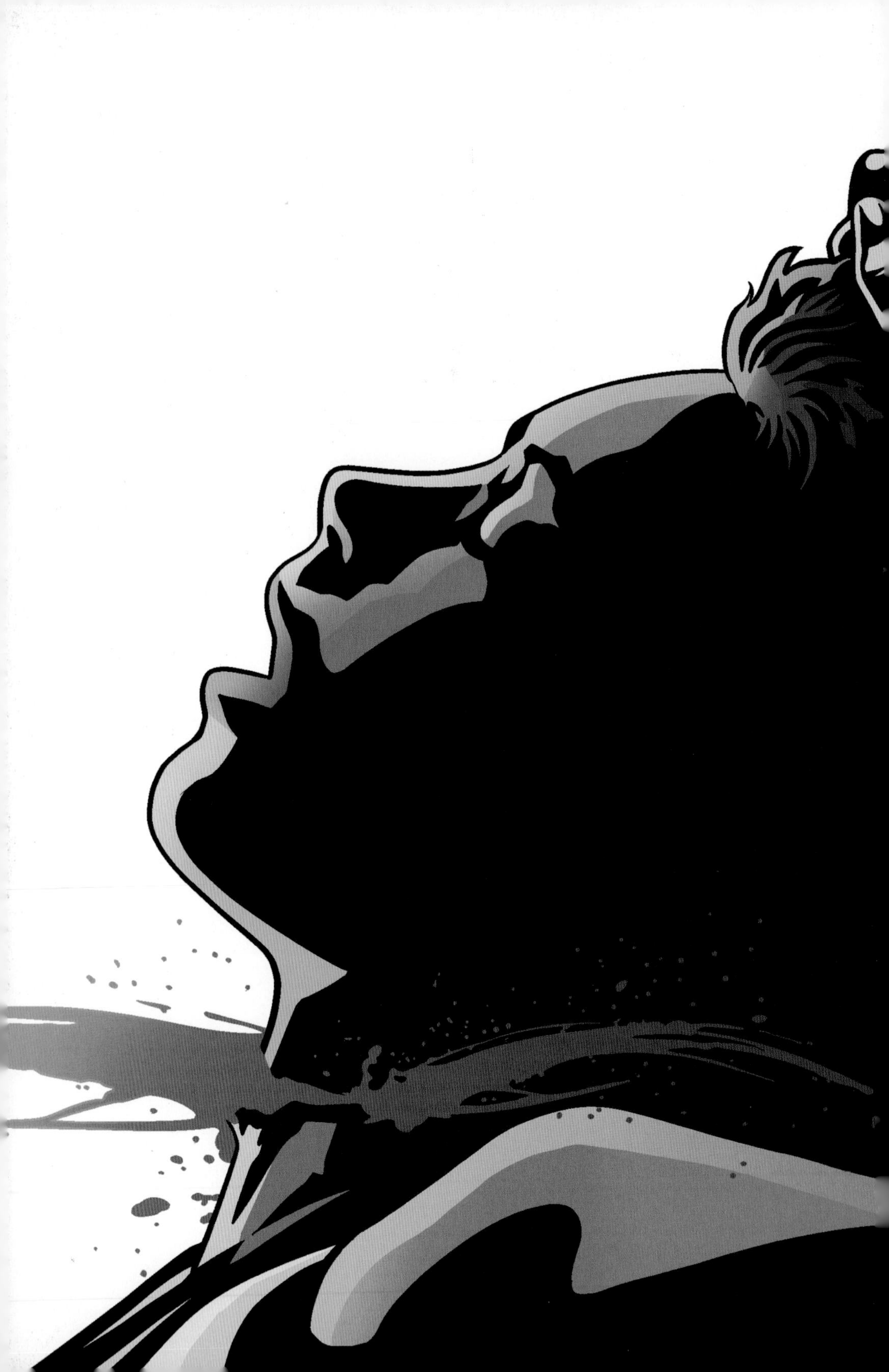

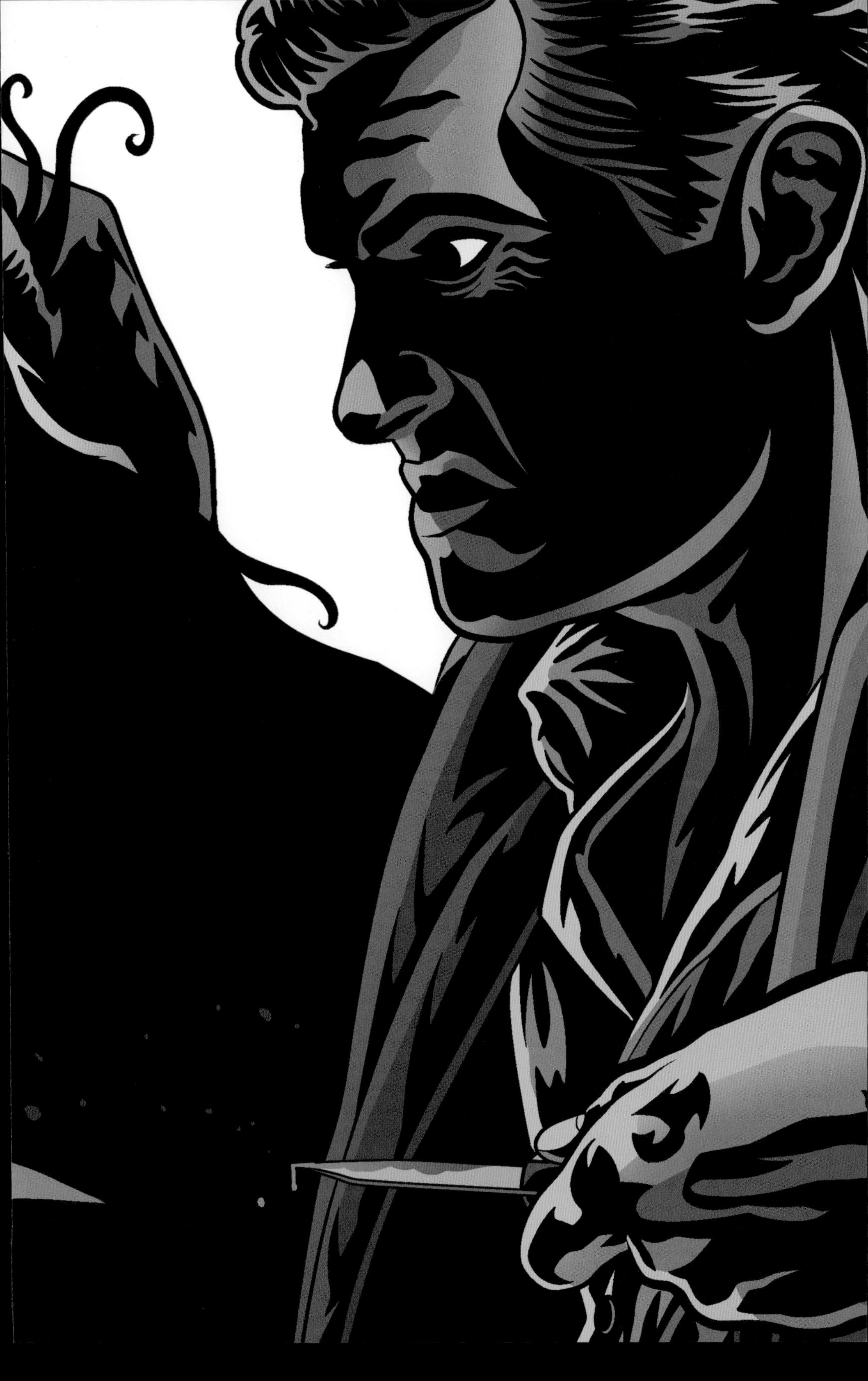

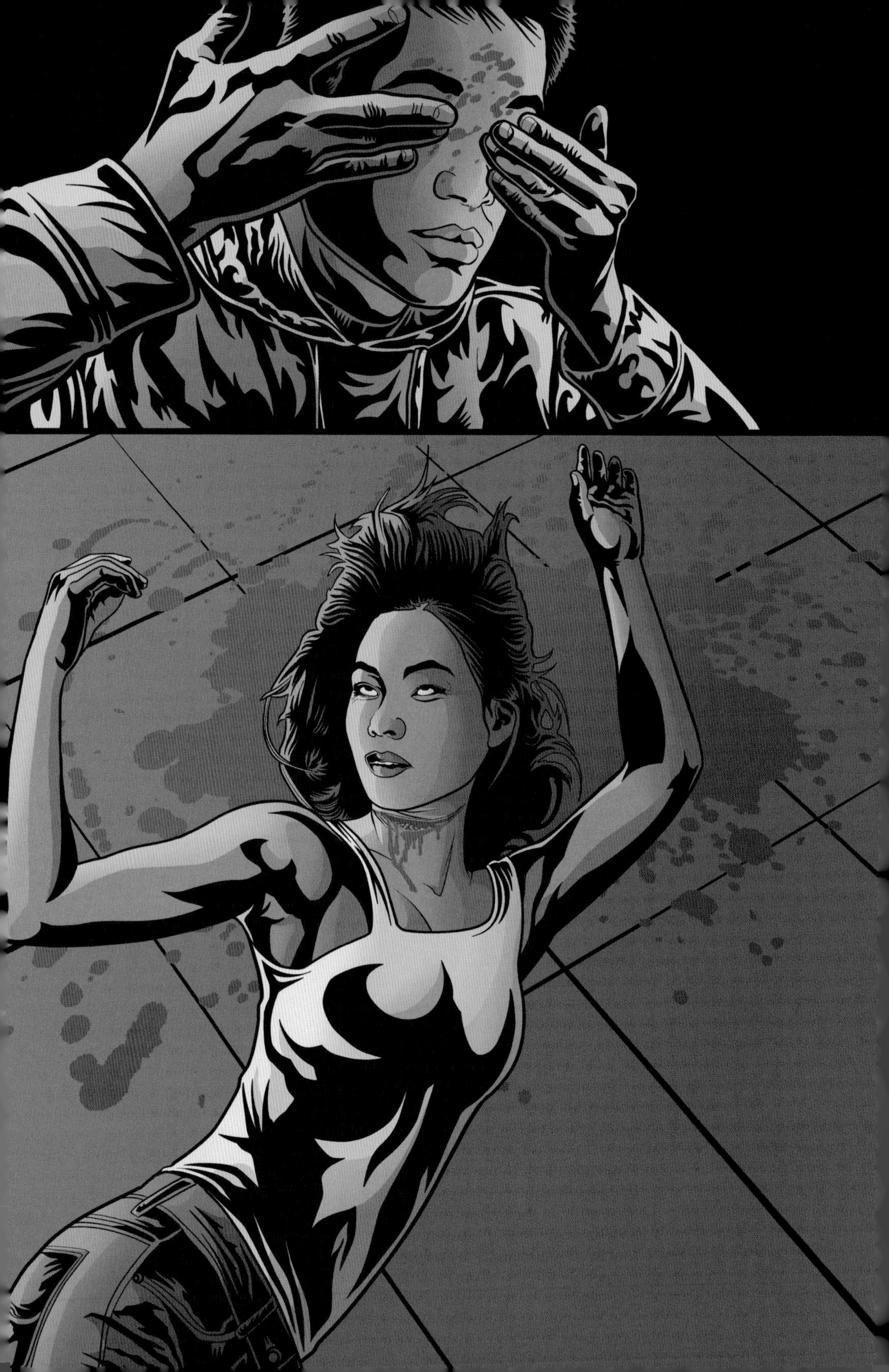

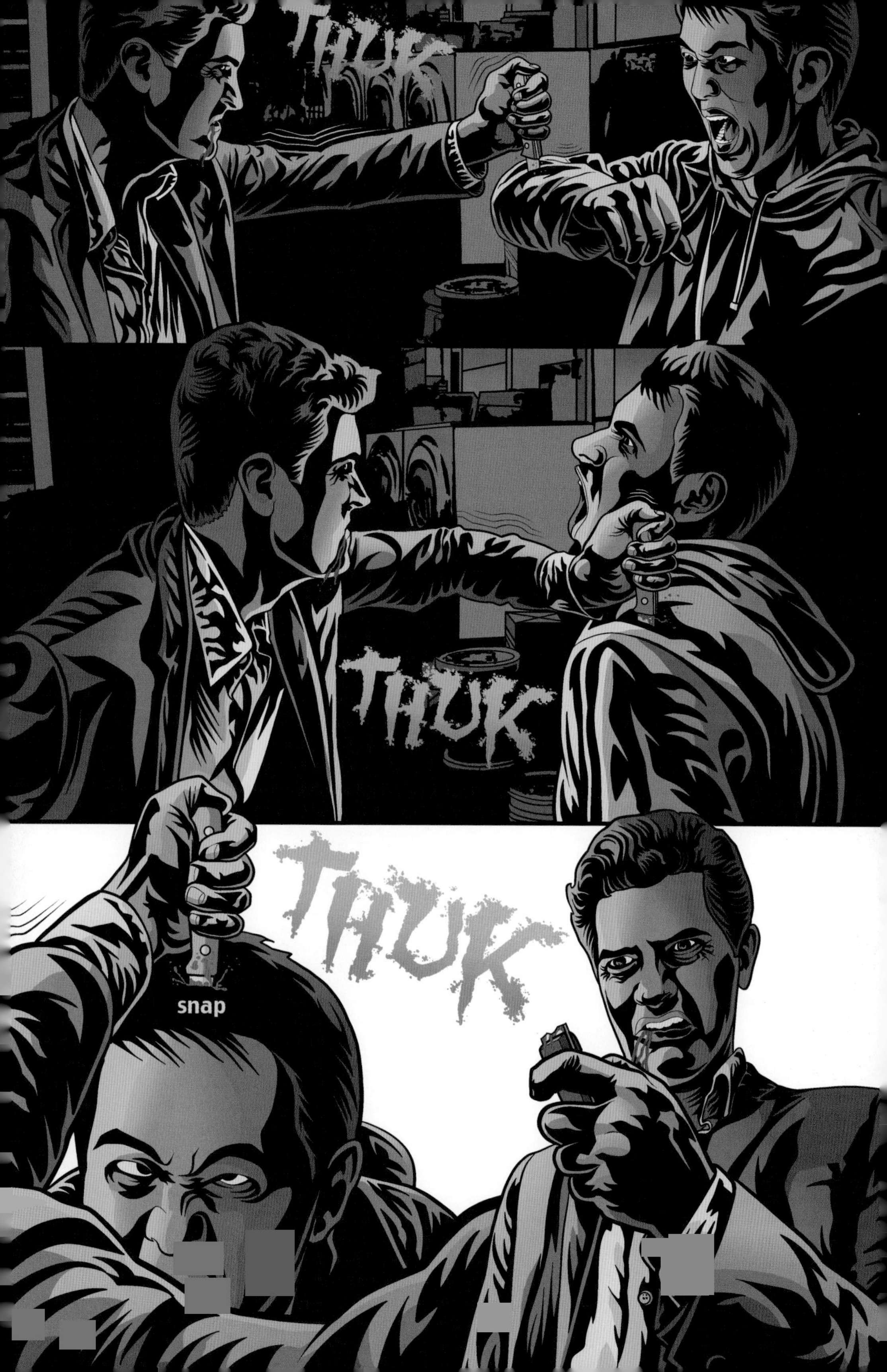
THUK
THUK
THUK
snap

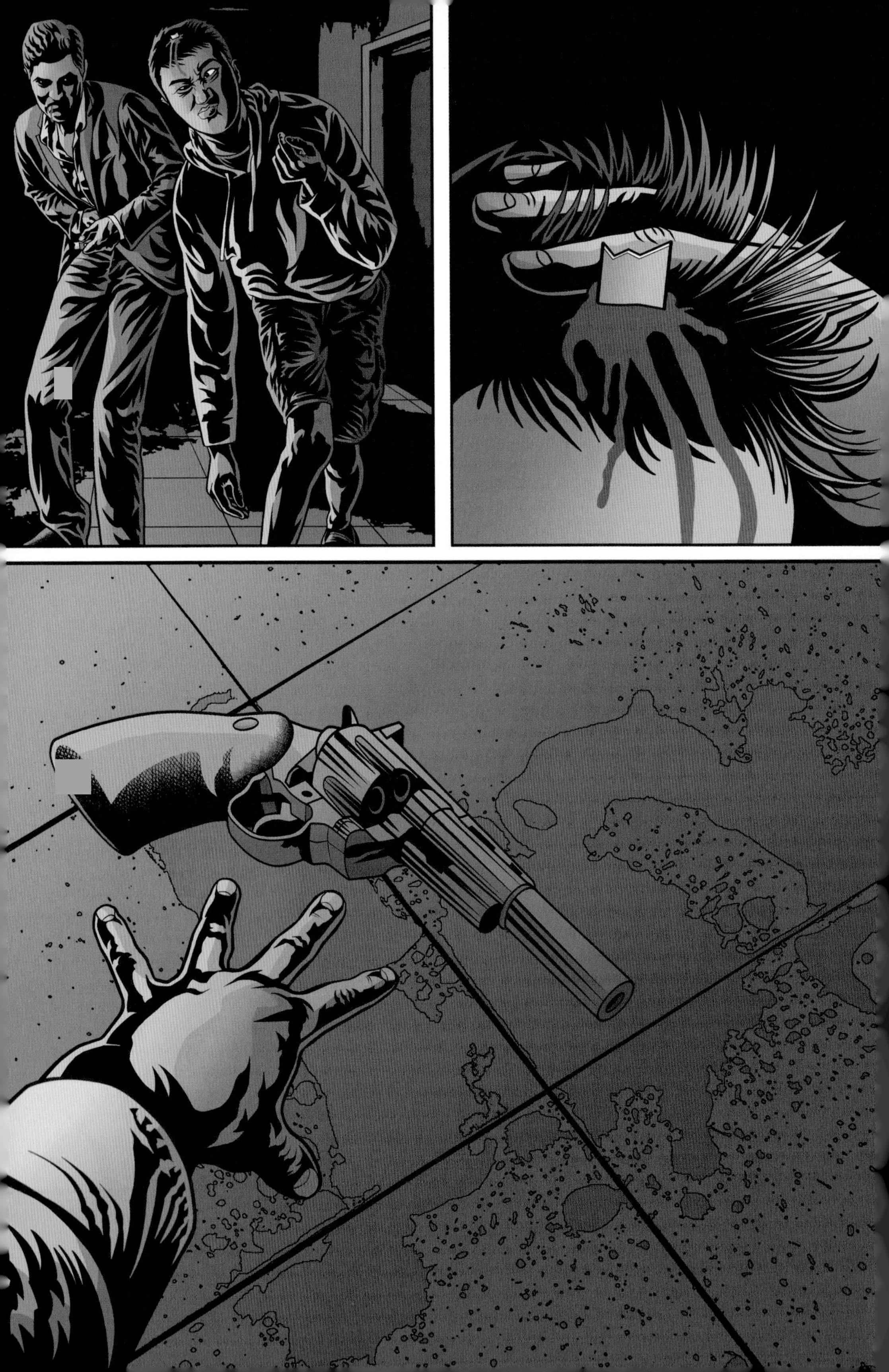

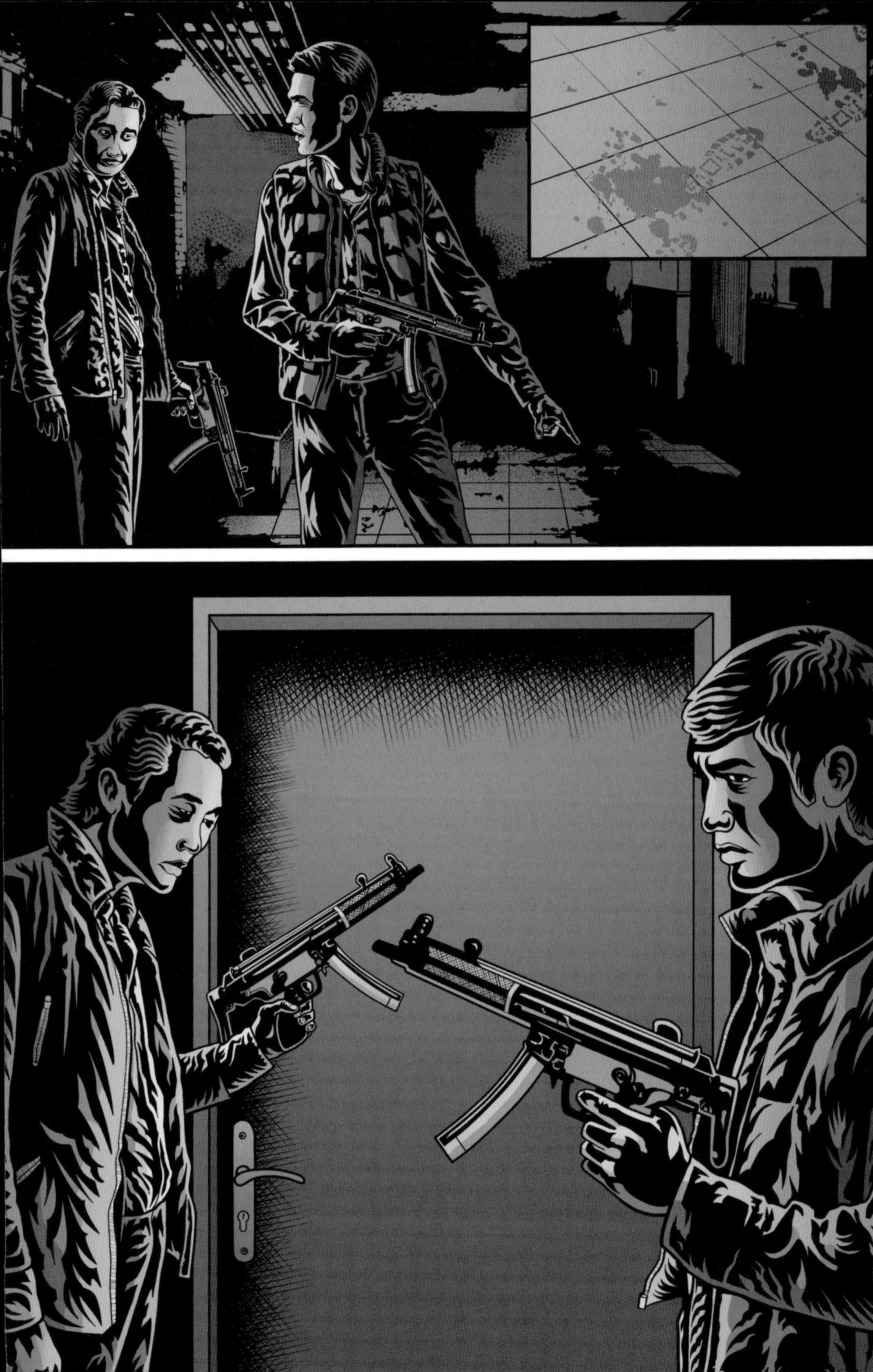

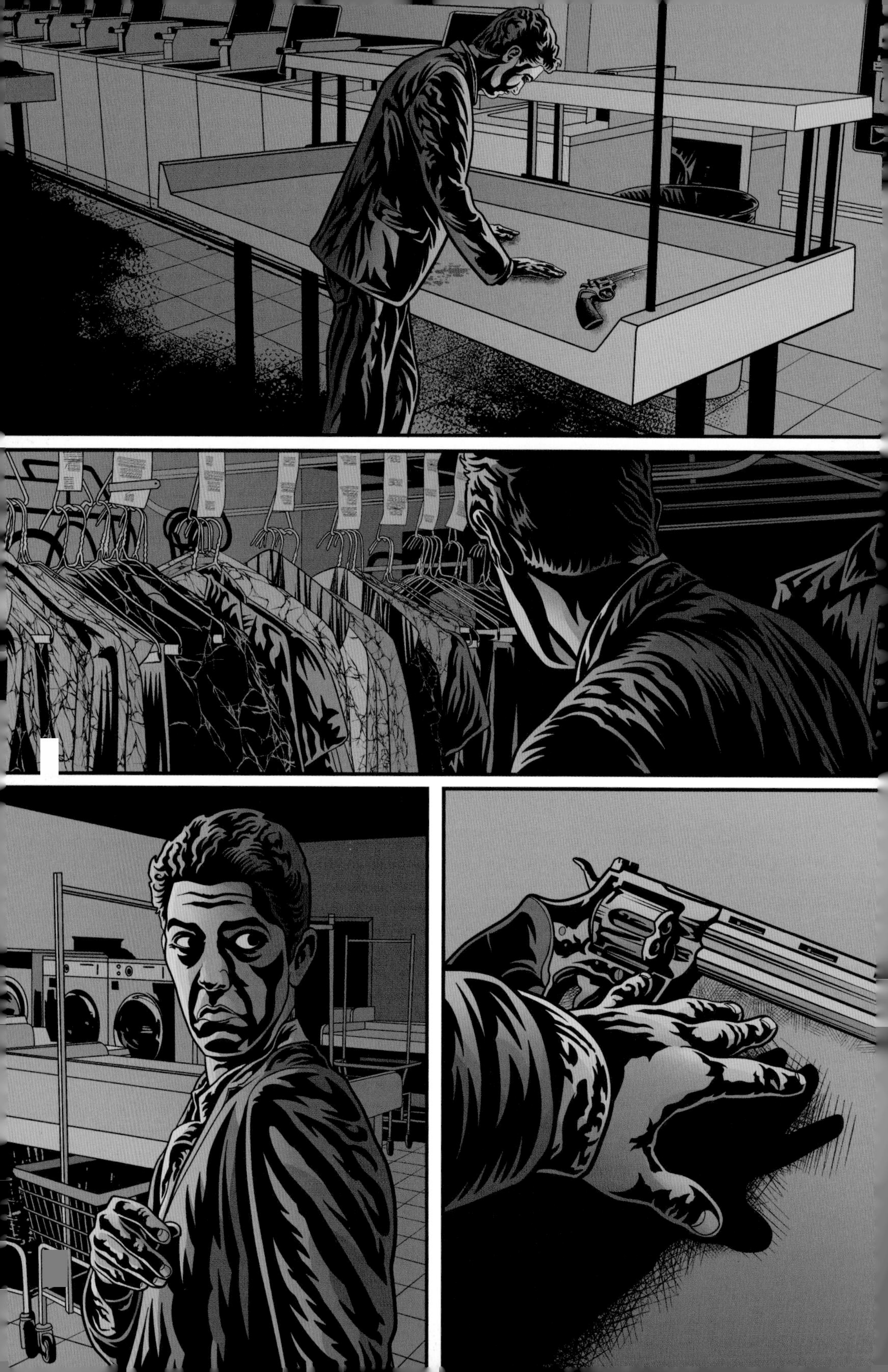

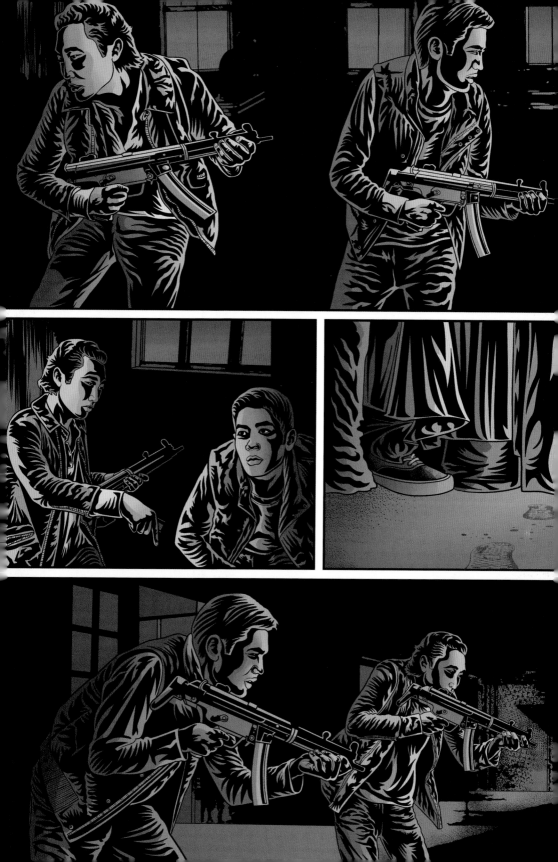

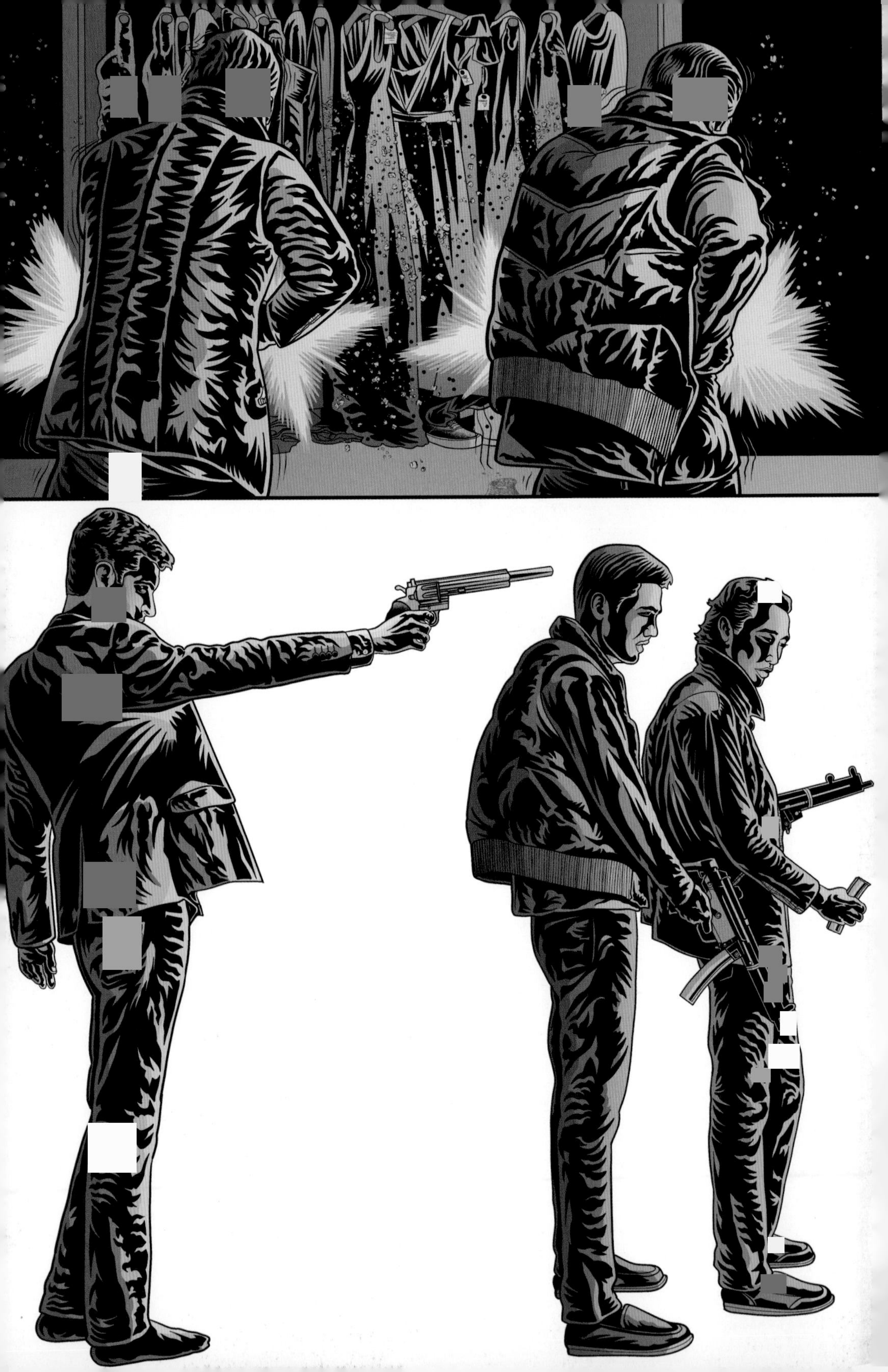

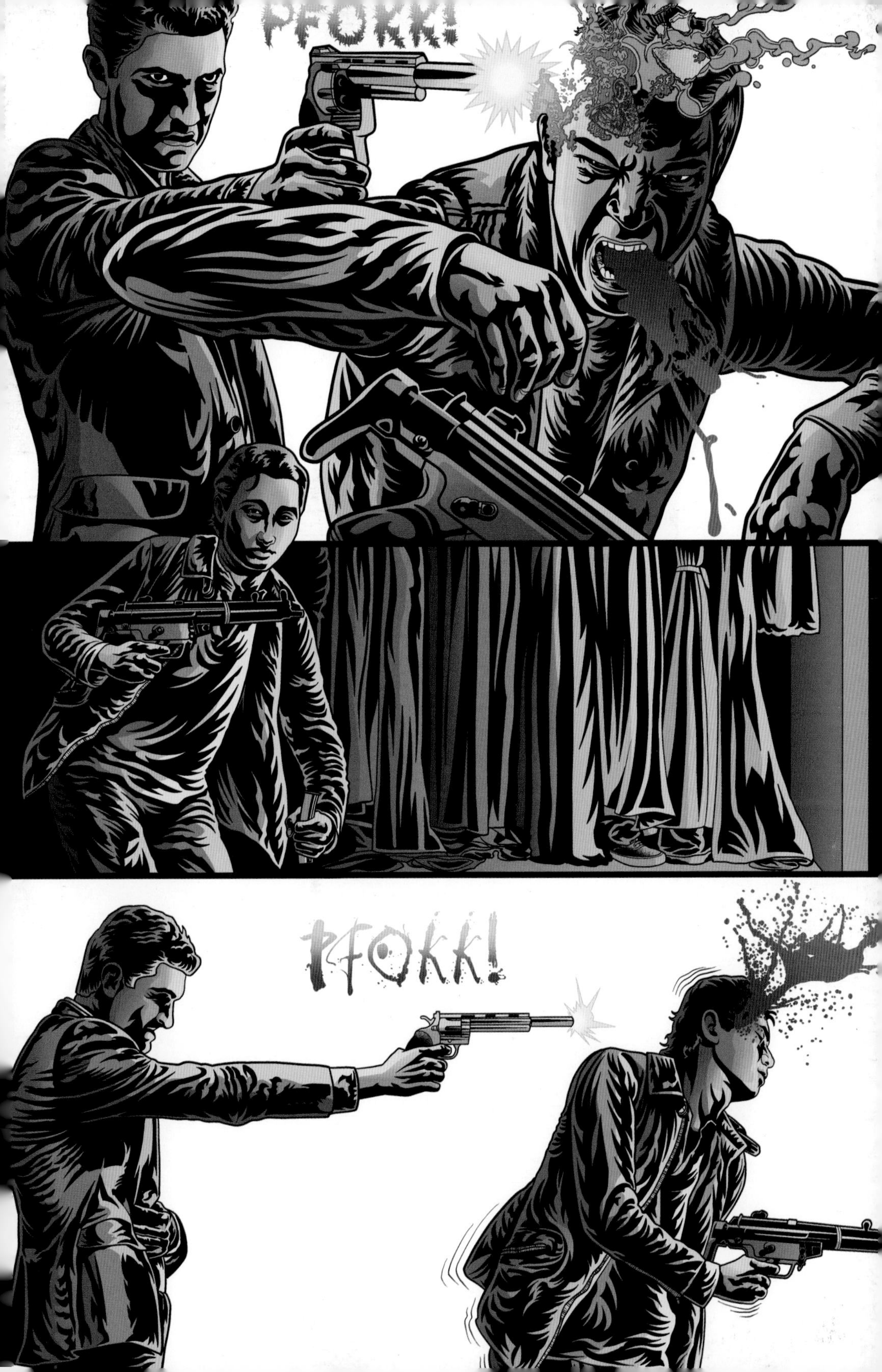
PFOKK!
PFOKK!

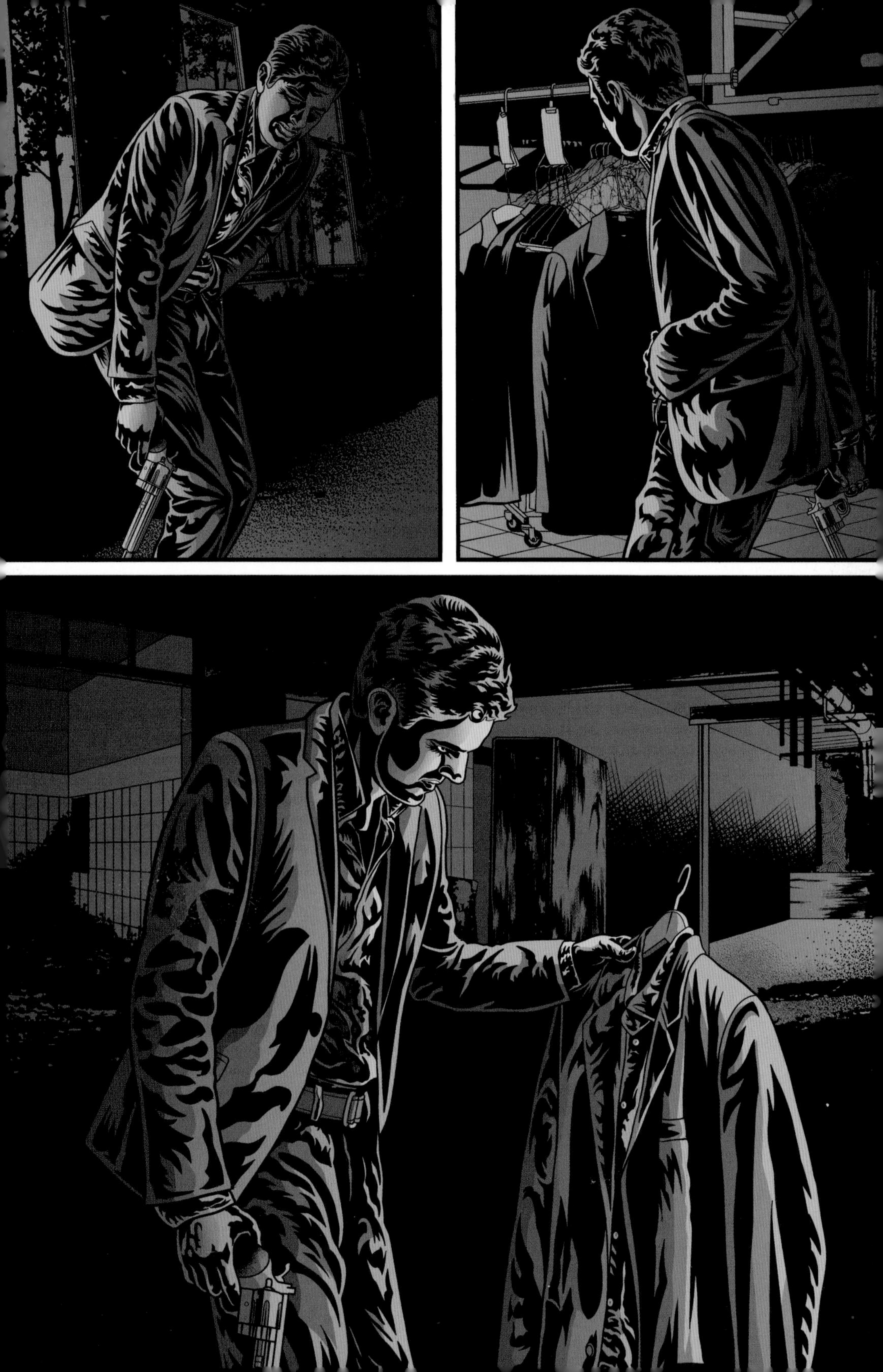

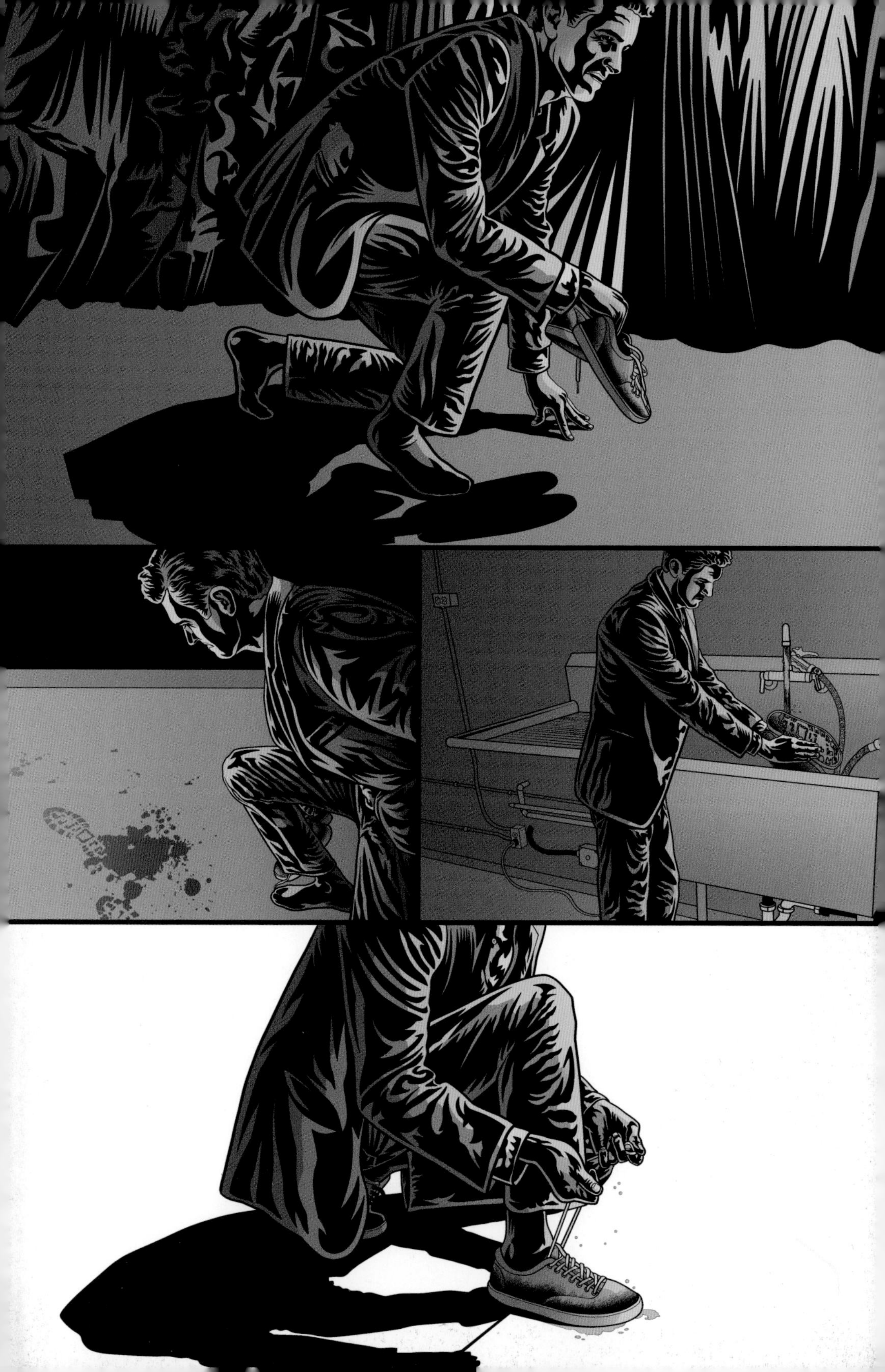

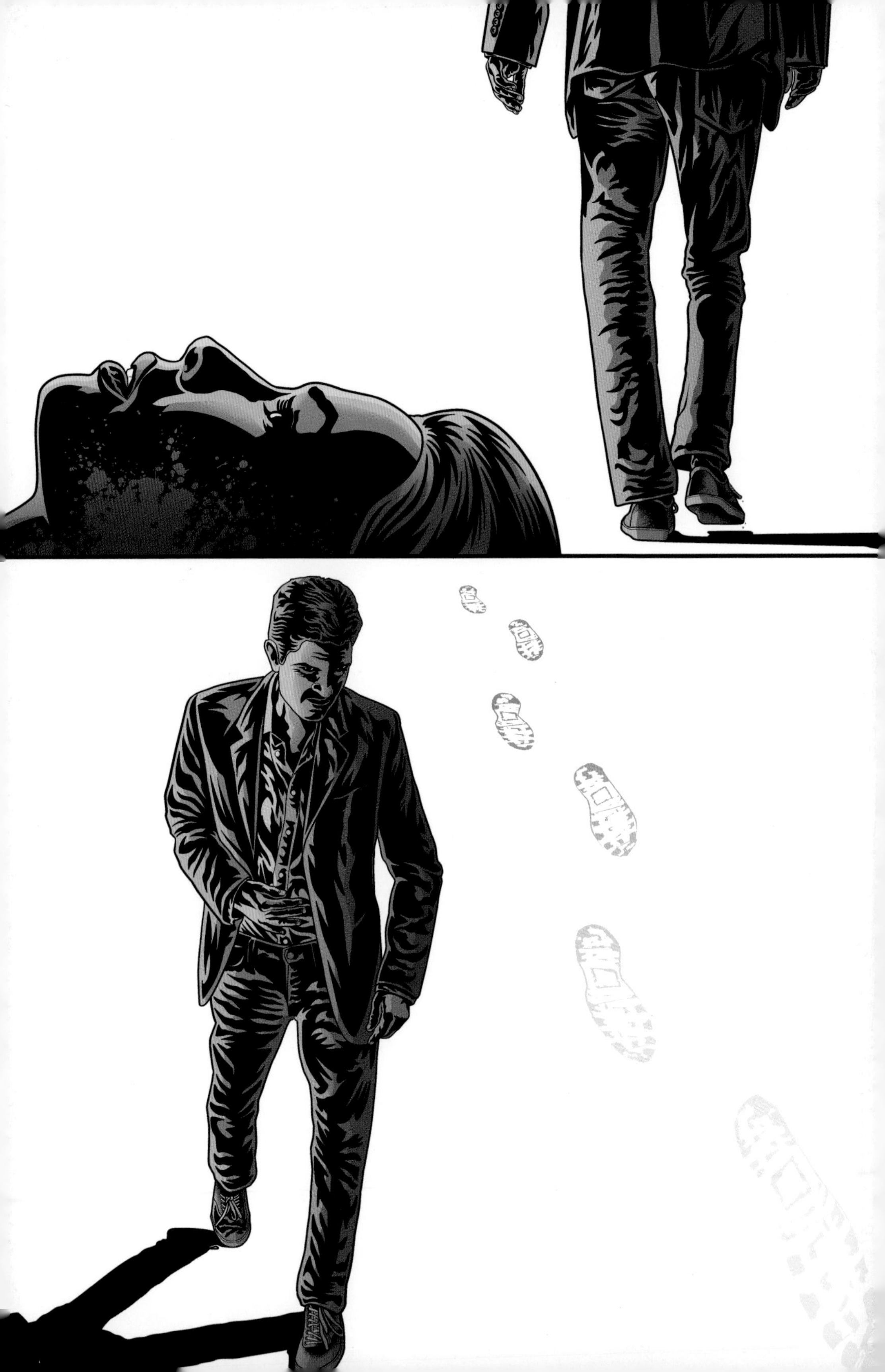

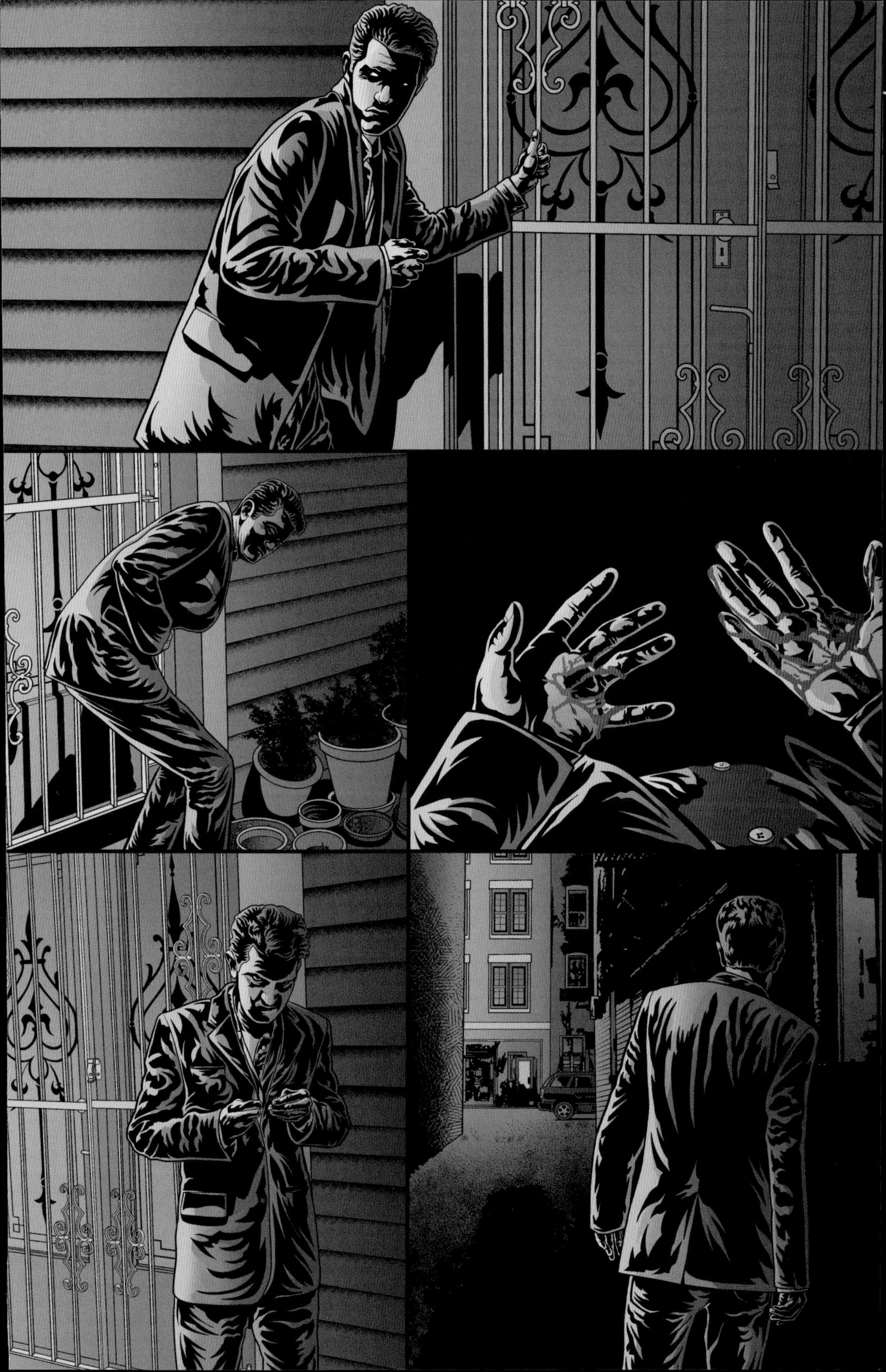

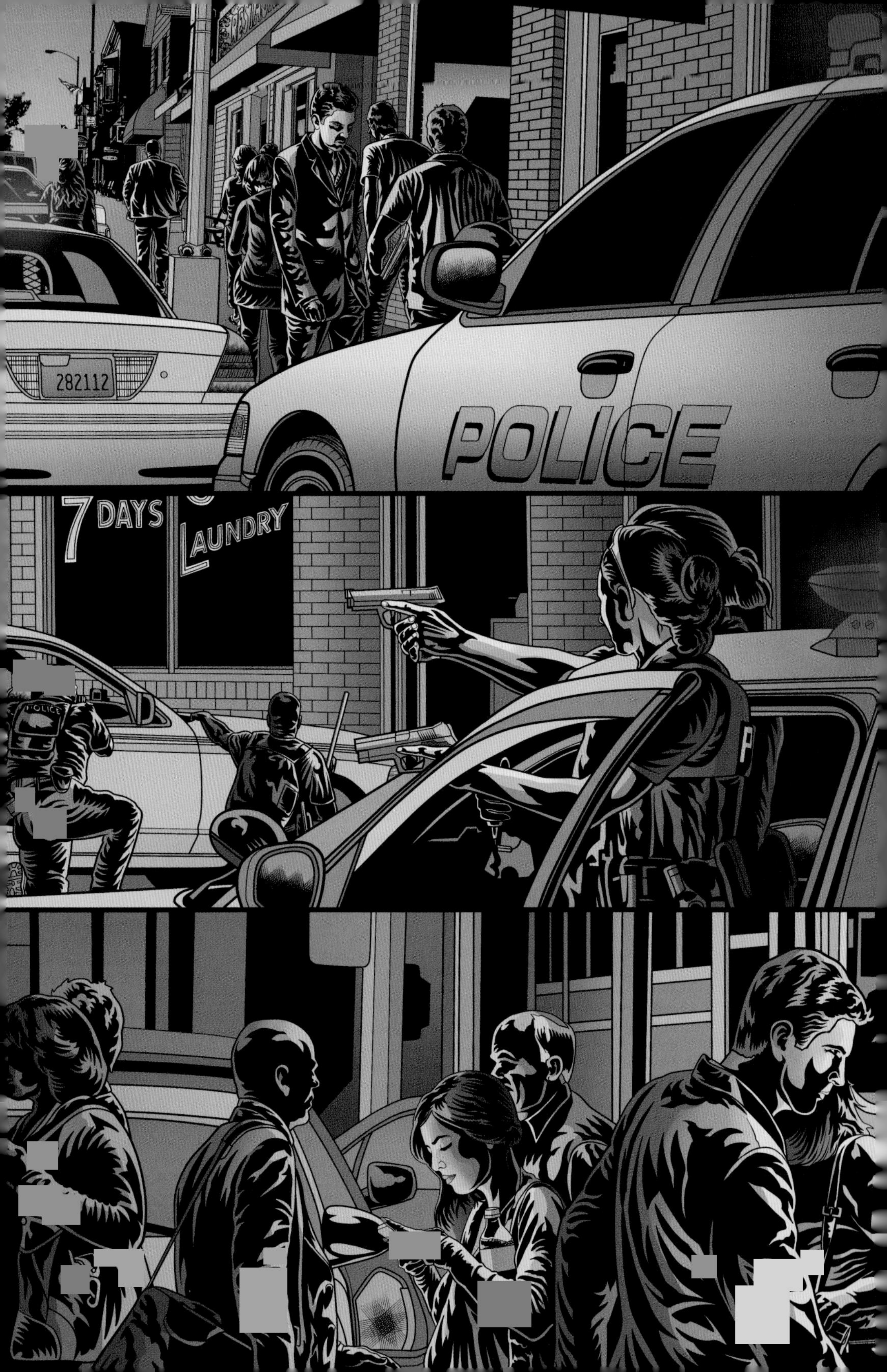
282112
POLICE
7 DAYS
LAUNDRY
POLICE
P

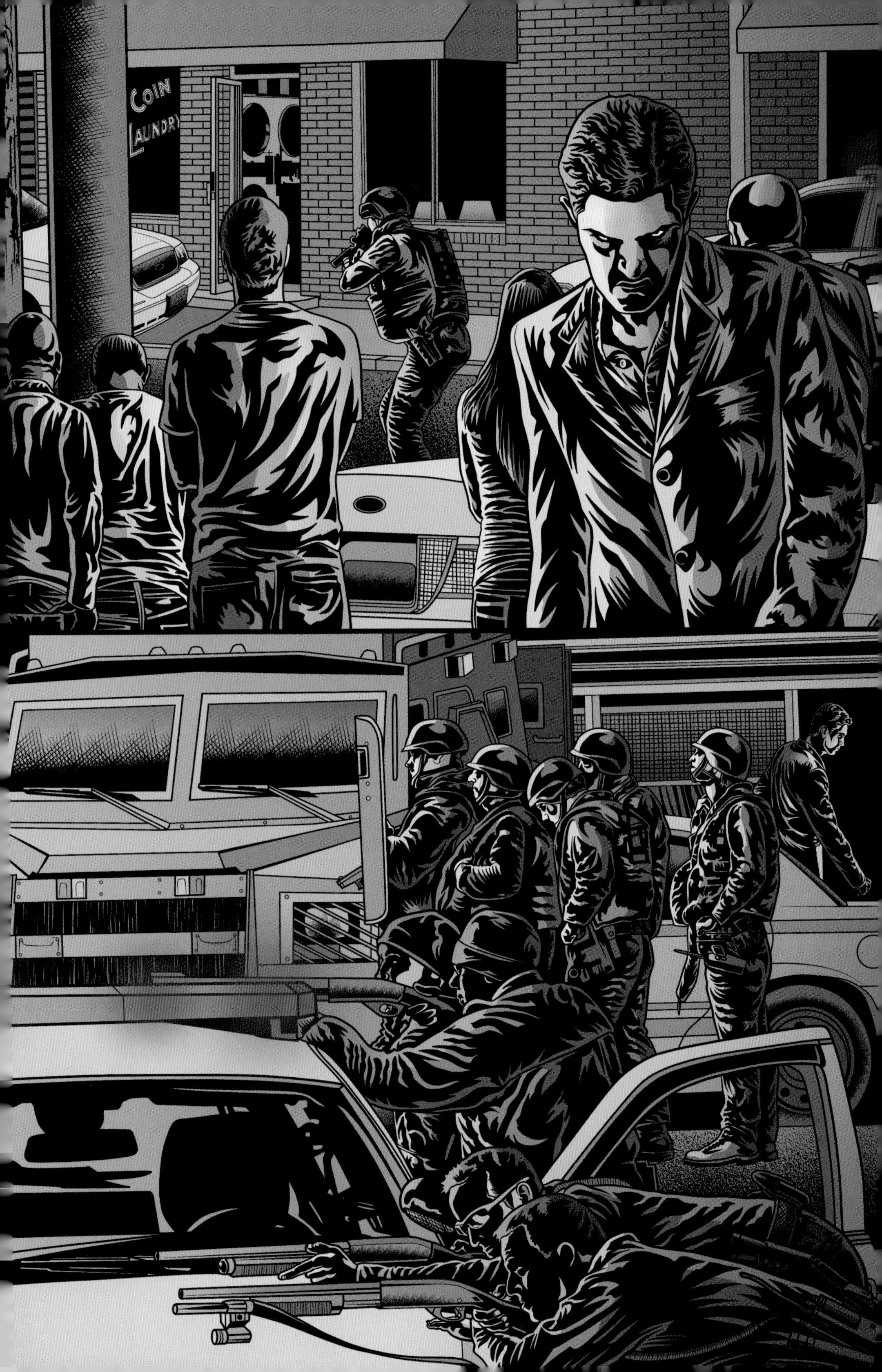
COIN LAUNDRY

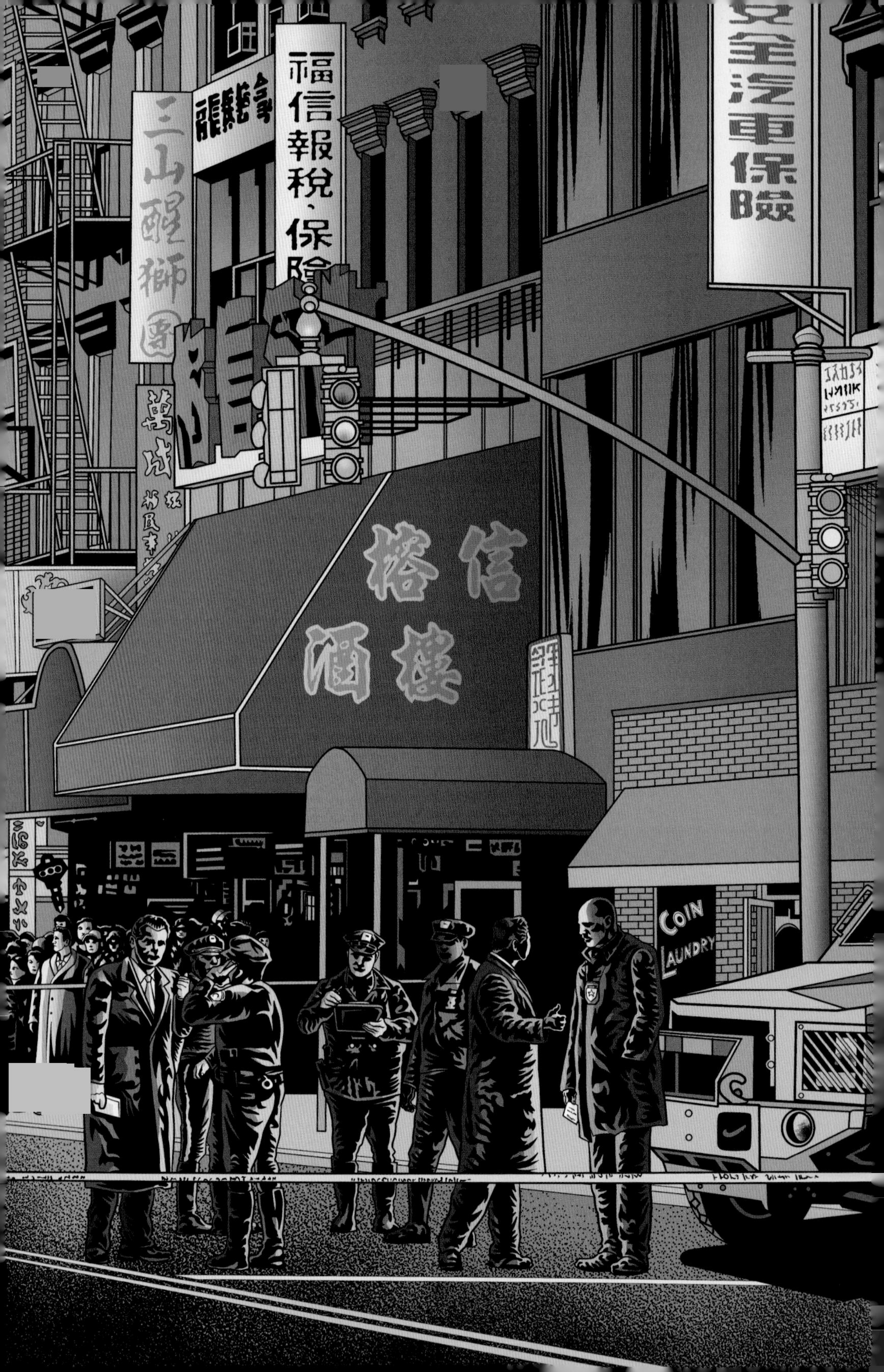
三山醒獅團
福信報稅
酒樓
COIN
LAUNDRY

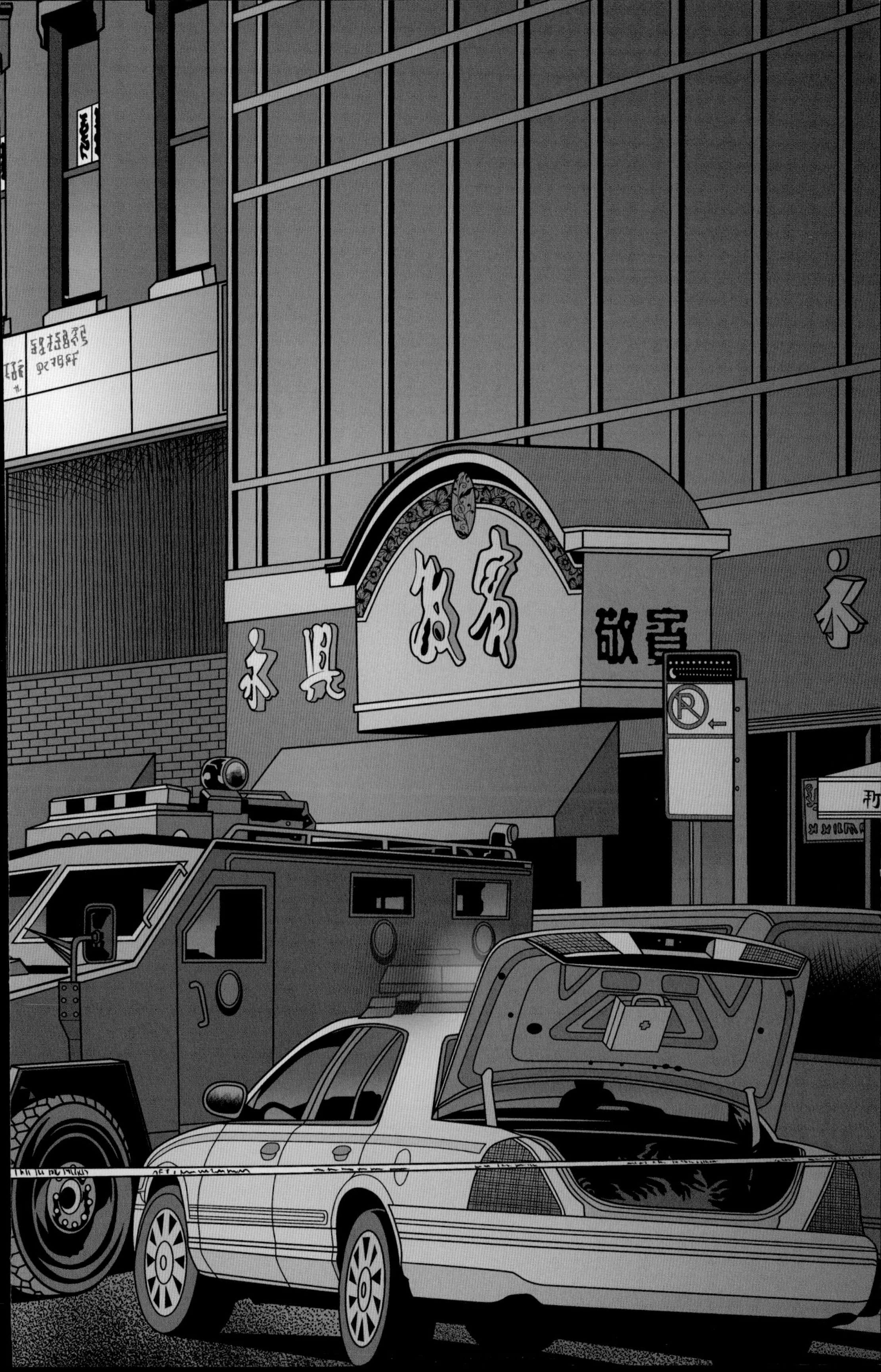

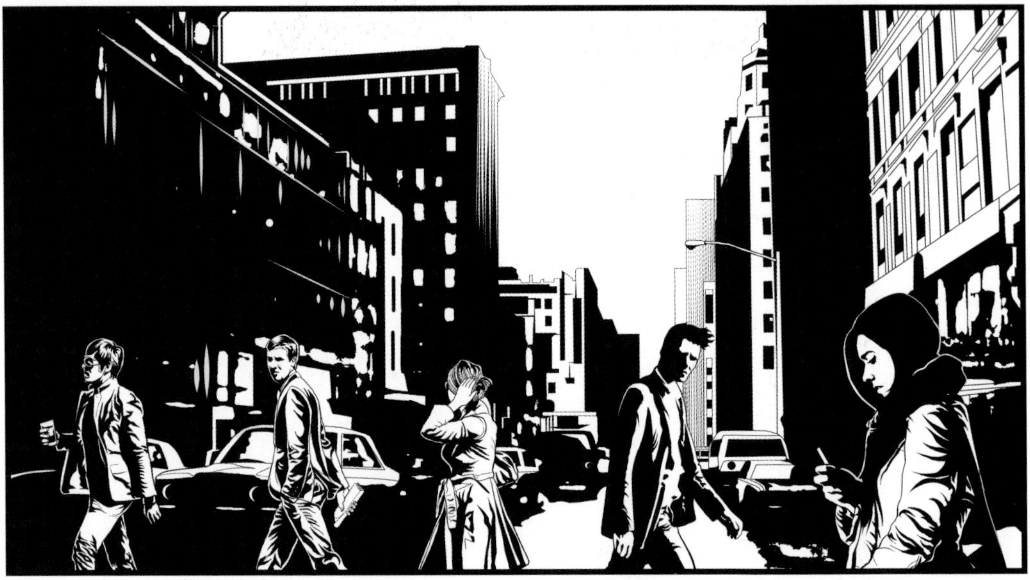

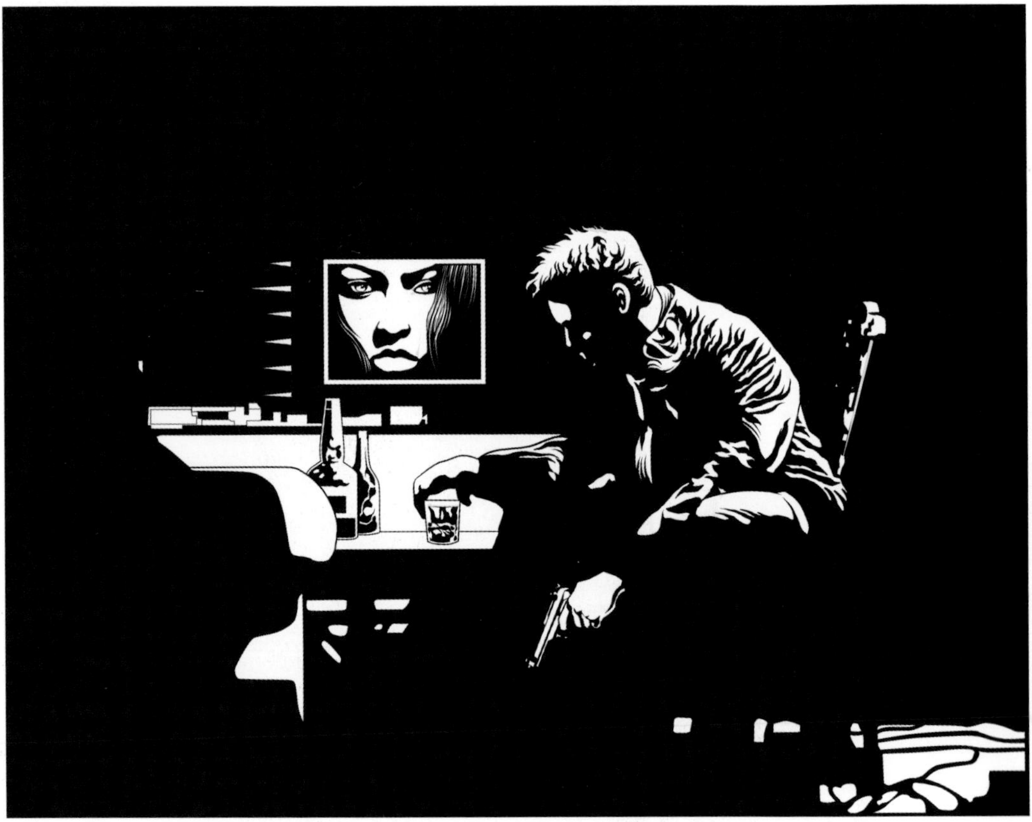

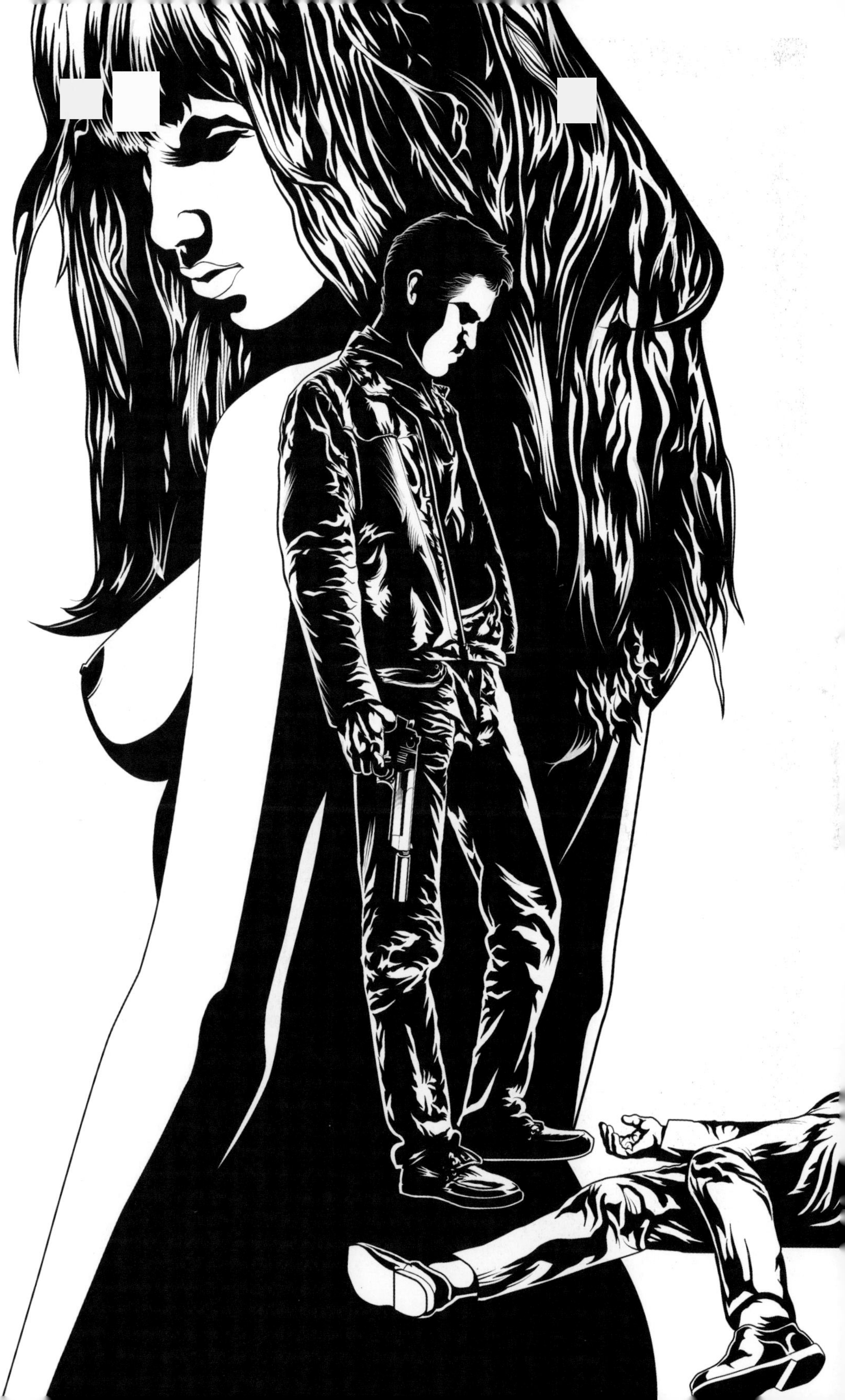

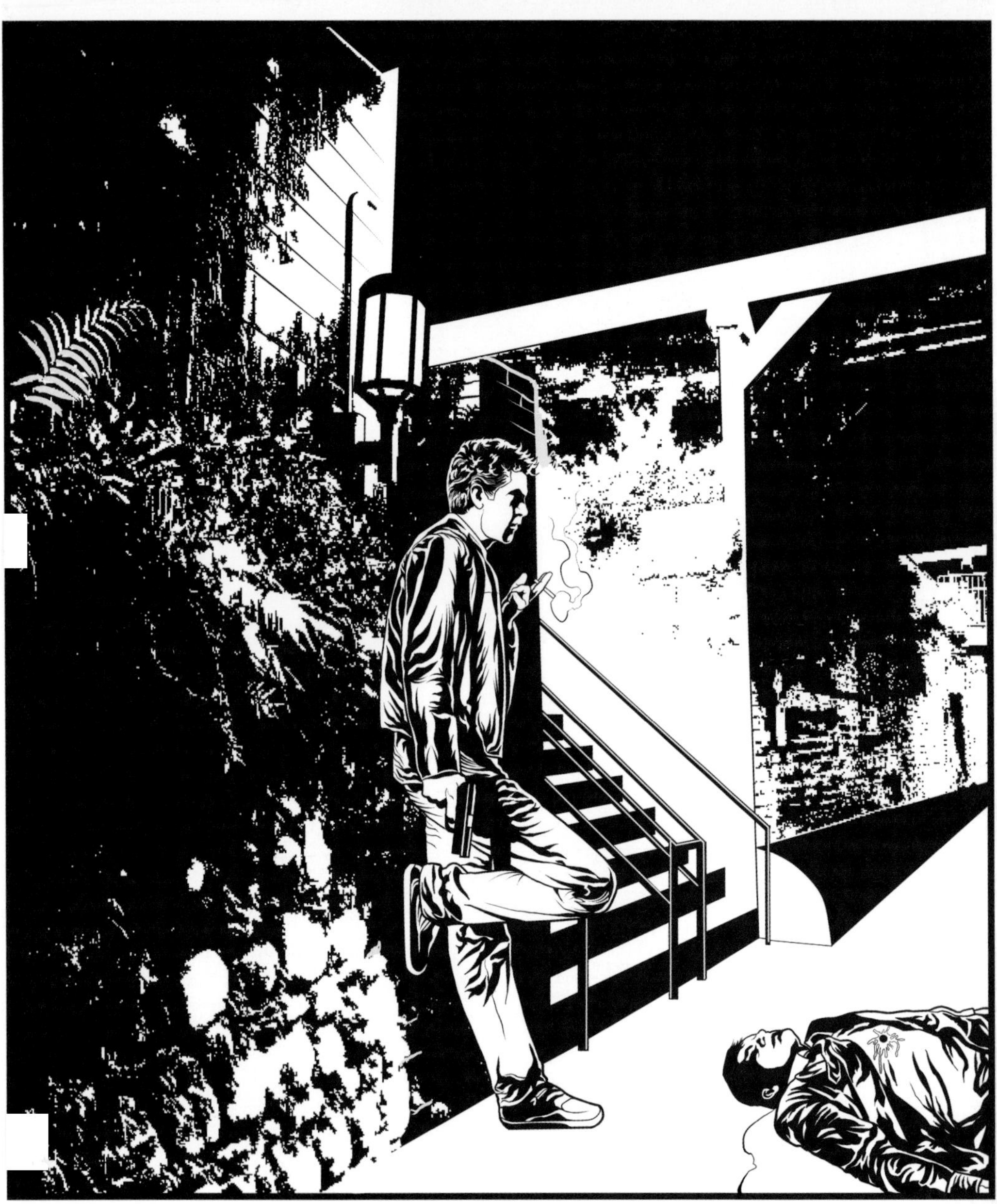
`15

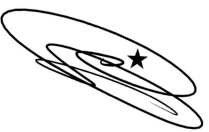

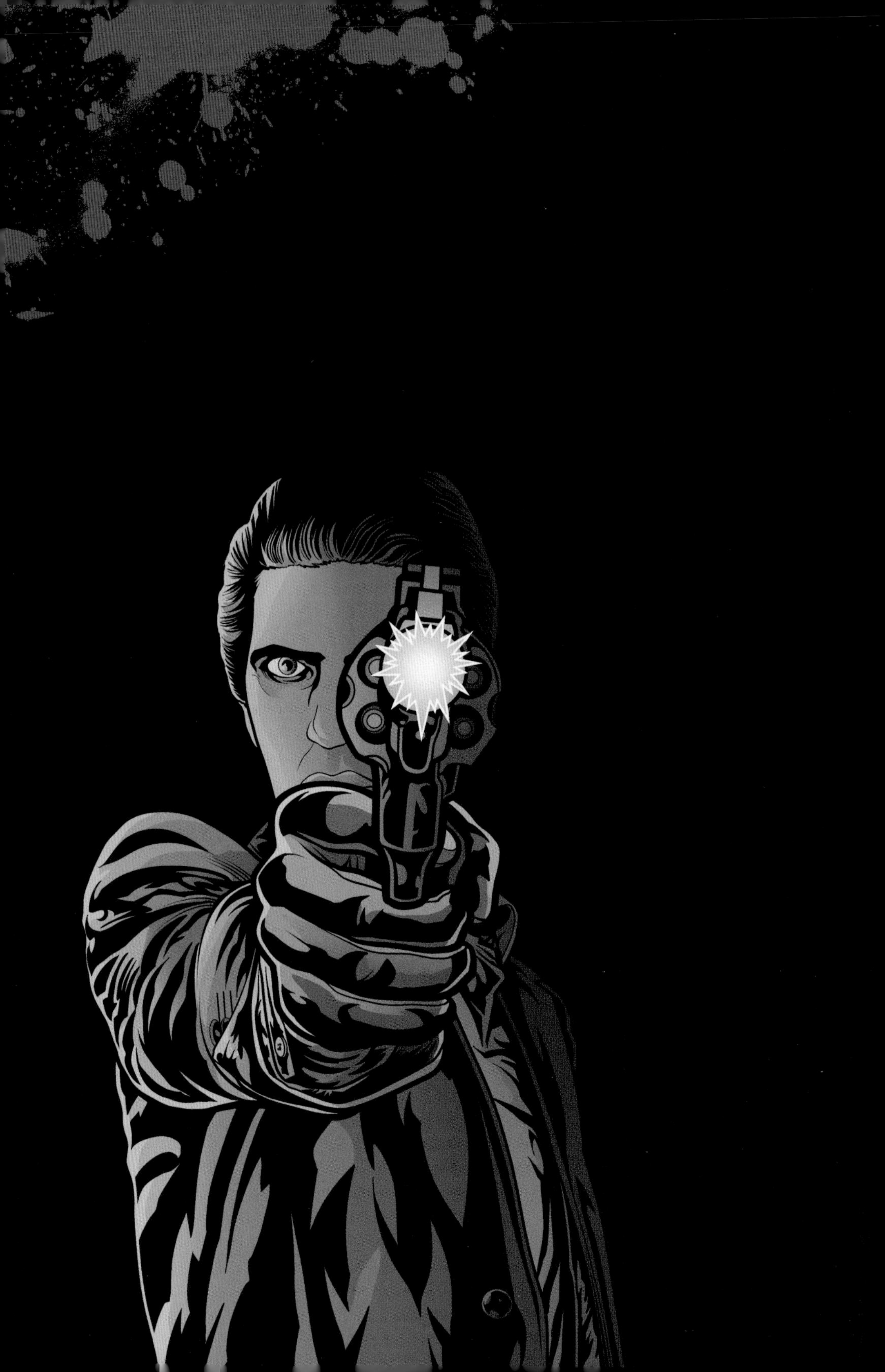

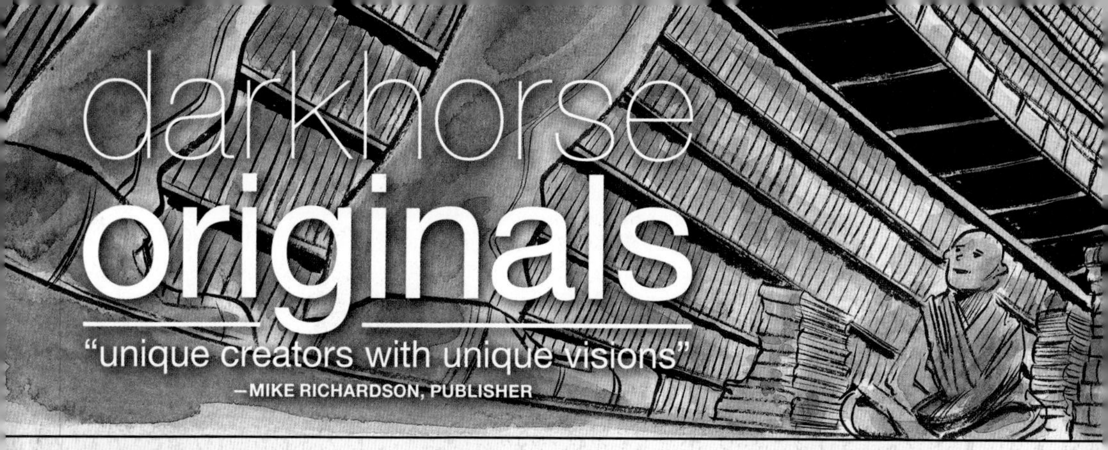
darkhorse
originals
"unique creators with unique visions"
—MIKE RICHARDSON, PUBLISHER

3 STORY: THE SECRET HISTORY OF THE GIANT MAN
978-1-59582-356-4 | $19.99

365 SAMURAI AND A FEW BOWLS OF RICE
978-1-59582-412-7 | $16.99

THE ADVENTURES OF BLANCHE
978-1-59582-258-1 | $15.99

APOCALYPTIGIRL: AN ARIA FOR THE END TIMES
978-1-61655-566-5 | $9.99

BEANWORLD
Volume 1: Wahoolazuma!
978-1-59582-240-6 | $19.99
Volume 2: A Gift Comes!
978-1-59582-299-4 | $19.99
Volume 3: Remember Here When You Are There!
978-1-59582-355-7 | $19.99
Volume 3.5: Tales of the Beanworld
978-1-59582-897-2 | $14.99

BLACKSAD
978-1-59582-393-9 | $29.99

BLACKSAD: A SILENT HELL
978-1-59582-931-3 | $19.99

BLOOD SONG: A SILENT BALLAD
978-1-59582-389-2 | $19.99

THE BOOK OF GRICKLE
978-1-59582-430-1 | $17.99

BRODY'S GHOST COLLECTED EDITION
978-1-61655-901-4 | $24.99

BUCKO
978-1-59582-973-3 | $19.99

CHANNEL ZERO
978-1-59582-936-8 | $19.99

CHERUBS
978-1-59582-984-9 | $19.99

CHIMICHANGA
978-1-59582-755-5 | $14.99

CITIZEN REX
978-1-59582-556-8 | $19.99

THE COMPLETE PISTOLWHIP
978-1-61655-720-1 | $27.99

CROSSING THE EMPTY QUARTER AND OTHER STORIES
978-1-59582-388-5 | $24.99

DE:TALES
HC: 978-1-59582-557-5 | $19.99
TPB: 978-1-59307-485-2 | $14.99

EVERYBODY GETS IT WRONG! AND OTHER STORIES: DAVID CHELSEA'S 24-HOUR COMICS
978-1-61655-155-1 | $19.99

EXURBIA
978-1-59582-339-7 | $9.99

FLUFFY
978-1-59307-972-7 | $19.99

GREEN RIVER KILLER
978-1-61655-812-3 | $19.99

HEART IN A BOX
978-1-61655-694-5 | $14.99

INSOMNIA CAFÉ
978-1-59582-357-1 | $14.99

THE MIGHTY SKULLBOY ARMY
Volume 2
978-1-59582-872-9 | $14.99

MILK AND CHEESE: DAIRY PRODUCTS GONE BAD
978-1-59582-805-7 | $19.99

MIND MGMT
Volume 1: The Manager
978-1-59582-797-5 | $19.99
Volume 2: The Futurist
978-1-61655-198-8 | $19.99
Volume 3: The Home Maker
978-1-61655-390-6 | $19.99
Volume 4: The Magician
978-1-61655-391-3 | $19.99
Volume 5: The Eraser
978-1-61655-696-9 | $19.99
Volume 6: The Immortals
978-1-61655-798-0 | $19.99

MOTEL ART IMPROVEMENT SERVICE
978-1-59582-550-6 | $19.99

THE NIGHT OF YOUR LIFE
978-1-59582-183-6 | $15.99

NINGEN'S NIGHTMARES
978-1-59582-859-0 | $12.99

NOIR
978-1-59582-358-8 | $12.99

PIXU: THE MARK OF EVIL
978-1-61655-813-0 | $14.99

RESET
978-1-61655-003-5 | $15.99

SACRIFICE
978-1-59582-985-6 | $19.99

SINFEST: VIVA LA RESISTANCE
978-1-59582-424-0 | $14.99

SPEAK OF THE DEVIL
978-1-59582-193-5 | $19.99

UNCLE SILAS
978-1-59582-566-7 | $9.99

DARK HORSE BOOKS

AVAILABLE AT YOUR LOCAL COMICS SHOP OR BOOKSTORE!
To find a comics shop in your area, call 1-888-266-4226

For more information or to order direct:
On the web: DarkHorse.com
E-mail: mailorder@darkhorse.com
Phone: 1-800-862-0052 Mon.–Fri. 9 AM to 5 PM Pacific Time.

OMNIBUS COLLECTIONS FROM DARK HORSE BOOKS

ALIENS
Volume 1
ISBN 978-1-59307-727-3

Volume 2
ISBN 978-1-59307-828-7

Volume 3
ISBN 978-1-59307-872-0

Volume 4
ISBN 978-1-59307-926-0

Volume 5
ISBN 978-1-59307-991-8

Volume 6
ISBN 978-1-59582-214-7

ALIENS VS. PREDATOR
Volume 1
ISBN 978-1-59307-735-8

Volume 2
ISBN 978-1-59307-829-4

ALIEN LEGION
Volume 1
ISBN 978-1-59582-394-6

Volume 2
ISBN 978-1-59582-494-3

PREDATOR
Volume 1
ISBN 978-1-59307-732-7

Volume 2
ISBN 978-1-59307-733-4

Volume 3
ISBN 978-1-59307-925-3

Volume 4
ISBN 978-1-59307-990-1

THE TERMINATOR
Volume 1
ISBN 978-1-59307-916-1

Volume 2
ISBN 978-1-59307-917-8

INDIANA JONES: THE FURTHER ADVENTURES
Volume 1
ISBN 978-1-59582-246-8

Volume 2
ISBN 978-1-59582-336-6

X OMNIBUS
Volume 1
ISBN 978-1-59307-939-0

Volume 2
ISBN 978-1-59307-940-6

INDIANA JONES
Volume 1
ISBN 978-1-59307-887-4

Volume 2
ISBN 978-1-59307-953-6

GHOST
Volume 1
ISBN 978-1-59307-992-5

Volume 2
ISBN 978-1-59582-213-0

Volume 3
ISBN 978-1-59582-374-8

Volume 4
ISBN 978-1-61655-080-6

Volume 5
ISBN 978-1-61655-383-8

CRIMINAL MACABRE OMNIBUS
Volume 1
ISBN 978-1-59582-746-3

Volume 2
ISBN 978-1-59582-747-0

Volume 3
ISBN 978-1-61655-648-8

BARB WIRE
ISBN 978-1-59307-993-2

THE MASK
Volume 1
ISBN 978-1-59307-927-7

Volume 2
ISBN 978-1-59307-937-6

ADVENTURES OF THE MASK
ISBN 978-1-59307-938-3

DARK HORSE HEROES
ISBN 978-1-59307-734-1

GRENDEL OMNIBUS
Volume 1: Hunter Rose
ISBN 978-1-59582-893-4

Volume 2: The Legacy
ISBN 978-1-59582-894-1

Volume 3: Orion's Reign
ISBN 978-1-59582-895-8

Volume 4: Prime
ISBN 978-1-59582-896-5

BUFFY THE VAMPIRE SLAYER
Volume 1
ISBN 978-1-59307-784-6

Volume 2
ISBN 978-1-59307-826-3

Volume 3
ISBN 978-1-59307-885-0

Volume 4
ISBN 978-1-59307-968-0

Volume 5
ISBN 978-1-59582-225-3

Volume 6
ISBN 978-1-59582-242-0

Volume 7
ISBN 978-1-59582-331-1

AGE OF REPTILES
ISBN 978-1-59582-683-1

NEXUS
Volume 1
ISBN 978-1-61655-034-9

Volume 2
ISBN 978-1-61655-035-6

Volume 3
ISBN 978-1-61655-036-3

Volume 4
ISBN 978-1-61655-037-0

Volume 5
ISBN 978-1-61655-038-7

Volume 6
ISBN 978-1-61655-473-6

Volume 7
ISBN 978-1-50670-002-1

$24.99 EACH